SHRIMP, COLLARDS & GRITS

PAT BRANNING

www.mycarolinacooking.com

SHRIMP, COLLARDS & GRITS

Recipes, Stories and Art from
the Creeks and Gardens of the Lowcountry

PAT BRANNING

Carolina Oak, watercolor on paper by Nancy Ricker Rhett.

Previous Page: The Live Oak is a native species found throughout the Lowcountry. Notice how the limbs rest peacefully on the ground, weighed down by their venerable age. This painting resembles the Angel Oak on Johns Island just outside Charleston, believed to be between 500 and 1,500 years old. The shaded area covered by its foliage extends over 17,000 square feet!

Opposite Page: Kingfisher by William Rhett III

Shrimp, Collards & Grits
Recipes, Stories and Art from the Creeks and Gardens of the Lowcountry

Copyright © 2011 by Pat Branning, original content only.
All artwork copyright remains with the artists. See pages 142-144 for information.

International Standard Book Number: 978-0-9831519-0-6

All rights reserved. No portion of this book may be reproduced, stored in a retrieval system, or transmitted in any form or by any means—mechanical, electronic, photocopying, recording, or otherwise—without prior written permission from the publisher, except as provided by United States of America copyright law. Printed in China.

Published by Lydia Inglett Ltd.
www.lydiainglett.com

To order more copies of this book please visit: www.mycarolinacooking.com
or www.starbooks.biz

For the joys of my heart —
my husband, Cloide,
my children, Elizabeth, Margaret and Andrew,
my grandchildren,
and, the memory of my mother and dad.

CONTENTS

Come On In to the Kitchen 11

Cooking Southern 15

Beaufort – The Jewel of the Lowcountry 17

Life in the Lowcountry 23

Gracious Beginnings 26

Shellfish Chowder 28
Frogmore Stew 29
Seafood Gumbo 30
Oyster Bisque 31
Tuscan Bean Soup 32
Garden Fresh Tomato Basil Soup 33
Crab Bisque 33
Pimento Cheese 34
Creamy Muschroom Soup 35
Meeting Street Crab Tassies 35
Pan Seared Lowcountry Crab Cakes 36
Bay Street Mushroom Puffs 36
Sea Island Crab Stuffed Mushrooms 36
Seafarer's Oyster and Crab Cake 37
Carolina Pickled Shrimp 37
Seafood Ceviche 38
The Great Bruschetta Caper 38
Cheese en Croute 38
She Crab Soup 39
Savannah Cheese Straws 40
Vidalia Onion Dip 40
The Perfect Mint Julep 40
Wassail Punch 40
Stuffed Artichoke Bottoms 40
Sweet Tea 41
Broiled Figs with Prosciutto and Gorgonzola 42
Black-Eyed Pea Hummus 42
Bacon-Mushroom Dip 43
Mixed Greens with Truffle Oil Dressing 44
Goat Cheese and Truffle Oil Crostini 44
Lowcountry Shrimp Cocktail 45
Caramel Pecan Brie 45
Best Ever Queso Dip 45

Breads and Brunches 47

Heritage Breakfast Puffs 48
Apple Bacon Sausage Balls 48
Farm Stand Peach Freezer Jam 49
Pecan-Apple Bread 50
Puffed Apple Pancake 50
Apple Fritters for Fall 51
Hot Baked Fruit with Granola Nut Topping 51
Roasted Vegetable Frittata 52
Corn Strata 53
Spinach Cheese Strata 53
Rise and Shine Breakfast Strata 53
Sweet Potato Biscuits 54
Spoon Bread 54
Cowan Creek Sweet Potato Cornbread 54
Fried Okra Pancakes 54
Zucchini Pineapple Bread 55
Cheddar Bay Biscuits 55
Fruit Nut Pumpkin Bread 56
Dixie-Style Hoe Cakes 57
Deep South Hush Puppies 57

Hot from the Oven Entrees 59

Deep South Buttermilk Fried Chicken 60
Lemony Chicken Piccata 60
Chicken Marsala with Pancetta 61
Sesame Chicken Wings 61
Chicken Divan 61
Vegetarian Lasagna 62
Chicken, Onion, and Pineapple Kebobs 62
Chicken Tostadas 62
Deep Fried Turkey 63
Chechessee Standing Rib Roast 64
Taco Salad 65
Land's End London Broil 65
Sizzlin' Flank Steak 66
Filet Mignon with Mushroom Marsala Sauce 67
Best Barbecued Ribs 68
Penne with Asparagus and Proscuitto 69
Roasted Rack of Lamb 70
Rustic Chicken with Mushrooms and Gruyere Polenta 71
Lowcountry Chicken Parmesan 71
Chicken Fricassee 72
Southern-Style Barbecued Chicken 73

www.mycarolinacooking.com

Tailgate Pulled Pork Barbecue 74
Pierre's Shrimp and Crab Gravy 75
Scalloped Oysters 76
Shrimp Curry 76
Pan Fried Steaks 77

From the Garden 79

Vidalia Onion Tart 80
Twice Baked Potato Casserole 80
Our Best Macaroni and Cheese 81
Fried Green Tomatoes 82
Buttermilk Fried Okra 83
Lucille Wright's Tomato Pie 83
Putting-on-the-Ritz Pineapple 83
Risotto with Creamy Scallops and Tomatoes 84
Autumn Salad with Balsamic Roasted Pears 85
Potato Gratin with Truffle Oil 85
Deep South Penne Pasta 86
Cranberry-Pineapple Gelatin Salad 86
Big Mama's Collard Greens 86
Savory Acorn Squash 87
Wild Rice Salad 88
Crisp Tybee Salad 88
Honey Balsamic Vinaigrette 89
Asparagus and Arugula Salad with Garbonzo Beans 89

Sensational Seafood 91

Louis' Fried Oysters 92
Daufuskie Island Oyster Stuffing 93
Beaufort's Best Shrimp Burgers 94
Blackened Redfish 95
Lowcountry Shrimp and Mussel Paella 96
Shrimp and Crab Salad 97
Mahi with Lemon and Capers 98
Ginger Glazed Mahi-Mahi 98
Macadamia Crusted Mahi-Mahi with Crab Relish 99
Seafood Ceviche on Cucumber Rounds 100
Grilled Fresh Cobia 101
Seared Scallop Salad 102
Crispy Oven Fried Fish 103
Shrimp Tempura with Soy Sake Dipping Sauce 104
Ogeechee Shad Roe with Bacon 105
Grilled Lowcountry Shrimp 106
Fish Casserole Au Gratin 107
Grilled Savannah Salad 107
Lowcountry Shrimp and Grits 108
Baked Mackerel with Herb Crust 109
Tideland Soft-Shell Crabs 110
Charleston Crab au Gratin 111
Crab Ogeechee 111
Grouper Oscar 111

Gullah Fixin's 112

Mullet Stew 118
Hoppin' John 118
Gullah Lowcountry Shrimp Pilau 118
Mama's Sweet Potato Poon 119
Broomfield Cabbage Soup 119
Fresh Specker Butter Beans 119
Dye's Country Corn Pone 119
Buttermilk Hush Puppies with Onions and Bell Peppers 120
Daufuskie Crab Fried Rice 120
Purloo 121
Boiled Peanuts 121
Lowcountry Red Rice 121
Carolina Country Hobo Bread 122
Corn Skillet Fritters 122
Buttermilk Pie 123
Old Country Pound Cake 123
Benne Seed Cookies 123

Sweet Splurges 125

Peach and Blueberry Trifle 126
Blueberry and Peach Crisp 127
Coconut-Pecan Chocolate Bars 128
Cranberry Toffee Walnut Tarts 128
Christmas Divinity 129
Mocha Surprise Truffles 129
Double Treat Toffee 129
Shaker Lemon Pie 130
Mama Green's Banana Pudding 131
Lucious Lemonade Layer Cake 132
Caramel Crème Brûlée 132
Huguenot Torte 132
Maple Sweet Potato Pie 133
Strawberry Cream Pie 134
Strawberry Torte 134
Pumpkin Mousse Parfaits 135
Soda Cracker Bark 135
Bite Sized Peppermint And Chocolate Chip Cheesecakes 136
Sweet Potato Streusel Tarts 136
Chocolate Chip Pecan Pie Bars 137
Palm Beach Brownies 137
Benne Wafers 139
Chocolate Raspberry Truffle Torte 138
Not So Humble Fudge Pie 138
Key Lime Pie with Grand Marnier Whipped Cream 138
Polenta Pudding with Caramel 139

Index 140

About the Artists 142

More diverse than the ingredients that simmer and blend together in my recipes are the friends through the years who have gathered around my kitchen table to eat, laugh and enjoy the results of our collective culinary creations. Enthusiastic tasters are to be commended for throwing calorie and cholesterol care to the wind during my many experiments.

I truly appreciate their unselfish expansion of both tastebuds and waistlines and the enrichment they have added to my life.

Throughout all these years, so many have touched my life and kitchen that to try to name them would be impossible. I most likely would forget someone. This book is largely about home cooking in the Lowcountry, so I have left the work of many of our brilliant chefs for another time.

Those precious friends and acquaintances who have inspired my culinary imagination, nurtured me with stockpots of love, and shared favorite recipes with me over a lifetime, deserve at least a clinking together of a goblet of very good cabernet.

My heartfelt appreciation goes to the artists and photographers who have agreed to warm the interior pages of this book with their incredible photographs and paintings. A huge thank you especially to Ray Ellis, who agreed to grace the covers of this book both front and back with his extraordinary works.

I have been touched by all who have taken time to write me through my web site, www.mycarolinacooking.com. It fuels my culinary energies just as much as my adventures to gastronomic places.

Gay Fish Company Docks, watercolor on paper by Nancy Ricker Rhett.

Acknowledgements

Follow me on www.mycarolinacooking.com as I travel through the Lowcountry on culinary adventures.

With the support of so many people from Savannah to Hilton Head, from Beaufort to Charleston, I'll be putting together an in-depth view of the food and beverage industry here.

Throughout all, my publisher, Lydia Inglett, has remained a steady and gentle voice of sound guidance.

I wish to thank George Trask, publisher of the Beaufort-Tribune.com, for inviting me to write for his newspaper each week, www.BeaufortTribune.com.

For inspiration, I thank the Lowcountry and especially the town of Beaufort who is worthy of the highest recognition, especially during this, her Tricentennial year! She stands proud today as a grand lady who has it all: blustery cumulus days, waters that sparkle and enchant, cozy harbors, duned beaches, inland secluded ponds, gorgeous antebellum homes and a sun that shines bright and often.

For this is the land of billowing spinnakers to sail, warming rays of sunshine to absorb, wild yellow, pink and red roses to inhale, ripening tomatoes, blueberries and blackberries to enjoy.

While every little aspect of Beaufort seems to strike my fancy with magical power, it was in truth the creations and flavors of my mother's kitchen on Lady's Island, that were to linger the most indelibly. I learned from her that great food and exciting people go together! Hers was a cuisine and a form of entertaining that represented the very soul of the place I fell in love with so many years ago, the place that has filled my heart and imagination for a lifetime. Here, on these pages, in the art, the stories and the recipes, is its story.

It is my wish that this collection of recipes and memories will give you a sense of this extraordinary place, with all its richness, and you will feel inspired to re-create them in your own home for a little taste of what life is like below the Mason Dixon line down in the deep South.

- Pat Branning

Come On In to the Kitchen And Make Yourself at Home

*I love good food, the kind you want to share with special friends and those you love.
I like remembering the taste of food sampled once in a faraway place
and having that memory stay with me for years to come.*

WELCOME TO THE LAND OF shrimp, collards and grits! Among the many islands of Beaufort County is one that bears the name Lady's. This is where Pleasant Point Plantation stretches along the twists and turns of the Beaufort River.

It was 1971 when I first crossed the little causeway at Pleasant Point leading up to a small wooden structure with a sign outside reading, "clubhouse." My husband and I had just driven in from Atlanta, parked the car and were getting out when a jovial man drove up in his golf cart. Upon seeing the Georgia tag on the back of the car and realizing we were not locals, he greeted us with, "Welcome to the land of shrimp, collards and grits! My name's Willie. I own the place, so if you see anything you like, let me know. Don't fool with the alligators and just beat the ground with a stick if you want the snakes to leave you alone."

Before we could respond, he spun off toward a group of men waiting on the first hole to tee off.

Despite this somewhat abrupt introduction to the place, there was a gentle spirit about it in contrast to the fast paced life we had in Atlanta. Rows of Palmetto trees lined the

Pat Branning

Everywhere I went, whether it was an oyster roast, a church gathering or a political supper, there was some sort of shrimp-corn-sausage stuff. One night I approached a man with a toothpick in his mouth and asked him what it was. Looking in disbelief and trying not to lose patience with me, he said, "Frogmore Stew."

Did that mean they put frogs in their stew?

*With appreciation to Karin Jurick for her painting of a Charleston carriage ride titled "Mosey Along."
Some of my very best food memories are of fabulous dinners in Charleston.*

IT HAS TO DO WITH driving down dirt roads with sleeping dogs, houses painted blue to ward off evil spirits, natives picking vine ripe tomatoes in the vast fields of St. Helena Island, and the sounds of Gullah hymns rising from a nearby church. It's about Wednesday nights at the infamous Beaufort Yacht Club, the sounds of laughter and dice games, and Larry Taylor fixin' everything there was to fix — especially loved for his fried chicken. Then there was that notorious fella named Skeet who mastered the art of traveling through town with his long legs jumping from roof top to roof top. It's remembering how local fishermen stood on the river banks gathering up pluff mud, mixing it with fish meal, getting ready for their nightly trip down the river to bait shrimp.

Intracoastal Waterway that meandered around the property, standing stately like soldiers guarding the shoreline as shrimp boats, barges, sailboats, and yachts passed by on their way to distant harbors. Walking up to the water's edge, we scattered marsh hens into the air, observed the massive wingspread of the great blue herons in flight, and watched egrets searching for fish among the rocks in shallow waters. There was something special here, unique and set apart. Standing at the point we could look across the river at the town of Beaufort standing like a true Southern Lady. We decided to stay.

Many of the activities and recipes described in this book took place in and around our home on the waterway. We owned Pleasant Point in the '70s and lived in the Arthur Barnwell House. The food and festivities presented are authentic and based on ideas from generations of Southern cooks and graciously served at oyster roasts, fish fries, barbecues, ladies luncheons and teas as well as dinners and cocktail parties. Many recipes are updated but represent what hostesses served when they wanted to put their best foot forward. Flavorful food and elegant style were always an indispensable part of everyday life. This book is all about the food but also the memories of how things were.

EVERYWHERE I WENT whether it was an oyster roast, a church gathering or a political supper, there was some sort of shrimp-corn-sausage stuff. One night I approached a man with a toothpick in his mouth and asked him what it was. Looking in disbelief and trying not to lose patience with me, he said, "Frogmore Stew." Did that mean they put frogs in their stew? It kept happening — those funny sounding words kept coming up. Words like Purloo or was it pilau and was it related to Kentucky Burgoo? Of course there was this chatter about chicken bog or hog and what was that?

Best I could figure out it was a chicken "bogged" down in rice and a boggy, soggy mess. Folks in town loved it and served it often!

Venturing over to to Bay Street, Harry's restaurant is where you could order the blue plate special. These were local fixins at their finest…the best "mess of collard greens" and catfish chowder you ever ate, biscuits with cream gravy, and of course, shrimp gumbo. When you ate fried chicken at Harry's, you picked it up with your fingers and ate it right off the bone. At one of the tables several men were talking about ribmeat and fatback and things like streak-o-lean. They got into a heated argument with one of the waitresses about the superiority of one over the other. Experiencing Lowcountry cuisine at Harry's must rank as high on most tourists' to-do

www.mycarolinacooking.com

Our home, the Arthur Barnwell House on Pleasant Point — painted by Beaufort artist Nancy Ricker Rhett — typifies Southern elegance and life on the Carolina coast in our much loved Lowcountry.

list as a horse-drawn carriage ride through Beaufort's historic district. But putting your finger on what, exactly, constitutes this distinctly Southern cuisine can be a bit tricky. Is it the frogmore stew, fried green tomatoes or gumbo with okra and hoppin' john?"

At one of the tables several men were talking about ribmeat and fatback and things like streak-o-lean. They got into a heated argument with a waitress about the superiority of one over the other.

WHEN ALL IS SAID and done, it's rice that signifies the real food culture of the Lowcountry. Rice is what made plantation owners wealthy in the 1700s after it was brought over from East Africa, probably Madagascar, to South Carolina, making South Carolina the major rice growing state until the Civil War.

Tomatoes, corn and hominy — the hulled and dried kernels of corn from which the bran and germ have been removed — were also significant, with hominy served daily.

*What joy to have beautiful raw ingredients
from our beloved islands; to cook fish fresh from the sea,
to arrange tomatoes in splashes of red, yellow and orange in tribute
to our sunsets and to seal memories of spring in jars of strawberry jam.*

Cooking Southern

*The Lowcountry is the embodiment of all that is Southern —
an amalgam of traditions, culture, folklore, art and great food.
Throughout this book, the art tells the story of the true South.*

My cooking philosophy is very simple. Find the finest and freshest ingredients possible and prepare them in a way that is delicious, uncomplicated and pleasing to the eye. To me there are no "must do" rules in cooking — try anything at least once. There is just nothing that compares to the rich and enticing color, aroma, and flavor of produce at its peak.

Of the dozens of seductive dishes filled with summer's bounty, all taste better with seasonal ingredients, locally produced. With those first nippy days of autumn, fresh produce still remains a major player in the kitchen. That first frost is no longer my signal for cool weather cooking, rather it begins with the late August exodus of summer vacationers. The sunlight hours begin to wane, nights are somewhat cooler and darker earlier as the thermometer dips into the 60s. The abundance of farm vegetables is augmented by the arrival of oyster season, fall squash, and luscious pumpkin desserts and breads.

Sun ripened garden tomatoes in tasty vinaigrettes give way to vegetable soups and casseroles. Picnics now take place in woodlands, and in the shelter of beach dunes. As the colors of the marsh grass turn from bright summer greens to autumn's gold and russets, so too does our table reflect autumn hues with red cabbage, acorn, and butternut squash and parsnips.

Thoughts now turn to Thanksgiving as the air has the crispness of a ripe apple and snuggly warm things are moved into drawers and closets in preparation for cooler days ahead. With the Christmas season fast approaching, we are spurred into a frenzy of flamboyant decorating and entertaining that can leave us breathless!

My Christmas kitchen transforms into a sugarplum fairyland with twinkling lights and glittering decorations, mulled cider simmering on the stove and cookies warm from the oven covering countertops. After all, December's early sunsets are the best time for baking and simmering those delicious cold weather soups and stews.

Pat in the kitchen with chef Phil Barnes.

Moon River, oil on canvas by Ray Ellis.

*Whether we are born and raised here, or come later in life as strangers,
the Lowcountry captures our hearts and imaginations
with a hold that can never be broken.*

Beaufort
The Jewel of the Lowcountry

There is a place abounding in wildlife and natural beauty, with rivers, streams, marshes, and islands, where daily life revolves around the ebb and flow of the tides. It's a road less traveled into one of our country's last unspoiled places, rich in folklore, history, and spectacular beauty. These pages capture the very essence of this place we affectionately call the Lowcountry.

While the tide surges twice daily to every corner of Beaufort County, it continues to insulate and distinguish this area from other counties within the state. It is this very isolation that has forged Beaufort's strong and unique character. The tide's bounty is legendary. Shrimp, oysters, and crabs have sustained this area for generations, elevating Beaufort County to prominence making it the "Jewel of the Lowcountry."

As early as 4,000 B.C. native Indians were living in the Lowcountry. A walk through the forest preserve in Sea Pines on Hilton Head Island reveals an old "Indian shell ring" which is the remains of one such early settlement.

Written history began about 500 years ago with the discovery of the area by the Spanish. Beaufort County was one of the earliest landings on the North American continent, second only to St. Augustine.

Because the seaport of Beaufort is located at the head of one of the largest natural harbors along the Atlantic coast, it was an ideal spot for the Spanish and French explorers to land. These French explorers visited this area long before the English arrived. In 1562, Captain Jean Ribaut and his Frenchmen entered the sound which he named Port Royal. They settled near the present town of Port Royal. However, when Ribaut returned to France for reinforcements, the soldiers who were left behind revolted, built themselves a ship and sailed for France the next year.

The Spanish then built a fort on Parris Island and called the new settlement there Santa Elena. It was about 1576, under attack from Native Americans, that Santa Elena was abandoned. Archeologists have determined the location to be on what is now the Parris Island golf course.

In 1587, England's Elizabeth I sent Sir Francis Drake to drive the Spanish out. They were successful and South Carolina was again left to the Indians. In 1711 Beaufort was

Tidalholm, also known as the Edgar Fripp House, 1 Laurens Street, Beaufort, watercolor on paper by Nancy Ricker Rhett.

Oppostie page: Sams House, watercolor on paper by Nancy Ricker Rhett.

established by the British and became the second oldest town in South Carolina, after Charleston. Both Beaufort County and its county seat of Beaufort were named for Henry Somerset, Duke of Beaufort, one of the Lords Proprietors of Carolina.

BEAUFORT IS A GRAND old Southern town who has maintained her magical charms of yesteryear. She's come through mighty wars, hurricanes, and earthquakes, and like many women with grit and determination, has emerged in all her finery, stronger than ever.

Walking beside the river, I feel the peacefulness that is Beaufort. The feeling continues on a stroll down shady streets in the Old Point, where stately homes exude a charm and elegance of a bygone era. This cozy town has not always known life so serene. Walking past the Berners Barnwell Sams house I notice the original slave quarters now converted to apartments. There is a blacksmith shop, a cookhouse and a laundry, but also I see it as the hospital it became during the Northern occupation. As I look up I can imagine a wounded Civil War soldier being carried inside.

Without a doubt, the most famous house is Tidalholm, the setting for movies like *The Big Chill* and *The Great Santini*, based on Beaufort resident Pat Conroy's book. Situated on the easternmost point in town with lawns sloping down to the river, its location is breathtaking. This was the summer home for the Fripp family, who built it in 1856 to escape the heat and mosquitoes plaguing them on their St. Helena Island plantation. Edgar's brother, James, owned the house at the time of the War. Upon his return, he found the house on the auction block being sold for taxes. According to the story told to me by Nancy Ricker Rhett, he was unable to raise the money and stood in the crowd with tears running down his cheeks. A Frenchman, sympathetic to the Southern cause, purchased the house, then presented the deed to Mr. Fripp. The Frenchman returned to France before Mr. Fripp could repay him. The family has a letter from the Frenchman documenting the story.

As the years went by, the home was used as a guest house for writers, artists, and other notables who wintered there in luxury. In those days one dressed for dinner, gathered for cocktails on the porch or in the drawing rooms, and dined on a superb gourmet meal that could last for hours. Today it is a private home.

St. Helena's Episcopal Church, established in 1712, watercolor on paper by Nancy Ricker Rhett.

ST. HELENA'S EPISCOPAL CHURCH, established in 1712, is one of the most picturesque in the country.

Construction began in 1724 using ballast brick from England which were covered with stucco. It was used as a hospital during the Civil War, and flat tombstones were placed across pews to serve as operating tables. Looking closely at the base of the church near the back gate, I discover the grave of one of Beaufort's founders, Col. "Tuscarora" Jack Barnwell. Captain Thomas Nairne was the original leader of the English settlement, but Barnwell took over after Nairne was killed by Indians. A walk inside reveals Capt. John Bull's silver communion service given in 1734 to the church in memory of his wife

The Castle, circa 1850, also known as the Joseph Johnson House, 411 Craven Street, watercolor on paper by Nancy Ricker Rhett.

who was killed by the Yemassee Indians. I am told that it still is used on special occasions.

The Baptist Church of Beaufort also served as a hospital during the Civil War, or the "Wah," as locals call it. Records show that in 1857, slave membership there was 3,317 while whites numbered just 182. It's a stunning example of Greek Revival Period architecture, featuring highly ornate and exquisite plaster work inside, all done by skilled slaves.

It doesn't take long to feel the connection here between the people, their land, the river, and their history. Simple pleasures and stories are everywhere and life becomes an adventure to be explored and discovered each day. Being still for a moment, I can hear the Spanish mission bells, and sense the presence of slaves in the vast fields of St. Helena Island picking cotton and dreaming of better days.

Continuing a walk up Craven Street I see *"The Castle,"* more formally known as the Joseph Johnson House. Built in 1850, stories around town say it is haunted by the ghost of Jean Ribaut's dwarf drummer boy. Occupants will never quite say for sure whether they've seen the ghost or felt his presence, but a childhood friend of Nancy Ricker Rhett's was locked in the basement for four hours. Nancy says, "Ask her!"

In November of 1861, the first major naval battle of the War Between the States was fought, the Battle of Port Royal. Two Confederate forts, Beauregard and Walker, were on either side of Port Royal Sound. Yankee ships circled and shelled the forts in what black folks call "the day of the big gun shoot." The Yankees won. Beaufortonians fled in "The Grand Skedaddle," even leaving food on the table in their haste. They grabbed only those valuables they could carry, buried some in the back yard and fled with their house slaves. Their field

The Hepworth House, circa 1720, 214 New Street. This is the oldest house in Beaufort and one of the oldest in the Lowcountry, built by Thomas Hepworth, Chief Justice of the Colony. In the rear wall of the basement are musket slits because during this era, attacks by Indians were a very real threat. Watercolor on paper by Nancy Ricker Rhett.

hands remained on the islands, more isolated than ever. In a way, this was a blessing, for it kept their Gullah culture intact.

Owners of "The Castle" buried their valuable crystal, china, and silver under the dirt floor of the wash house before they fled. The home was used as a hospital and the wash house became a morgue. After the War, the owners returned and dug up all their valuables intact; no one wanted to disturb the dead.

As I drive away from town past heavily wooded areas, I can almost see Francis Marion deep within, planning his next encounter with the British. At the plantation gates along the winding roads, I picture a team of trotting horses drawing a carriage beneath the graceful branches of moss-laden live oaks.

Cultivation of cotton, rice, and indigo in the 17th and 18th centuries brought great wealth to Beaufort, which was already rich in many ways. Its waters teemed with fish, oysters, crab, and shrimp, and the soil was rich for cultivation. Many were needed to work the land, so as the slave trade grew from the coast of Africa, so did the black population of the area. Our blacks here created their own language, a mix of Elizabethan English and African. It's called Gullah, and subsequently, so is their culture — unique to this area and in all the world.

Prior to the Civil War, Beaufort was one of the wealthiest towns in the United States and was commonly regarded as the Newport of the South by wealthy planters who built grand summer homes here. It was here that breezes were cooler and social life abounded.

With a wealth of servants to handle the housework, the residents of these grand homes enjoyed busy social lives, attending balls, the races and lovely dinner parties. The Hunting Club, too, offered hours of relaxation for the men who religiously enforced the club's rule that no man go home sober.

While the Civil War was raging throughout the South, Beaufort was spared because General Sherman's troops had occupied the town. Rather than destroy Beaufort, they turned churches and homes into offices, morgues and hospitals. Although she was spared, her prosperity came to a sudden halt. During Reconstruction, the economy was non-existent. Carpetbaggers and Scalawags ravaged the town. Confederate money was hardly worth saving, and many of the grand homes were sold for taxes, which few could raise.

AFTER THE PERIOD of Reconstruction, Beaufort began to recover a little. Mining for phosphate brought some prosperity. But the Great Storm of 1893 literally drowned all that, along with thousands of people. Then cotton farming was wiped out by the boll weevil in early 1919. World War I came along, then the Great Depression. World War II saw the expansion of the military in our area, bringing some economic relief.

It was not until the late '60s that tourists began to discover Beaufort's magic. Buildings got painted and restored, and the town began to realize they had something very special. And special it is.

THE BEAUFORT OF TODAY has a tranquility that is at variance with its past. Six flags have waved over its gentle terrain. The great water oaks saw the British set up their naval operations during the American Revolution and gazed down on young men who came to settle "honour" at the notorious dueling spots of the day. These are the same woods where tolled the Spanish mission bells and echoed the voices of slaves at work in the fields. This is where the Yemassee Indians made their camp and sat by the water's edge to eat snails and oysters.

To walk through this town, its woods and gardens, is to step into history. It's a place for patient viewing, to feel the richness of the past and imbibe in nature in all its splendor. To rush is to deprive oneself of a spiritual awareness that's here for the inhaling.

OVER SIXTY-EIGHT large islands lie just off the coast of Beaufort, and more than two hundred smaller islands, at least a half acre in size, speckle the salty tidal marshes. As the tide flows in and out, the tens of thousands of acres are visible at ebb tide and at high tide become invisible. This area has been called the Sea Islands since Europeans first set foot here almost five centuries ago. From the air, these islands appear to be sparkling little jewels as the water splashes against the marsh grass.

These islands are part of the great Sea Island complex that extends from the Santee Delta, north of Charleston, over one hundred miles South to the Savannah River. The largest island, Port Royal, so named by Jean Ribaut, supports the town of Beaufort on its easternmost tip. Other large islands include Hilton Head, Daufuskie, Hunting, Fripp, St. Helena, and Lady's.

The Lewis Reeve Sams House, 601 Bay Street, nicknamed "The Wedding Cake House," circa 1852. This is where Barbra Streisand and Nick Nolte filmed The Prince of Tides. *Watercolor on paper by Nancy Ricker Rhett.*

Marshlands, circa 1814, built by Dr. James Robert Verdier. Watercolor on paper by Nancy Ricker Rhett.

The Thomas Fuller house, "Tabby Manse," circa 1786. Tabby was a type of building material used in the coastal Southeast from the late 1500s to the 1850s. It is made of equal parts lime, water, sand, oyster shells, and ash and was used for foundations, walls and floors. It dries to a hard finish, with a grayish-white color. 1874 photograph by Mr. Wilson, Savannah, whose glass negatives are much prized. Photo courtesy of George Trask.

One thing for sure, no life on our sea islands is complete without at least one quail or dove shoot and a few fishing expeditions whether it be casting from the beach or braving a trip to the gulf stream on the high seas.

Life in the Lowcountry

From the earliest days, native Americans taught settlers in Beaufort how to hunt wild game, fish, gather honey, roast oysters and grow and use corn.

Hunting for Dove

For centuries, Southern boys have enjoyed glorious dove shoots when these small, migratory gray birds fly in. Springtime brings them to the Lowcountry on their way northward and fall brings them back south; they stop off here for a rest before proceeding on to Mexico for the winter. Dove are prized for their tastiness on the supper table. However, many come home empty handed because the dove dart out at 200 miles an hour, turning sideways flips just as the trusty shotgun is raised skyward! If you listen closely, you'll hear the whistling in their wings as they fly.

The Duck Hunt

There must be something magical about getting up at three o'clock in the morning, climbing into a fourteen foot bateau, a faithful black lab in the bow, turning on the engine and traveling down to one of the islands for a shoot at the break of dawn. In all the hunting tales I've heard, it's always been said that the finest hunting occurs as the winter storms blow through and the waters are their roughest. The rougher the weather, the more successful the hunt would be. I'll never forget being on Eddings Island one very cold December morning and hearing the wingbeat of ducks circling overhead just as the sun began to rise. To a duck hunter, there is no sound in the world quite so exciting!

It is incredible what tasty dishes can be prepared out of rice, onions, bacon and any one of a variety of wild meats. These dishes are known as pilau, with the name of the meat ingredient preceding the word pilau, as in marsh hen pilau, duck pilau, or oyster pilau. In the old days, many dishes were created out of necessity — one being duck over rice. The Gullah people on Lady's Island would take two large wild ducks, pick and clean them thoroughly, cut them into small pieces, season them well with salt and pepper, roll them in flour and brown them in a cast iron skillet. After all pieces were browned on all sides, the excess cooking oil would be discarded from the skillet. Then the duck pieces would be returned to the skillet. One large white onion, chopped up, would then be added. Next, two cups of water and a teaspoon of Tabasco were added. The flour that the duck pieces were rolled in sufficed to thicken the liquid into a wonderful gravy. The meat would then cook with a lid on very low heat for a couple of hours until tender. Always, this was served over white rice so that delicious gravy could be absorbed.

Opposite Page Top: Steady to Wing, oil on canvas by Julie Jeppson. Bottom: After the Hunt, oil on canvas by Julie Jeppson.

Bay Street, downtown Beaufort, looking East, Early 1900s. Photo courtesy of Richard & Gini Steele, Steele Studio, www.antiquepix.com

St. Phillip's Island Oyster Omelet

This recipe is that of Pierre McGowan, a sportsman and native of the Lowcountry, who learned it from a friend while on a camping trip to St. Phillip's Island. This dish was created purely by accident. One morning, as the men were preparing breakfast, one of them reached into his ice chest and produced a pint of raw oysters, asking, "How about adding these to the scrambled eggs?" Into a large hot skillet, with plenty of melted pure butter, he poured the raw oysters and allowed them to cook for two minutes until their edges began to curl. On top of the oysters, he poured eight well-beaten eggs mixed with half and half, salt and pepper, and six drops of Tabasco. When eaten with grits, toast, and coffee, this breakfast dish would satisfy even the most finicky eater. Other versions of this dish could include shredded sharp cheddar cheese and a few tablespoonfuls of chopped onion.

Pitchforking for Flounder

As the tide ebbs and exposes the oyster beds, the flounder seek refuge in the pluff mud. They feed on finger-length mullet, then bury themselves in the mud and silt at the bottom of these creeks to await the returning tide. As the tide ebbs, the water is muddy and the unwary flounder become unaware of their predators. This is when fishermen fish with pitchforks, a custom believed to have started during slavery, that was then passed down through the generations. It's a method where the fisherman walks through the muddy water sticking the pitchfork into the bottom in front of him, blind gigging. When the fisherman feels a quiver coming from the end of the pitchfork, he knows he has caught either a flounder or a stingray! Since the pitchfork has no barbs, when the fish is lifted out of the water, its wiggling can cause it to slip off and escape. Therefore the fisherman must carefully ease several fingers into the gills and, while holding it securely, raise the fish and the pitchfork out of the water at the same time. Next the fish is placed on a stringer, one end of which is secured to his belt.

Gigging for fish at night using a light and a spear is a form of gathering fish which predates the British coming to our coast. Records show that Native Americans used this method often and made spears out of wood; their light came from burning lightwood knots made from pine trees. Gasoline burning torches began being used in the early part of the twentieth century, and these were phased out about 1940 with the advent of Coleman lanterns. It's a sport still participated in today by natives and newcomers alike.

The English brought with them their taste for cream sauces, but the cooks in most English homes were African. They added their own exotic seasonings and culinary skills, creating dishes we still serve today, such as oyster pilau and okra and tomatoes.

It was these three forces combined – this meeting of native ingredients, English taste buds, and African culinary skill – that created the magic that exemplifies Lowcountry cooking today.

Bluffton Oysters

Bluffton oysters grow in the May River, which has 8 to 10 foot tides moving vast amounts of clean ocean water over its banks. This dramatic water exchange prevents heavy rains from diminishing the river's salinity as happens in the Chesapeake and Apalachicola bays, and more importantly, it prevents pollutants from accumulating near the delicate filter feeders.

Thus, our May River oysters have a distinctive wild and briny flavor that locals claim is unparalleled in the world.

Today, Larry and Tina Toomer operate the Bluffton Oyster Company. Larry is a third-generation oysterman from a tenacious family. Oyster pickers such as the one in this painting must face biting winds each winter and stay bent over for hours at a time swinging heavy culling hammers to break single selects, doubles or compact clusters from the dead shells that support them.

Oystering at Low Tide, oil on canvas by Michael Harrell.

Gracious Beginnings

Weathered rolling pins, rustic wooden mixing bowls, floral dish towels faded and worn from years of use, an old recipe box with dozens of 3 x 5 cards in mother's flowery script — welcome to the Southern kitchen!

SAVANNAH KNOWS HOW to throw a party and has been nicknamed the "Hostess City of the South" since Colonial times. She remains to this day a city proud of her hospitality, grace and style. There are two things Southern ladies take very seriously — Bridge and cooking! Life may be a game... but Bridge is serious business. The most popular "pick-ups" during these afternoon games are the cheese straws. These are quite delicate and crafted from flour, butter, cheese and red pepper. These are frequently served with pecans of all types, whether toasted, sugared or spiced. Some say "pee-cans" while others pronounce it "pah-khans"

On the Salts – Savannah Style

One does not have to travel far from the heart of downtown Savannah to reach wonderful residential areas on the banks of the rivers and creeks that wind their way through the Lowcountry. In times gone by these idyllic spots served as summer places for city residents trying to escape the torrid summer heat. It was called summering "on the salts."

Stories of life at these summer homes during the late 1800s describe fishing, crabbing, rowing, and berry-picking as favorite pastimes. Swimming was called "bathing," and was done mainly within the confines of a bathhouse, the men in long-sleeved jerseys and knee-length shorts and the ladies covered with clothing from head to toe.

Savannah is the first planned city to be based on a system of squares. The well-ordered arrangements of lots may still be seen, along with the squares and gorgeous broad avenues. James Oglethorpe's vision still gives Savannah a sense of orderly grace.

Spirited Savannah

There's an old Savannah saying that goes like this: In Charleston, people want to know who your people are; In Augusta, what your church is; And in Savannah, what you want to drink. Savannah is known as a city that loves its spirits. Nothing confirms this better than the Mint Julep. Mint Juleps should never be rushed, either in their preparation or their enjoyment. Served on the verandah, shaded by the branches of ancient moss covered live oaks, this beloved drink has long been a Southern tradition. Serve them in frosted sterling cups with silver spoon straws for a luxurious experience. And, always, always have plenty of fresh mint on hand from the garden.

By far the most spirited of Savannah's concoctions is the infamous Chatham Artillery Punch. The original recipe used equal parts of rum, brandy and whiskey, mixed with sugar and lemons. This was allowed to mature over several days in tubs or horse buckets! Finally, when the mixture was determined to be ready, ice was added, then champagne was poured over the ice completing the preparation.

Opposite Page Top: Morning Over Savannah;
Far Right: Ballast Stones - Factors Walk;
Right: By the Fountain.
All paintings watercolor on paper by Ray Ellis.

Savannah, "Hostess City of the South"

Moonlit Return, watercolor on paper by Ray Ellis.

Shellfish Chowder

One must never underestimate the power of soup. Just when we think we know all about it, we come across one that makes us rethink the whole subject. Reflecting back on the canned vegetable and tomato soup I grew up on, today's chowders, and bisques and hearty layered stews truly comfort and refresh us. They can be so soothing and gratifying that many times they become a complete meal.

For example, this shellfish New England-style chowder is delicious in a variety of different ways. Feel free to change the proportions of shellfish, depending on what is available at the market. Shrimp, scallops, lobster and crab mingle quite well with the diced potatoes and rich, smoky bacon.

¾ pound red potatoes, cut into ¾-inch pieces

½ cup finely chopped shallots

6 slices bacon, finely chopped

¾ cup bottled clam juice

2½ cups whole milk

⅛ teaspoon cayenne

¼ pound shrimp, shelled, deveined and cut into ½-inch pieces

½ pound sea scallops, quartered

1 teaspoon kosher salt

½ pound lump crabmeat, picked clean of ligaments and shells

2 tablespoons chopped fresh cilantro

2 tablespoons chopped fresh chives

Cook bacon in a heavy pot over moderate heat, stirring occasionally, until crisp. Transfer bacon with a slotted spoon to paper towels to drain. Pour off all but one tablespoon of fat from the pot and stir in potatoes, shallots, and clam juice.

Simmer, covered, until potatoes are tender, about 8 minutes.

Stir in milk and cayenne and return just to a simmer.

Add shrimp, scallops, and salt and simmer until shellfish is just cooked through.

Stir in crab or lobster and half of herbs and simmer one minute. Serve chowder topped with bacon and remaining herbs.

www.mycarolinacooking.com

Frogmore Stew

Frogmore Stew, watercolor on paper by Nancy Ricker Rhett.

FROGMORE STEW IS A FAVORITE WAY to commemorate all sorts of rites of passage, such as birthdays, engagements, graduations, retirements or the arrival of a new neighbor. The setting is almost always casual and outdoors, with wooden tables lined with newspapers.

This is a classic Lowcountry dish. It's also known as a Lowcountry Boil and Beaufort Stew. Local historians believe that the recipe was the invention of local shrimpers who used whatever food items they had on hand to make a stew. Richard Gay of Gay Seafood Company tells the story about how he invented the stew while on National Guard duty in Beaufort in the 1960s. He was preparing a cookout of leftovers for his fellow guardsmen; he brought the recipe home to the little community of Frogmore, putting out copies at his seafood market. That's how it all began, and today it has become a favorite at sophisticated restaurants in Charleston and up and down the coast.

You'll find Frogmore Stew served everywhere from weddings to school suppers to family reunions. This recipe is for the basic dish, but often onions, crabs and butter are added.

Note: All frogs are noticeably absent from this stew.

RECIPE

1 ½ gallons water

Juice of one lemon

Salt to taste

3 tablespoons Old Bay Seasoning

2 pounds kielbasa, cut into ½-inch slices

10 to 12 ears of corn on the cob, broken into 3-inch pieces

4 pounds of shrimp in the shell

In a large stock pot over medium high heat, add the water, lemon, salt and Old Bay Seasoning; bring to a boil.

Add the sausage and gently boil, uncovered, for five minutes. Add corn and cook and continue cooking an additional five minutes. (Begin timing immediately, don't wait until the water is boiling.)

Add shrimp and cook an additional three minutes longer. Remove from heat, drain immediately and serve. Yields: 8 servings.

Seafood Gumbo

Amanda Belle, oil on canvas by Michael Harrell.

For many years, New Orleans has received the credit for gumbo, but actually its roots are West African. When asked what best characterizes old Lowcountry cooking, many a native will tell you it's the gumbo. No one flavor dominates, but all are allowed to shine at their best. One secret is that the broth is allowed to simmer for a long time, but the gumbo is not. Therefore the crab, tomatoes, shrimp and okra are tender but still fresh and sweet tasting.

RECIPE

This recipe is inspired by an award winning gumbo from Charleston.

¼ pound spicy Italian chicken sausage links

32 ounces chicken broth

One 28-ounce can crushed tomatoes

3 bay leaves

1 tablespoon butter

1 tablespoon olive oil

1½ cups chopped sweet onion

2 celery ribs, chopped

⅓ cup chopped green bell pepper

2 tablespoons flour

½ cup water

Salt to taste

Freshly ground black pepper

1 teaspoon Old Bay Seasoning

½ tablespoon dried oregano

¼ cup fresh parsley

1 teaspoon Worcestershire sauce

6 cups sliced young, tender okra, trimmed and cut ½-inch thick.

½ pound fresh shrimp, deveined, peeled and cut into thirds

½ pound ocean fresh crabmeat (freshness makes all the difference in this dish)

Bring water to a boil in a saucepan and cook sausage links for about 4 minutes until cooked through and then drain. Chop into small pieces.

In a Dutch oven bring the chicken broth, tomatoes, bay leaves and sausage to a light boil over medium heat. Meanwhile, in a separate skillet, heat oil and butter and add the onion, celery and green pepper and sauté until they are soft and start to caramelize. Add vegetables to chicken broth mixture. Cover and bring back to a light boil. Continue cooking, covered, over medium heat for 5 minutes.

In a small bowl, whisk together flour and water. Stir flour mixture, spices, herbs and Worcestershire sauce into chicken broth mixture. Cover and cook over high heat for 10 minutes. Add the okra and allow to cook together with the broth for 10 more minutes.

Add shrimp and crab meat, reduce heat and cook for 5 minutes. Remove from heat and discard bay leaves. Cover and let it rest for 5 minutes before serving. Serves 6 to 8.

Oyster Bisque Savannah Style

RECIPE

If Lucille made it, it has to be good!

1 quart shucked oysters in their liquor
Salt and black pepper
4 stalks celery, cut in medium sized pieces
1 medium onion, chopped
4 cups whole milk
2 cups heavy cream
4 tablespoons butter
2 tablespoons all-purpose flour
Freshly grated nutmeg
Pinch of curry powder
1 tablespoon fresh lemon juice
1 tablespoon Worcestershire sauce
Cayenne pepper
Paprika
Chopped fresh parsley leaves

Pick over the oysters for shells and remove them. Simmer the oysters and the liqueur in a covered pot over low heat with some salt and black pepper. Stir once in awhile until the edges of the oyster begin to curl, about 5 minutes.

Lift the oysters out of the stock with a slotted spoon and put them in a colander with a bowl underneath to catch the pot liquor. Pour the stock from the pot into the bowl, being careful to discard any oyster dregs. Set the stock aside.

Cook the celery and onion in a little water until tender; drain, reserving the broth. Add the broth to the oyster stock (should measure about 2 cups) and then add the milk and cream (reserving a little cream to whip for garnish.) Heat the butter, then whisk in the flour to make a roux. Add the stock mixture to the roux, and stir briskly until thickened and smooth. Add a little nutmeg, a pinch of curry powder, the lemon juice, Worcestershire, and cayenne.

On a recent visit to the Bluffton Oyster Company, I was told we could not photograph the Gullah women oyster shuckers. They believe it takes their soul if their picture is taken. Photograph by Bob Ovelman.

THE LOWCOUNTRY CUISINE IS RICH with the bounty of its waterways; the celebrated blue crabs, the fresh ocean shrimp, the fish and those sweet briny oysters. For years, Lowcountry hostesses have gilded special dinners with oyster bisque.

Savannah's most sought after caterer, the late Lucille Wright, brought perfection to the most perfect party. For years party goers nibbled on her cheese straws, ate her marinated shrimp, and enjoyed her famous tomato pie. After a bite or two, guests would know this was made by Lucille. There was just something different – she added her special touches to all her recipes. Legend has it that if you were planning a party and couldn't get Lucille, you'd have to postpone the party. Her distinctive cuisine became the very heart and soul of this region, and its ambiance and flavors have stayed with me over a lifetime.

Mash the oysters with the celery and onions and mix well; add to oyster stock. Keep warm over hot water until time to serve. Whip the reserved cream. Pour bisque into individual bowls. Swirl an even portion of whipped cream into each bowl. Add a little paprika and chopped parsley to garnish. Add a little sherry, if desired. This is positively fabulous!

Government regulations have made the work of shucking oysters harder because they require shucking rooms to be kept cold. Standing on a sloping cement floor, the workers use small space heaters to warm their feet as they open the cold, sharp shells.

www.mycarolinacooking.com

Sunny Morning, oil on canvas by Marilyn Simandles.

Tuscan Bean Soup

½ cup navy beans, soaked overnight, drained and rinsed

½ cup cannelini beans, soaked overnight, drained and rinsed

3 tablespoons olive oil

2 cups sweet onions, diced

1 cup diced celery

1 cup diced carrots

4 cloves garlic, sliced

Salt and freshly ground black pepper

One 14-ounce can diced tomatoes

One 14-ounce can chick peas, drained and rinsed

2 quarts chicken stock, plus extra water if needed

2 sprigs rosemary

3 sprigs thyme

1 sprig oregano

2 bay leaves

1 teaspoon red chili flakes

4 cups fresh baby spinach

1 loaf crusty sourdough bread

Parmigiano-Reggiano, grated

Place the navy beans and cannellini beans in a pot, add water to cover by 2 inches and bring to a boil. Simmer for 45 minutes or until tender. Use the same process for the cannellini beans.

In a large pot, heat the olive oil and add the pancetta, rendering the fat and cooking until slightly crispy for about 3 minutes. Sauté the onion, celery, carrot and garlic for several minutes. Season with salt and pepper to taste. Add the diced tomatoes, the cooked and drained navy beans, cannellini beans, chick peas, and the chicken stock. Using kitchen twine, tie the herbs and the bay leaves into a bundle and add to the pot. Season with the red chili flakes, salt and pepper. Cook for 20 minutes, then add the spinach. Continue cooking until the beans are tender.

TO COOK THE BREAD: Preheat the oven to 350° and drizzle olive oil over the slices. Serve the soup in large bowls with grated Parmigiano-Reggiano and a slice of toast.

River Street Lights, oil on canvas by Ray Ellis.

Garden Fresh Tomato Basil Soup

When summer gives you a bumper crop of tomatoes, make soup! I have a big problem each summer – I grow too many tomatoes! Not willing to let anything so wonderful go to waste, I scour books and magazines trying to come up with a tasty way to use them all.

This soup is one I like to call "summer style" because I skip the cream. I found that by reserving a pound of chopped tomatoes to add to the finished soup just before serving, I end up with a soup bursting with flavor from the pieces of fresh tomato.

5 pounds sun ripened tomatoes, cored and quartered, plus one pound, cored and diced

2 sweet onions, chopped

6-8 garlic cloves, peeled and let remain whole; 1 clove minced

3 tablespoons extra virgin olive oil

Salt and freshly ground black pepper

Sugar to taste

1 cup chopped fresh basil

Heat oven to 450°. Combine the quartered tomatoes, onions, whole garlic cloves, oil, salt and pepper, and sugar in a large roasting pan. Roast, stirring once or twice until tomatoes are brown in spots, about 1 ½ hours. Let cool several minutes. Working in 2 batches, process roasted tomato mixture in food processor until smooth.

When ready to serve, combine the diced tomatoes, a clove of minced garlic, fresh basil and a little salt in a bowl to marinate for an hour.

Transfer to a large saucepan, add pureed tomato mixture and simmer over medium heat until diced tomatoes are slightly softened, about 5 minutes. Season with salt and pepper and sugar to taste. Serve. Yields: 4-5 servings.

Crab Bisque

No visit to Savannah would be complete without an evening spent at Elizabeth's on Thirty-Seventh, where award winning chef, Elizabeth Terry, elevates Southern cooking to a new level of excellence. In searching through mother's old wooden recipe box, I came across the recipe for crab bisque served at Elizabeth's, written many years ago in mother's distinctive flowery scroll. This sumptuous soup is a Lowcountry specialty and can serve as an elegant first course for a formal dinner or, with rolls and a salad, as a main dish for lunch or a family supper.

6 tablespoons butter

1 cup minced green onion

½ cup minced celery

1 tablespoon minced carrot

6 tablespoons flour

2 ½ cups milk

2 ½ cups chicken broth

¼ teaspoon nutmeg

¼ teaspoon white pepper

Dash of cayenne pepper

1 cup cream

¼ cup sherry

1 pound claw crabmeat

Fresh parsley or mint leaves for garnish

Melt butter over low heat in a saucepan. Add onion, celery and carrot and cover. Steam 5 minutes or until tender. Whisk in flour and cook 2 minutes. Whisk in milk and broth. Bring to a boil, whisking occasionally. Add nutmeg, white pepper, cayenne pepper, cream, sherry and crab. Garnish and serve immediately. Serves 12.

Pimento Cheese, Caviar of the South!

Private Thoughts, oil on canvas by Joe Bowler.

When marsh grass turns from green to gleaming gold and brightly colored pumpkins greet us at every turn, we know that autumn has arrived. I love that first crisp day of autumn after the long months of summer heat. It won't be long now until a drive through the country will show fields of neat bales of hay and pumpkins piled high at roadside stands.

Remember the days in the old South when ladies enjoyed afternoon tea and gathered with friends, relaxed, and caught up on the latest news in town? This is when the silver was polished and tea plates were neatly stacked with a folded napkin between each one. Tea sandwiches were always served, with pimento cheese on a variety of breads, without crusts, which were cut into neat little triangles.

Today you'd be hard pressed to find a church picnic or family reunion where pimento cheese isn't a part of the occasion. Lots of people know how to make it, but few know the real secrets to making the finest this side of the Mason Dixon line. Known as the Caviar of the South, it has a lot in common with grits. It's a food that's widely misunderstood and often unfairly maligned. Like grits, pimento cheese is little known outside the South. And folks who have never eaten it are reluctant to try even the tiniest bite.

Those who are brave enough to try it normally discover that they have been culturally — or, perhaps, culinarily — deprived.

RECIPE

This recipe has been handed down through the years and is delicious in a sandwich, on toasted wheat bread, on a hamburger or veggie burger in place of sliced cheese or simply served on a cracker.

One 3-ounce package cream cheese, room temperature

1 ½ cups grated sharp cheddar cheese

½ cup grated Monterey Jack cheese

½ cup good mayonnaise

¼ teaspoon freshly ground black pepper

¼ teaspoon garlic salt

4 tablespoons pimentos, crushed

3 teaspoons grated onion

cayenne pepper (optional)

Using a food processor or a mixer, beat cream cheese until it is smooth and fluffy. Add all the remaining ingredients and beat until well blended. Keep in the refrigerator.

www.mycarolinacooking.com

Creamy Mushroom Soup

Mushrooms used to be one item I could leave out of my grocery cart. I think I just didn't have any real good idea what to do with them. Then I tasted this incredible mushroom soup – unlike any of the tasteless ones I'd had before. This recipe is a luxurious, yet earthy, grand tribute to the mushroom. This soup will take center stage for just about any meal you wish to serve!

16 ounces white button mushrooms, sliced

8 ounces cremini mushrooms, sliced (baby Portobello)

1 large onion, diced

3 tablespoons olive oil

6 tablespoons butter, divided

2 stalks celery, diced

2 sprigs fresh thyme

7 tablespoons all purpose flour

6 cups chicken stock

½ cup heavy cream

½ cup chopped parsley

Heat oil and 4 tablespoons of butter in a large soup pot set over medium heat. Add the onion and celery, season lightly with salt and pepper, and cook until softened. Add remaining butter, thyme and mushrooms, and cook until just softened, about 3 minutes. Season again with salt and pepper.

Remove a few mushroom slices and set aside to reserve for a garnish. Add flour, and stir forcefully until completely combined, and cook another 3 minutes or until the flour turns a light blond color. Add stock, bring to a boil, and then reduce to a simmer.

Let simmer uncovered for 15 to 20 minutes. Remove and discard thyme sprigs. Remove from heat, and puree soup until smooth by using either an immersion blender or a food processor. Return pureed soup to heat. Add cream and parsley; heat through. Taste and season again with salt and pepper. Serve with reserved mushrooms as garnish. Yields: 6 servings.

Girl Star, photograph by Bob Ovelman.

Meeting Street Crab Tassies

Tassies are little cream cheese pastry tarts. Most are filled with a rich, golden pecan custard, but in this case they are little savory and highly addictive tarts filled with crab, herbs and cheese. They absolutely melt in your mouth with their rich goodness.

1 stick unsalted butter, softened

3 ounces cream cheese, softened

4 ounces all purpose flour

1 pound claw crabmeat

¼ teaspoon salt

½ teaspoon seasoning salt

½ cup mayonnaise

1 tablespoon freshly squeezed lemon juice

½ cup grated Swiss cheese

¼ cup fresh dill weed, chopped

¼ cup minced flat leaf parsley

2 medium green onions, minced

½ teaspoon Worcestershire sauce

Dash of Tabasco sauce

1 teaspoon good sherry

Paprika

Cream the butter and cream cheese together until light and fluffy. Stir in the flour and shape the dough into 24 equal balls, Chill for 1 hour, then press into the cups of a non-stick or lightly buttered mini pan to form shells.

Position a rack in the center of the oven and preheat it to 350°. Pick over the crabmeat for bits of shell and mix it with the remaining ingredients except the paprika. Divide the filling among the prepared pastries, mounding it in the center and sprinkle lightly with paprika. Bake until golden brown, about 30 minutes. Let cool somewhat before taking them from the pan. They can be made ahead, covered and refrigerated or frozen. Reheat on an ungreased baking sheet at 350°.

Crab, watercolor on paper by Nancy Ricker Rhett.

Pan-Seared Lowcountry Crab Cakes.

Pan-Seared Lowcountry Crab Cakes

1 pound crab meat, drained and flaked

1 egg, lightly beaten

¼ cup minced red bell pepper

4 teaspoons mayonnaise

2 teaspoons prepared mustard

⅛ teaspoon cayenne pepper

Salt and freshly ground black pepper

2 tablespoons plain bread crumbs

Unbleached all-purpose flour for coating

Olive oil for sautéing

In a large bowl combine the crab meat, egg, bell pepper, mayonnaise, prepared mustard, cayenne pepper, salt and pepper and gently mix. Use just enough of the bread crumbs to bind the crab meat mixture together. Shape into four cakes and coat with the flour.

Heat a small amount of olive oil in a skillet until very hot. Add the crab cakes to the skillet and cook until golden brown on both sides. Serve warm with Lowcountry Aioli (page 101). Yields: 4 crab cakes.

Bay Street Mushroom Puffs

Two 8-ounce cans crescent rolls

8-ounces cream cheese, softened

One 4-ounce can mushrooms, drained and chopped

2 green onions, chopped

1 teaspoon salt

1 egg, beaten

2 tablespoons poppy seeds

Once you unroll the crescent roll dough, you will see the perforations. Press to seal, forming two rectangles. Mix the cream cheese, mushrooms, green onions and seasoned salt in a bowl until combined. Spread the cream cheese mixture evenly over the two rectangles and roll like a jelly roll to enclose the filling. Cut each roll into 1 inch slices.

Arrange the slices cut side up in a single layer on a baking sheet. Brush with the egg and sprinkle with poppy seeds. Bake at 375° for 10 minutes. Serve hot. Yields: 4 dozen puffs.

Sea Island Crab Stuffed Mushrooms

Morel mushrooms are the "king" of all mushrooms. They have a thick stem, bulky cap, and are absolutely delicious! Use them whenever you can.

12 ounces mushrooms, cleaned and stems removed

1 pound lump crabmeat, picked clean of shells and ligaments

1 garlic clove, minced

¼ pound pepper jack cheese, grated

1 teaspoon Worcestershire sauce

½ teaspoon salt

¼ cup mayonnaise

2 ounces Parmigiano-Reggiano cheese, grated

Preheat oven to 350°. Place mushroom caps on a baking sheet lined with parchment paper. In a large bowl, mix together crabmeat, garlic, and pepper jack cheese, Worcestershire sauce, cayenne pepper, salt, mayonnaise and Parmigiano-Reggiano cheese. Place a heaping tablespoon of the crab mixture into the cap of each mushroom. Bake the mushroom caps for 30 minutes. Serve at once.

> When serving hors d'oeuvres on a platter, it's better to serve small platters which can easily be refilled rather than one large platter that will look sparse as it is depleted.

Seafarer's Oyster and Crab Bake

One 8-ounce package cream cheese

1 cup Parmesan cheese

1 pound crabmeat, picked clean of cartilage

Salt and freshly ground black pepper

1 clove garlic, minced

1 small onion, minced

1 cup cooked and chopped crispy bacon

¼ cup chopped fresh basil

1 dozen oysters on the half shell

Preheat oven to 350°. Combine the cream cheese, Parmesan, crabmeat, salt, pepper, garlic, onion, bacon and basil. Place oysters on a baking sheet and carefully spoon the mixture onto the oysters in the half shell, putting a rounded mound on each. Bake for 10 minutes until nicely browned and bubbly.

Carolina Pickled Shrimp

4 pounds fresh shrimp

8 large sweet onions, sliced thin

1½ cups canola oil

2 cups white vinegar

⅓ cup capers, drained

1½ tablespoons tomato paste

1½ teaspoons sugar

⅓ cup prepared horseradish

Salt and freshly ground black pepper

¼ teaspoon red pepper

In a very large glass container, place a layer of shrimp and a layer of onion rings, alternating layers until all are used. In a bowl, combine the oil, vinegar, capers, tomato paste, sugar, horseradish, salt and pepper and red pepper until well blended. Pour all the sauce over the shrimp; cover the jar and refrigerate overnight. Pickled shrimp will last up to one week in the refrigerator.

> Shrimp season runs from mid-June until mid-January. The S.C. Department of Natural Resources determines specific opening and closing dates each year. Oysters, clams, and mussels are in season from mid-September to mid-May. Crabbing is done year round.

May River Morning, oil on canvas by Michael Harrell.

Seafood Ceviche

3-6 cucumbers

1 pound bay scallops

⅛ cup extra virgin olive oil

1 tablespoon freshly chopped cilantro leaves

½ papaya, peeled, seeded and diced very small

1 mango, peeled, seeded, and diced very small

1 lemon, juiced

3 limes

¼ red onion, diced very small

Dash of cayenne pepper

Salt and freshly ground black pepper, to taste

Caviar - optional

In a large mixing bowl, mix the onion, lime juice, lemon juice, mango, papaya, cilantro and olive oil. Season mixture with the cayenne pepper, salt and pepper and stir in the scallops immersing them completely in the marinade. Cover and refrigerate for at least 8 hours. The acids in the marinade will actually "cook" the scallops.

Peel cucumbers and cut into ¼-inch thick slices. Strain scallop mixture and spoon onto cucumber disks. Dot with caviar, if desired.

This recipe is one I treasure from my years living in South Florida, where we enjoyed the very freshest seafood the year round. Mangos and papayas were always plentiful and delicious. However, when these fruits are not available, peaches and other seasonal fruits may be substituted and this appetizer retains its wonderful refreshing flavor!

The Great Bruschetta Caper

Olive oil

1 red bell pepper, seeds removed and sliced into thin strips

1 yellow bell pepper, seeds removed and sliced into thin strips

¾ teaspoon sugar

1½ tablespoons capers, drained

3 tablespoons julienned fresh basil leaves

3-4 ounces blue cheese

Salt and freshly ground black pepper

1 baguette

Preheat the oven to 375°. Heat several tablespoons olive oil in a sauté pan over medium heat. Add the pepper and cook until soft, about 15 minutes. Sprinkle with the sugar and continue cooking for several more minutes. Stir in the capers and basil, and season to taste with salt and pepper. Set aside.

Slice the baguette crosswise into 18 thin round slices. Brush the bread rounds lightly with olive oil on one side. Arrange them in rows, oil side up, on a sheet pan lined with parchment paper and toast in the oven until lightly browned.

Top each toast round with a teaspoonful of the pepper mixture. Place blue cheese on top and return to the oven for a couple minutes to warm through. Serve immediately.

Cheese en Croûte

Flavorful herb cheese spread encased in savory puff pastry.

1 teaspoon Dijon mustard

One 12-ounce package Havarti cheese

1 teaspoon dried parsley

½ teaspoon dried chives

¼ teaspoon dried dill weed

¼ teaspoon dried basil

¼ teaspoon fennel seeds

Half (17¼-ounce) a package frozen puff pastry, thawed

Assorted crackers

Spread Dijon mustard over top of Havarti cheese and sprinkle with parsley, chives, dill weed, basil and fennel. Place cheese, mustard side down, in center of puff pastry. Wrap package style, trimming excess pastry. Gently press along seam to seal. Place seam side down on lightly greased baking sheet. Brush with egg and chill for 30 minutes. Bake at 350° for 20 minutes. Brush with egg and bake an additional 10 minutes or until golden brown. Serve with assorted crackers.

Cheese Wheel, oil on linen by Shannon Smith.

www.mycarolinacooking.com

She Crab Soup

McClellanville Oak, oil on linen by Betty Anglin Smith.

THE NAMES OF SOME of our Lowcountry dishes are as colorful and exciting as the fresh local ingredients that go into them: names like Frogmore stew, she-crab soup and hoppin' john.

She-crab soup is considered by many to be Charleston's quintessential dish. The soup is so named because eggs from the female crab give it a unique taste. This creamy delicacy is almost always flavored with a generous helping of sherry.

She-crab soup is said to have originated with Blanche Rhett, wife of South Carolina Governor Goodwyn Rhett. She asked her butler William Deas to dress up his crab soup in honor of President Taft. He made this simple bisque into a legend by stirring in crab roe. She-crab, as it came to be called, became Deas' trademark when he later cooked at Everett's Restaurant, and has since been indelibly associated with Charleston.

The recipe for this soup I've enjoyed for so many years is from the original Charleston Receipts cookbook, published by the Junior League of Charleston in 1950. I haven't found a recipe yet that's any better!

RECIPE

1 tablespoon butter
1 quart whole milk
¼ pint cream (whipped)
Few drops onion juice
⅛ teaspoon pepper
½ teaspoon Worcestershire
1 teaspoon flour
2 cups white crab meat
Several tablespoons crab eggs
½ teaspoon salt
4 tablespoons dry sherry

Melt butter in top of double boiler and blend with flour until smooth. Add the milk gradually, stirring constantly. To this add crab meat and eggs and all seasoning except sherry. Cook slowly over hot water for 20 minutes. To serve, place one tablespoon of warmed sherry in individual soup bowls, then add soup and top with whipped cream. Sprinkle with paprika or finely chopped parsley. Secret: if unable to obtain "she-crabs," crumble the yolk of hard boiled eggs in the bottom of soup plates. Serves 4 to 6.

Savannah Cheese Straws

1 pound New York sharp cheddar cheese, grated

½ cup butter, softened

1 ½ cups all-purpose flour

1 teaspoon baking powder

¼ teaspoon baking powder

¼ teaspoon salt

¼ teaspoon cayenne pepper or to taste

Preheat oven to 300°. Cream together cheese and butter. Sift together flour, baking powder, salt and cayenne pepper. Add dry ingredients to creamed mixture. Knead well. Shape dough into logs, cover and chill 8 hours. Cut into ¼ inch slices and place on ungreased baking sheets. Bake at 350° for 15 minutes. Cool on wire racks. Store in an airtight container.

Vidalia Onion Dip

From the Vidalia Onion Cookbook, Vidalia, Georgia

12 ounces Jarlsburg cheese, shredded

2 cup sliced Vidalia onions

2 cup mayonnaise

Combine the cheese, mayonnaise and onions in a bowl and mix well. Spoon the cheese mixture into a baking dish. Bake at 350° for 25 minutes. Serve warm with your favorite crackers. Serves 8.

NOTE: Back before Vidalia onions became available in our local markets, we'd buy them from a local gentleman from Lucy Creek who drove his pickup truck to Georgia each spring and came back to town with the back of the truck filled with bags of those sweet, sweet onions.

The Perfect Mint Julep

3 cups water

3 cups mint leaves fresh from the garden, lightly packed

2 cups sugar

1 cup bourbon

Sprigs of fresh mint for garnish

To make syrup, combine water, mint and sugar in a heavy saucepan. Bring to a boil over medium heat, stirring constantly until sugar dissolves. Boil gently for 3 minutes. Remove from the heat, cover and chill at least 3 hours. When ready to serve, strain syrup into a bowl or pitcher, pressing into leaves to extract flavors. Discard the mint.

For individual drinks, fill tall frosted glasses or silver julep cups with finely crushed ice. Add 1 to 1 ½ jiggers of syrup and 1 to 1 ½ jiggers of bourbon to each glass. Stir gently and garnish with fresh mint. Yields: 8-10 servings.

Wassail Punch

Cloves and cinnamon dress up a blend of fruit juices for special occasions. This is a recipe I was given on a Christmas Tour of Homes in Charleston.

2 quarts apple cider

2 cups orange juice

2 cups pineapple juice

½ cup sugar

½ cup lemon juice

12 whole cloves

4 cinnamon sticks

Orange slices and cranberries for garnish

Bring the first seven ingredients to a boil in a large kettle. Reduce the heat and simmer, uncovered for about 15 minutes.

Discard cinnamon and cloves. Garnish with orange slices and cranberries, if desired. Serve warm in your favorite Christmas cups. Yields: 3 ½ quarts or 14 servings.

Stuffed Artichoke Bottoms

Makes a delicious brunch served with salad and bread.

One 7 ½-ounce can artichoke bottoms

¼ cup butter

2 shallots, finely chopped

2 fresh mushrooms, thinly sliced

2 ounces prosciutto, finely chopped

2 teaspoons parsley, minced

2 teaspoons flour

⅓ cup milk

Freshly ground black pepper

Sherry

2-3 ounces shredded Gruyere cheese

Butter

Sauté artichoke bottoms in butter briefly on each side. Remove artichokes from the pan and sauté shallots and mushrooms, and prosciutto. Add parsley, stir in flour, and cook over low heat for 2 minutes, stirring constantly. Remove from heat and stir in milk. Return to heat and stir until thickened and smooth. Season to taste with pepper and sherry. Fill artichoke bottoms with mixture, sprinkle with cheese, and dot with butter. Run under the broiler until cheese is melted and bubbly. Yields: 5 -7 servings or may be cut in half and served as appetizers.

Sweet Tea – Champagne of the South

Cat Island Marsh, oil on linen by Peter Rolf.

HERE IN THE SOUTH where good manners are still considered an important part of everyday life, we can say just about anything about anybody as long as we follow the comment with, "Well, bless her heart."

If you're in South Carolina and you purchase your sweet tea in a can – well, bless your heart! It's a sure sign you're not from here. The North and the South are not divided so much by the Mason-Dixon Line as we are by the sweet tea line. Sweet tea is as basic to our way of life as our magnolia trees.

South Carolinians love their iced tea and are pretty much fanatical about it. Why, I've known folks to judge a restaurant as desirable or not based upon the way they make their sweet tea. A barbecue place without sweet tea doesn't even qualify as authentic anything. Sweet tea, white bread and slaw – that's the key to a good barbecue place.

A cold glass of iced tea is the first thing we offer a guest in our home. It's how we make friends, family and neighbors feel welcome. I believe it was Prohibition that marked the start of the iced tea era, when we did away with most of the alcohol. Think about the 1930s when ice delivery came about, and a nice cold glass of tea became as common on the South Carolina table as white linen.

Now, just because we love iced tea doesn't mean we know how to make it. I've been to many restaurants where they serve up a liquid that is barely amber in color with a few fast melting ice cubes and, worst of all, a thin circle of lemon perched on the rim of the glass. Just try to squeeze that little lemon circle. It's an impossible task! I just want to impress upon those north of the Mason-Dixon Line and west of Texas, that making great iced tea is a simple thing.

Here's an easy formula I learned from Nathalie Dupree. Pat Conroy calls her "the Queen of the Southern kitchen."

RECIPE

Take 6 small tea bags and a pot of water. Bring the water to a boil but just barely; turn off the stove and let it steep for several hours. Add a pinch of baking soda to keep it from turning cloudy. Squeeze the tea bags to extract all the goodness, pour the tea in a cold pitcher. Add enough water to make 2 quarts.

To sweeten the tea, make a syrup by bringing 1 cup sugar and 1 cup water to a boil and turn off the stove. Stir until sugar dissolves. Pour this into the pitcher of tea and add lemon and a touch of mint, if desired. Serve over ice and enjoy! Yields: 2 quarts.

www.mycarolinacooking.com

A La Carte, oil on canvas by John Carroll Doyle.

Broiled Figs with Prosciutto and Gorgonzola

Enjoy fresh figs when they are in season, from the end of July through about the middle of August. This is a delicious way to enjoy them.

1 cup balsamic vinegar

20 large figs

5 ounces gorgonzola

10 thin slices prosciutto, cut into halves lengthwise

Bring the vinegar to a boil in a small saucepan and reduce the heat. Simmer until reduced to the consistency of syrup. Cool to room temperature.

Cut an X in the top of each fig, cutting halfway through the fig. Stuff with the cheese. Wrap each fig with a piece of prosciutto and arrange on a greased baking sheet. Broil in a preheated oven until the cheese melts. Drizzle with the balsamic reduction to serve and garnish with parsley. You can prepare these a day in advance and simply place under the broiler at serving time.

Black-Eyed Pea Hummus

Hummus is one of my all-time favorite foods. It's something I can eat on almost anything, including raw veggies, pita chips, some endive leaves or straight out of the bowl! For years I made it with chickpeas, but now that I've tried the version with black eyed peas — that's it! It is so flavorful, but still has that true taste of hummus. Sweet potato chips with black-eyed pea hummus is a winning combination.

2 cloves garlic

4 cups cooked black-eyed peas, rinsed and drained

¼ cup fresh lemon juice

¼ cup olive oil

1 teaspoon salt

½ teaspoon ground black pepper

½ cup tahini

In a food processor with the motor running, add the garlic. When chopped, add the black eyed peas, lemon juice, olive oil, salt and pepper. Process until smooth. With the processor running, add tahini and process until all ingredients come together. Taste and adjust seasonings. If too thick, add additional lemon juice or oil.

Daffodil picking time is how we know it's nearly spring in the Lowcountry. Fields in Bluffton and Beaufort open for public picking each year and it's a rite of spring in this region. In Beaufort the Trask family opens their fields of daffodils planted on Cane Island in the late 1960s. In Bluffton, the Merricks open their fields on Calhoun Plantation in Pinckney Colony. On a walk through the cemetery surrounding the Parish Church of St. Helena in Beaufort, I noticed a tribute to the lifetime achievements of John M. Trask Sr. His tombstone reads: "He's noted as a farmer, landowner, businessman, political figure, respected employer, hunter and saltwater fisherman. And then this: "Near the end of his life he grew daffodils on Cane Island and enjoyed opening his fields to the community." Daffodil Farm, oil on canvas by Ray Ellis.

Bacon-Mushroom Dip

3 dried porcini mushrooms

½ cup boiling water

8 slices thick cut bacon

1 large leek (white and pale-green parts only, halved lengthwise, thinly sliced crosswise, and washed

4 cloves garlic, minced

1 pound cremini, white, or shitake mushrooms, cleaned and chopped

1 teaspoon salt

¼ teaspoon freshly ground pepper

1½ teaspoons finely chopped fresh thyme

1 package cream cheese, softened

2 cups sour cream

3 tablespoons sliced scallions, dark green parts only

In a bowl, soak porcini in the boiling water until soft, about 20 minutes. Working over the bowl, lift out porcini, and squeeze out liquid. Coarsely chop porcini. Pour liquid through a fine sieve into another bowl, and reserve.

Cook bacon in a large skillet over medium heat until crisp, about 5 minutes per side. Drain on paper towels. Pour off rendered bacon fat, reserving ¼ cup. Wipe skillet clean. Coarsely chop bacon.

Return 3 tablespoons bacon fat to skillet. Add leek and garlic and cook over medium heat, stirring occasionally, until translucent, about 2 minutes. Add fresh mushrooms and porcini, then the salt and pepper. Raise heat to high, cook, stirring until mushrooms are tender 5 to 8 minutes. Add thyme; cook 2 more minutes. Transfer to a plate and cool.

With an electric mixer, whisk cream cheese in a bowl until smooth. Gradually add sour cream, whisk until smooth. By hand, stir in mushrooms, three quarters of the bacon, scallions, and 2 tablespoons porcini liquid. If necessary, add more porcini liquid to reach desired consistency.

Garnish dip with scallions and remaining bacon. If desired, cook sliced mushrooms in remaining tablespoon of bacon fat in a medium skillet over medium heat, stirring occasionally, until golden brown, about 2 minutes. Use these as a garnish on top. Serve with chips or your favorite crackers or pita bread.

Mixed Greens with Truffle Oil Dressing

TRUFFLE OIL DRESSING
(I use white Truffle Oil)

2 tablespoons white truffle oil

1 ½ tablespoons extra virgin olive oil

1 tablespoon champagne wine vinegar

¼ teaspoon fresh squeezed lemon juice

½ teaspoon sea salt

Freshly ground black pepper to taste

SALAD INGREDIENTS

2 small heads of baby spinach leaves, stems removed and torn into bite sized pieces

1 small bunch fresh basil leaves, stems removed and torn into bite sized pieces

Onion slices – optional

Sea salt

In a large bowl, toss the spinach and basil leaves with the truffle dressing. Place salad mixture on individual plates and sprinkle with sea salt and freshly ground black pepper.

Photograph by Bob Ovelman.

ADD SOME PIZZAZZ to your everyday cooking with truffle oil! My friend, photographer Bob Ovelman of Hilton Head, advised me about all the delicious truffle oils he's discovered and how he uses them. Mixed green salad made with truffle oil dressing gives a whole new meaning to salads. There's something about it that makes you want to throw away your fork and eat the salad with your fingers! Flavors become sensual and utterly irresistible and command a magical place in your culinary palette.

Did you know truffle oil is top quality olive oil that has been infused with either white or black truffles? Both types of truffles have an earthy, mushroom like flavor. Originally, it was created when truffles were soaked in olive oil. Before commercial truffle oil was introduced in the 1980s, chefs in Italy and France traditionally made their own by steeping tiny bits of truffles in high quality olive oil. It's a finishing oil as opposed to a cooking oil. In other words, it's more of a flavoring or seasoning – it adds a burst of flavor – and should only be used lightly on your foods or dishes. For instance, it can be drizzled over foods. Experiment by adding a little truffle oil to some of your favorite dishes.

Goat Cheese and Truffle Oil Crostini

24 (1 ¼ inch thick) diagonally cut baguette bread slices

Extra virgin olive oil

1 clove garlic

8 ounces goat cheese

Truffle oil

Freshly ground fresh thyme leaves

black pepper, freshly ground

Arrange bread slices on a baking sheet. Brush with olive oil and bake about 6 minutes. Remove from oven and rub the toasted bread with the garlic clove on the cut side. Cool. Just before serving, spread each slice of toasted bread with a thin layer of goat cheese. Pour a small amount of truffle oil into a teaspoon and tilt the spoon to sprinkle several drops on each toast. Sprinkle black pepper over the top and garnish with a few thyme leaves.

If you have difficulty finding truffle oils and butters locally, you may order them from amazon.com, cooking.com, DeanDeluca.com or, if you are fortunate enough to live in the Lowcountry, stop by the Village at Wexford and visit the Oilerie, a fascinating new olive oil bar.

Lowcountry Shrimp Cocktail

Here's a delicious way to prepare those fresh-from-the-sea shrimp when you want to preserve as much of their natural taste as possible. This method is from Bob Ovelman who swears by it and has been fixing shrimp this way for years, with rave reviews!

1½ pounds of shrimp

3 cans of beer

1 (10 ounce) bottle of white vinegar

1 cup chopped celery

A dash of dry mustard

2 tablespoons Old Bay Seasoning

2 tablespoons Black Pepper

Note that there is no water used in this recipe. Bring all ingredients except the shrimp to a boil; add shrimp and cook just until it begins to boil again. Pour off liquid and drain in a colander. Refrigerate several hours before serving. Serve chilled with your favorite sauce.

COCKTAIL SAUCE

1 (6 ounce) bottle of chile sauce

1 tablespoon horseradish

1 tablespoon Worcestershire sauce

Juice of ½ lemon

Caramel Pecan Brie

1 4 inch Brie round

4 sheets frozen phyllo pastry, thawed

¼ cup hot caramel topping (Smuckers works well)

4 tablespoons butter melted

¼ cup chopped, glazed pecans

Your favorite crackers, graham crackers and Granny Smith apple slices

Preheat oven to 350°. trim rind from top of Brie round; set aside.

Cut 1 (9 inch) square of heavy duty aluminum foil and place it on a baking sheet. Unfold the phyllo dough. Cut phyllo into an 8½ inch square, cutting through all layers. Place 1 sheet of phyllo on aluminum square. Brush sheet with some of the melted butter. Repeat process with remaining phyllo and butter to make 4 layers on the aluminum square. Place Brie round in the center of the phyllo square. Bring the edges of foil up, pressing lightly against Brie, to form a phyllo bowl for Brie, using the foil to hold up the phyllo.

Spoon the caramel topping over the Brie round, spreading to the edges. Sprinkle evenly with pecans. Bake for 10 minutes, or until phyllo is lightly browned. Remove from the oven, and let it stand for 5 minutes.

Gently peel back the foil. Using a wide spatula, transfer phyllo wrapped Brie to the serving dish. Serve with graham crackers, Granny Smith apple slices and your favorite crackers.

Best Ever Queso Dip

2 (8 ounce packages) cream cheese

2 (8 ounce) blocks Fontina cheese, shredded

1 (8 ounce) block white Cheddar cheese, shredded

1 (4 ounce) package goat cheese, softened

2 tablespoons butter

1 tablespoon minced garlic

4 large poblano peppers, seeded and chopped

1 (24 ounce) jar roasted red peppers, drained and chopped

1 (12 ounce) jar roasted red peppers, drained and chopped

1 bunch green onions, chopped

1½ cups heavy whipping cream

1 teaspoon red pepper

1 teaspoon garlic powder

1 teaspoon salt

In a heavy pot, heat butter over low heat until melted. Add garlic and cook for one minute while stirring constantly. Add peppers and green onions. Cook over medium high heat for 8 minutes, stirring frequently, until tender. Add cream, red pepper, garlic powder, and salt, stirring to combine. Reduce heat to medium-low. Add cheeses, stirring until cheese is melted. Serve with your favorite tortilla chips. Yields: 10 to 12 servings.

Alligator, photograph by Bob Ovelman.

This amazing, docile looking predator has skills and abilities that have allowed it to outlive dinosaurs, mammoths and saber-toothed cats.

Being a cold blooded animal, the gator's body temperature reflects the environment which he inhabits. So, when it's cold, he's cold and vice versa. Their presence often signals the end of winter when they climb out of hibernation.

Don't be surprised if you see alligator tail on the menu at some local restaurants!

Breads and Brunches

The simple act of tying on an apron connects us to the generations of Southern women who have shown love to their families with delicious home cooked meals. Every recipe card splattered and yellowed with age is a treasured keepsake that connects us to our mothers and grandmothers and cherished friends.

When I was growing up, I truly loved my grandmother's big, Southern country breakfasts. She would put out salty country him, sausage cream gravy, bacon, eggs, fried apples, homemade apple butter, biscuits, and just about anything else you could think of to put on a biscuit. I've always been mystified by how she made these biscuits without ever measuring a single ingredient. She mixed them up in a big wooden bowl using only her hands. Flour would be flying all over the place as she calmly went about her task. Just anticipating that first piece, hot and dripping with farm fresh butter, was a sheer delight! Then she'd pinch off pieces of dough and shape them in her hands, never using a cutter. I tried to use her technique many times but could never quite get it down.

The heavenly aroma of baking bread drifting throughout the house takes me back to that place where time moved more slowly. Mother always made her own hushpuppies and they were delicious!

Hushpuppies are truly some of the finest Southern fixins' you'll ever eat. There are several versions of how the name "hush puppy" came to be. Most I've read have to do with keeping a dog quiet with fried cornmeal balls. Legend says that hunters and trappers traveling with their hunting dogs would keep them quiet with cornmeal batter fried in their iron pots over an open fire. As they threw these to the dogs they said, "Hush puppy."

Still another version comes from the time when Atlanta was occupied by Federal troops. There, a cook at one of the hotels used a plateful of fried cornmeal balls to hush a puppy. The name was cute, so it stuck.

Most likely, the name and the practice came about in the old days from the need to transport food from the kitchen to the main houses. In those days, kitchens were detached to help prevent fires from spreading to the main houses. Everyone had dogs loose in the yards for protection. Therefore, it was quite difficult to carry the food without being knocked down. Fried cornmeal balls carried in pockets could be tossed out as far as possible, allowing enough time to get across the yard. As the balls were tossed, the cooks called out "Hush puppy, Hush puppy."

To this day, cornmeal is a staple in the South. The Southern preference for cornbread over wheat is said to have developed during the Civil War, or simply the "Wah." At that time Union blockades kept wheat from the Southern region. Since corn, which originated in Mexico three to four thousand years ago, had been cultivated for some time by the Southern colonists, this was no real hardship.

Mother knew that comfort food was all about home cooking - those special dishes that warm our souls and put smiles on our faces.

Opposite Page: Going to Church, oil on canvas by John Carroll Doyle.

Heritage Breakfast Puffs

Year after year, these have been a real crowd pleaser for brunch during the Heritage Golf Tournament, held each spring on Hilton Head Island at the famous Harbor Town Golf Course.

Two 8-count cans refrigerator crescent rolls

1 pound hot pork sausage

¼ cup minced onion

8 ounces fresh mushrooms

One 4-ounce can chopped green chiles

1 teaspoon fresh thyme

8 ounces cream cheese, chopped

1 egg white, lightly beaten

Poppy seeds to taste

Open cans of the crescent roll dough and press it over the bottom of a baking dish, pressing the perforations to seal. Brown the sausage in a large skillet, stirring until crumbly. Add the onion and sauté until tender. Add the mushrooms, green chiles, and thyme. Sauté until the mushrooms are tender; drain. Add the cream cheese to the vegetables in the skillet and cook until melted and smooth, stirring constantly. Spread the mixture over the roll dough. Roll and chill in the refrigerator until ready to bake. Brush with the egg white and sprinkle with poppy seeds. Bake at 375° for 30 minutes or until golden brown. Slice and serve while hot. Serves 12.

> November 27-30, 1969, Thanksgiving weekend, innovative Sea Pines designer Charles Fraser gave the first tournament on the newly created Harbour Town Golf Links a traditional twist by calling it the "Heritage Classic."
>
> That first tournament was won by Arnold Palmer and the course and Arnold's victory became the talk of the media.
>
> Now the tournament is played each year the week after the Masters in April. It is recognized as one of the premier golf events in the country.

Harbour Town Lighthouse, watercolor on paper by Nancy Ricker Rhett.

Apple Bacon Sausage Balls

½ cup butter or margarine

1 cup water

3 cups herb seasoned stuffing mix

4 ounces breakfast sausage, crumbled

4 ounces turkey sausage, crumbled

¼ cup shredded apple

2 cups chopped pecans

1½ pounds sliced bacon

Heat the butter or margarine in the water in a saucepan until melted. Add to the stuffing mix in a bowl and mix well. Add the breakfast sausage, turkey sausage and apple; mix well. Chill for 1 hour.

Shape by tablespoonfuls into balls and roll each ball in the chopped pecans. Cut the bacon crosswise into thirds. Wrap one piece of bacon around each ball and secure with a wooden pick. Place on a baking sheet and bake at 350° for 35 to 45 minutes or until cooked through. You can cut one of the balls in half to test for doneness. This can also be served as an appetizer.

www.mycarolinacooking.com

Farm Stand Peach Freezer Jam

Remember the days when folks sat out on front porches after dinner, greeted neighbors and simply passed away the hours before sleep with quiet conversation? They didn't bring out their Blackberry or their iPhone or answer dozens of e-mails. They just sat in their rocking chairs and talked. It's a quality of life I believe we've lost to a world of electronics and flashing screens. Maybe it's the same for canning things. While the front porch people have mostly left us, my guess is that many of the women who wore floral aprons and canned summer's produce are now sitting in front of walls of wired components.

Every summer I bring home baskets of summertime fresh peaches, blueberries, strawberries, or whatever happens to be in season at the farmers' market. There's so much goodness packed into these few months, that the desire to stretch these delicious fruits into the colder months ahead is always on my mind.

Perhaps I should stash some of summer away in jars filled with my own jams and jellies and master the art of preserving. Each year I think about standing over a hot stove sterilizing jars and it's overwhelming! What if I did something wrong and all the jars explode in the heat? The "what-ifs" have kept me mired in doubt while each summer passed by along with all its wonderful fruits and vegetables. When winter came along, I always regretted my fear of canning and started planning to conquer the fear when summer rolled around. Well, it never happened.

But I have broken through my preserving paranoia just enough so that I can take a small step along the road to heat-processed canning. I put away my Blackberry long enough to discover freezer jam!

Making freezer jam follows the same process as heat canning, with one primary thing missing – the heat. Since you store freezer jam below zero degrees, you don't need to bring the jars to a boil. What a relief to find out we can enjoy making our own jam without the element of danger that goes along with sterilization and storing at room temperature.

Besides helping my canning phobia, I discovered there was another benefit to not boiling your jam. Uncooked fruit stays much fresher than cooked preserves. When you crack open your treasure in mid-December, it will taste more like the fresh summer fruit you picked up from the farmers' market. There are a few brands of pectin that require that you use boiling water in the initial step on the stove, but isn't enough to affect the flavor or texture of your fruit.

Pectin is the fruit derived gel that holds jam together and creates a thick consistency. It's important to buy a brand of pectin that is compatible with no cook freezer jam. Read the instructions carefully, as recipes can vary from brand to brand. Different kinds of pectin call for different amounts of sugar. Freezer jams always run a little thinner than heat processed preserves, but they should still set to a nice, spreadable consistency. If you prefer a thicker jam, just heat the fruit to a boil for two minutes before freezing.

Photograph by Pat Branning.

RECIPE

This recipe yields 4 pint jars of freezer jam, truly fresh tasting and delicious.

2 ¾ cups finely chopped, peeled and pitted ripe peaches

6 ½ cups sugar (I use superfine)

2 pouches Sure Jell Liquid Pectin

½ cup fresh lemon juice

¼ teaspoon almond extract

1 vanilla bean, seeds scraped and cut into small pieces

Combine the peaches and sugar in a large mixing bowl and stir. Set aside for 10 minutes, stirring occasionally. The sugar should be nearly dissolved. In a separate bowl combine the pectin and lemon juice. Pour the pectin mixture into the peach-sugar mixture and stir constantly until the sugar is no longer grainy and is completely dissolved, about 3 minutes. Add the almond extract and the vanilla bean seeds and stir to combine. Spoon the jam into clean ½ pint or pint size jars. Place one piece of vanilla bean inside each jar. Cover the jars and let stand at room temperature until the jam is set, up to 24 hours. Place the jam in the freezer and use as needed. Freezer jam should be consumed within 1 year. Jam may also be stored in the refrigerator for up to 3 weeks.

Fallen Apples, oil on canvas by Shannon Smith.

Pecan-Apple Bread

A rich, moist texture - outstanding! Tastes like pralines on the top!

1½ cup chopped pecans, divided

1 (8 ounce) container sour cream

1 cup granulated sugar

2 large eggs, room temperature

1½ tablespoons vanilla extract

2 cups all-purpose flour

2 teaspoons baking powder

½ teaspoon baking soda

½ teaspoon salt

1½ cups finely chopped, peeled tart apples

½ cup butter

½ cup brown sugar

Preheat oven to 350°. Bake the pecans in a single layer in a pan for about 10 minutes. Beat in sour cream and next 3 ingredients with an electric mixer for 2 minutes or until blended. Stir together flour and next 3 ingredients. Add to the sour cream mixture, beating just until blended. Stir in apples and ½ cup toasted pecans. Spoon batter into a greased and floured 9x5-inch loaf pan. Sprinkle with remaining 1 cup chopped pecans. Bake at 350° for 1 hour or until a wooden pick inserted into center comes out clean. Cool before serving.

FOR TOPPING: Bring the butter and brown sugar to a boil in a 1 quart heavy saucepan over medium heat, stirring constantly. Boil for 1 minute. Remove from heat and spoon over top of bread. Cool completely. May be frozen up to 3 months.

NOTE: The toasted pecans baked into the top of this bread make it especially good. This goes well with ham and baked pineapple for brunch or a special breakfast.

Puffed Apple Pancake

Every late August, we'd take a trip to the mountains. On the way home, we'd stop at the small town market and buy North Carolina apples for this recipe.

6 large eggs

1 cup milk

2/3 cup flour

½ teaspoon salt

4 large apples, peeled, cored and sliced

4 tablespoons lemon juice

5 tablespoons butter

½ cup brown sugar, lightly packed

1 teaspoon cinnamon

Maple syrup, warmed to serve

Mix together the eggs, milk, flour, and salt. Toss the apple slices with 2 tablespoons of the lemon juice. Melt butter in a 12-inch quiche dish in a preheated oven at 415°. Remove the dish from the oven and lay the apple slices evenly over the bottom. Return to the oven until the butter sizzles. Do not let the apples brown.

Remove from the oven and immediately pour the batter over the apples. Mix together the brown sugar and cinnamon and sprinkle the mixture over the batter.

Put back in the oven for 25-30 minutes then drizzle the remaining 2 tablespoons of lemon juice over the top. Cut into portions and serve immediately with the warm maple syrup. This is truly a delicious dish! Yields: 6 to 8 servings.

BREADS AND BRUNCHES 51

Apple Fritters For Fall

Apple fritters are guaranteed to make you smile! I made a batch late yesterday – those delicious fried nuggets of cinnamon-flavored batter stuffed with flavorful Granny Smith apple chunks and dusted with powdered sugar. Serve them as a breakfast treat or as an incredible dessert with vanilla ice cream.

2 cups Granny Smith apples, peeled and diced

2 cups self rising flour

½ cup brown sugar

2 large eggs

1 cup milk

3 tablespoons melted butter

1 teaspoon cinnamon

Mix flour, sugar and cinnamon together using a fork to break up any lumps. Add in milk, melted butter and eggs. Stir well to combine. Peel and dice apples, add to batter, stirring in. Drop, by ⅛ cup fulls into hot oil and turn to allow to brown on both sides. Drain on a paper towel lined plate. Dust with confectioner's sugar, if desired. Serve hot and enjoy!

Hot Baked Fruit with Granola Nut Topping

Hot baked fruit is a perfect side dish for roasted pork and ham and lends a sweet-tart taste of four kinds of my favorite fruit. The topping gives the dish a crispy crown of yummy goodness that makes it irresistible.

2 Granny Smith apples, cored and diced

2 Sweet Delicious apples, cored and diced

2 green Anjou pears, cored and diced

One 5-ounce package dried cherries

1 cup firmly packed light brown sugar

¼ cup all purpose flour

1 teaspoon ground cinnamon

6 tablespoons butter, melted

2 cups applesauce

1 recipe Granola Nut Topping

Preheat oven to 350°. In a medium bowl, combine apples, pears, and dried cherries. In a separate bowl, combine brown sugar, flour, and cinnamon. Add melted butter to brown sugar mixture, stirring to combine. Add applesauce to brown sugar mixture, stirring to mix well. Combine brown sugar mixture and fruit mixture. Spoon into an ungreased 13 x 9-inch baking dish. Bake for 45 to 50 minutes, or until fruit is tender. Top with Granola Nut Topping.

GRANOLA NUT TOPPING
Makes 4½ cups

1 cup old fashioned oats

½ cup chopped pecans

½ cup slivered almonds

½ cup chopped walnuts

½ cup sweetened flaked coconut

1 teaspoon ground cinnamon

¼ cup butter

3 tablespoons honey

3 tablespoons light brown sugar

Preheat oven to 275°. Line a rimmed baking sheet with aluminum foil. Spray foil with nonstick cooking spray and set aside.

In a medium bowl, combine oats, pecans, almonds, walnuts, coconut, and cinnamon.

In a small saucepan, combine butter, honey, and brown sugar. Bring to a boil over medium heat, stirring until sugar is dissolved. Add butter mixture to oat mixture, stirring to combine well. Spread oat mixture in an even layer on prepared baking sheet. Bake for 35 minutes, until browned, stirring at 10 minute intervals. Store in an airtight container.

Shoreline, Low Tide, photograph by Bob Ovelman.

Roasted Vegetable Frittata

1 small zucchini, diced and sliced

2 red bell peppers, diced

1 red onion, peeled and diced

⅓ cup olive oil

Kosher salt and freshly ground black pepper

2 cloves garlic, minced

1 tablespoon butter

12 eggs

1 cup Half and Half

¼ cup Parmigiano-Reggiano cheese

⅓ cup chopped scallions, white and green parts

½ cup grated Gruyère cheese

¼ cup dry roasted pine nuts (optional)

Preheat oven to 425°. Place the zucchini, peppers, and onions on a sheet pan and drizzle with olive oil and sprinkle with 1½ teaspoon salt and about ½ teaspoon pepper. Toss well. Bake for 15 minutes. Add the garlic, toss with a spatula and bake for another 15 minutes. Once the vegetables are tender, turn the oven down to 350°. In an omelet pan, heat the butter and sauté the scallions over medium low heat for a minute. Add the roasted vegetables to the omelet pan and toss with the scallions. In a large mixing bowl, whisk together the eggs, Half and Half and the Parmigiano-Reggiano cheese. Pour the egg mixture over the vegetables and cook for 2-4 minutes in the skillet. Using a rubber spatula, lift the cooked edges and allow the uncooked eggs to flow underneath, until the eggs are almost set. Then place the skillet in the oven and bake the frittata for 20 to 30 minutes until puffed and set in the middle. Sprinkle Gruyère cheese on the top and bake a few more minutes until the cheese melts. Top it off with a sprinkling of dry roasted pine nuts. Yields: 8 servings.

Beaufort Seawall, oil on canvas by Peter Rolfe.

IT'S FUN TO MAKE frittatas and stratas because there are as many varieties as your imagination will allow. Best of all, they're simple and quick to make, nutritious and they allow you to put neglected ingredients from your refrigerator to good use. One of the most healthful foods, eggs, are perfectly proportioned protein powerhouses encased in handy little packages. They are also incredibly versatile, whether used in savory dishes, eaten on their own or used as the building block for countless fabulous dishes.

A frittata is simply a quiche minus the crust or an Italian version of an omelet. They are a snap to make and chock full of fresh vegetables, herbs, cheeses, and meats, making a simple yet hearty meal. Frittatas can be as casual or dressed up as you want them to be — they can be served directly out of the pan, or transferred to a platter and garnished with cheese, herbs, or vegetables for a more sophisticated presentation.

Usually a frittata is cooked on the stove like an omelet and then baked in the oven to finish, whereas stratas are egg, cheese, and bread casseroles, cooked entirely in the oven, that puff up when baking.

Breakfast, lunch, or dinner — if you have a carton of eggs on hand, a simple, satisfying meal is never more than a few minutes away. This particular frittata was inspired by a recent trip to the farmer's market where I purchased some red onions, a small bunch of scallions, a few red bell peppers, and some zucchini squash. The magic of this frittata lies in roasting the vegetables with olive oil, salt and pepper, and fresh minced garlic. Everything bakes together in a pan of deliciousness, topped off by a wonderful Gruyère cheese. Roasted pine nuts add just the right amount of crunch in contrast to the creaminess of the eggs. I wish you could have been there when it came out of the oven; yum.

This roasted vegetable frittata can be layered and presented in a number of ways, and I encourage you to experiment with your own favorite assortment of vegetables and cheese to produce the results you and your guests will love.

Corn Strata

Here's a strata I'm glad I finally tried. It packs lots of nutrition with its whole grain bread, more flavor than you can imagine and boasts a wonderful, light consistency. It works well anytime - breakfast, lunch or for a delicious change of pace at the dinner table.

9 slices whole grain bread with crusts removed and cut into cubes

2 scallions, chopped

About 6-7 ounces extra sharp cheddar, grated

7 ounces Pepper Jack cheese, grated

11 ounces frozen white corn kernels or 2 ears of fresh corn, when in season

2 tablespoons butter

2 tablespoons fresh chopped basil

8 large eggs

2 cups whole milk

½ cup buttermilk

Salt and freshly ground black pepper to taste

Preheat oven to 350°. Butter a 13 x 9-inch baking dish. Sauté the corn with a little butter until corn begins to change color and set aside to cool. It becomes slightly translucent. Layer the bread cubes, scallions, corn, cheddar, Pepper Jack cheese, basil, and salt and pepper, repeating the layers in the baking dish until all ingredients are used. End with a layer of cheese on top. In a large mixing bowl, whisk the eggs, milk, and buttermilk until thoroughly combined. Pour over the top of the layered casserole baking dish. Cover and refrigerate overnight. Bake at 350° in a preheated oven for one hour, or until lightly golden brown on top. Remove from the oven and run a knife around the edges to loosen it from the baking dish. Cut into squares and serve hot. Yields: 8-10 servings.

Adding a garnish will give your strata a bit of elegance and freshness. Once on a serving platter, add a sprinkle of chopped fresh herbs.

Spinach Cheese Strata

6 slices whole grain bread

2 tablespoons butter, softened

1 cup shredded cheddar cheese

½ cup shredded Monterey Jack cheese

1¼ cups milk

6 eggs, slightly beaten

1 package (10 oz.) frozen spinach, thawed and drained and squeezed dry

¼ teaspoon salt

⅛ teaspoon freshly ground black pepper

½ teaspoon freshly ground nutmeg

4 slices of bacon, cooked crispy and crumbled on top

Spread bread with butter. Arrange buttered slices in a single layer in a greased 9x11 baking dish. Sprinkle with cheese. Combine remaining ingredients and pour over bread and cheese. Cover and refrigerate overnight (at least 8 hours). Bake at 350° about 1 hour until puffy and golden. Sprinkle crispy, crumbled bacon on top once the strata is out of the oven. Serve warm. Yields: 6 servings.

Egret, photograph by Bob Ovelman.

Rise and Shine Breakfast Strata

Here's a strata you can whip up a day ahead and bake the next day.

½ stick butter, melted

1 loaf French bread (another bread of your choice may be substituted)

1 pound cooked sausage, ham or chicken, crumbled or diced

2 cups shredded sharp cheese

5 eggs, well beaten

2 cups Half and Half

1 teaspoon dried mustard

The night before, melt butter in a 9x11 casserole dish. Tear the bread into cubes and coat in the melted butter, leaving it in the bottom of the dish. Sprinkle with cooked meat, then the cheese. Mix egg, Half and Half, and mustard and pour over the cheese. Pat with fingers until the mixture in the pan is completely wet. Cover and refrigerate overnight. The next day, uncover and bake at 350° for 45 to 50 minutes.

Spinach baked with 2 types of cheese and whole grain bread makes this a real standout for breakfast, brunch, or dinner!

My recipes often call for roasted nuts because roasting intensifies flavor. But nuts are mighty delicate things –they can go from tasty to charred in a matter of seconds. I know because I burned a bunch of them before realizing baking in a 350° oven is a whole lot safer than toasting in a pan on top of the stove. Stir frequently so the nuts toast evenly. They tend to brown on the bottom quickly. Do not walk away while they're in the oven. If you should burn them, it's best to toss them away!

Sweet Potato Biscuits

2 cups self rising flour

1/4 cup sugar

3 tablespoons shortening

2 tablespoons butter

1 cup cooked and mashed sweet potatoes

1/3 cup milk

Softened butter for topping

Preheat oven to 400°. Combine flour and sugar in a medium bowl. Cut in shortening and butter with a pastry blender until mixture resembles coarse meal. Add potatoes and milk and mix until dry ingredients are just moistened. Turn dough out onto a lightly floured surface and knead 4 to 5 times. Roll dough to 1/2-inch thickness. Cut with a 2-inch biscuit cutter and place biscuits on lightly greased baking sheets. Bake 15 minutes or until golden brown. Remove from the oven and brush tops with softened butter. Yields: 12 biscuits.

NOTE: One large sweet potato yields about 1 cup mashed.

Spoon Bread

1 cup quick cooking grits

1 cup uncooked corn meal

1 teaspoon salt

1 cup Half and Half

4 eggs

3 teaspoons baking powder

1/2 stick butter, melted

Combine cornmeal, grits, and salt in a mixing bowl. Stirring constantly, gradually add boiling water. Stir in the melted butter. In a separate bowl beat eggs until thickened and pale in color. Add Half and Half and beat to combine. Add milk and egg mixture to the cornmeal mixture with the baking powder. Beat with an electric hand-held mixer or whisk to blend. Turn into a generously buttered 8-inch square glass baking dish. Bake for 30 minutes at 350°. Mixture should be firm. Serve with plenty of butter.

NOTE: A real Southern classic! Its pudding-like texture calls for this bread to be eaten with a spoon.

Cowan Creek Sweet Potato Cornbread

Make this homey cornbread and enjoy the aroma as it wafts throughout the house.

1 cup stone-ground cornmeal

3/4 cup white whole wheat flour

1 teaspoon cinnamon

1/2 teaspoon salt

1 teaspoon baking soda

1 cup mashed sweet potatoes

1/2 cup maple syrup

1 egg white

1/2 cup skim milk

Preheat oven to 350° and spray an 8-inch loaf pan with cooking spray and set aside. In a large bowl, mix together sweet potatoes, maple syrup, egg white, and skim milk. In a separate bowl, mix cornmeal, white whole wheat flour, cinnamon, salt, and baking soda. Stir the dry ingredients into the sweet potato mixture until just blended. Pour into prepared pan and bake for about 40 minutes.

NOTE: Ahh…I can smell an oven seeping with the sweet smell of autumn as I type! Butter them while hot. Those melted puddles of butter send up puffs of pure Southern incense.

Fried Okra Pancakes

Described by all who've tasted 'em to be "lip-smackin' good."

1/2 cup stone-ground cornmeal

1/2 cup all purpose flour

1 1/2 teaspoons salt

1 teaspoon baking powder

Oil for frying

1/2 cup water

Fresh black pepper

1/2 cup finely chopped onion

2 cups thinly sliced okra (about 1/4 inch)

1 egg, lightly beaten

In a mixing bowl, combine cornmeal, flour, 1 teaspoon of the salt and baking powder and stir well to blend. In a separate bowl, whisk together egg and water, then stir into the dry ingredients, mixing only until moistened. Lumps are okay. Sprinkle remaining 1/2 teaspoon salt, and pepper over onion and sliced okra and toss lightly. Fold seasoned vegetables into the batter. Pour 1 inch of oil into a heavy skillet and heat to 340°. Spoon okra batter by heaping tablespoons into hot oil. Do not overcrowd pan. Fry until golden brown on one side, and with a slotted spoon or tongs, carefully turn and continue frying until second side is browned, about 3 minutes. Remove from oil and drain well on paper towels. Keep in a warm oven until ready to serve. Yields: about 16 - 2-inch pancakes.

NOTE: Because they only spend 3 minutes in hot oil, the okra stays green and it crunches in your mouth, feeling fresh rather than oily. I first ate these pancakes on Pawley's Island with lots of maple syrup.

Zucchini Pineapple Bread

Out of this world good!

2½ cups white flour
½ cup whole wheat flour
2 teaspoons baking soda
¼ teaspoon baking powder
1 teaspoon salt
1 cup chopped pecans
1¼ teaspoons cinnamon
¾ teaspoon nutmeg
3 eggs, beaten
⅔ cup vegetable oil
2 teaspoons vanilla
2 cups shredded zucchini
One 8¼ ounce can crushed pineapple, drained

Combine baking soda, baking powder, salt, sugar, cinnamon, and nutmeg in a large bowl. Make a well in the center. In a separate bowl, mix eggs, oil, and vanilla. Pour into well in dry ingredients and stir until just moistened. Stir in zucchini, pecans, and pineapple. Spoon batter into two greased 9x5-inch loaf pans. Bake at 350° for 55 minutes or until a toothpick inserted in the center comes out clean.

If bread is crumbly and hard to slice when it's fresh, cool it for an hour and place in the freezer for 30 minutes. It should slice easier.

Cheddar Bay Biscuits

These are the best biscuits a country ham could ever meet!

4 cups Bisquick baking mix
¼-½ cup shredded cheddar cheese
1⅓ cup water
½ cup butter, melted
1 teaspoon garlic powder
¼ teaspoon salt
⅛ teaspoon onion powder
⅛ teaspoon dried parsley

Preheat oven to 375°. Lightly grease a baking sheet or line with parchment paper. In a medium mixing bowl, combine Bisquick, cheddar cheese and water. Mix until dough is firm. Using a small scoop, place dough on prepared baking sheet. Bake for 10 to 12 minutes, until golden brown. In a small bowl, combine melted butter, garlic powder, salt, onion powder, and dried parsley. Remove biscuits from oven and immediately brush with melted butter mixture. Serve warm. Yields: 20 biscuits.

Oyster Landing, oil on canvas by Ray Ellis.

Church on Prince Street, oil on canvas by Peter Rolfe.

Fruit Nut Pumpkin Bread

2 2/3 cups sugar

One 15-ounce can of pumpkin

1 cup canola oil

4 eggs

1 teaspoon vanilla extract

3 1/2 cups all purpose flour

1 1/2 teaspoons ground cinnamon

1 teaspoon salt

1 teaspoon baking soda

1/4 teaspoon ground cloves

1 1/2 cups coarsely chopped walnuts

2/3 cup golden raisins

2/3 cup raisins

2/3 cup dried cranberries

CRANBERRY CREAM CHEESE SPREAD

1/2 cup dried cranberries

1 1/2 cups boiling water

One 8-ounce package cream cheese, softened

1/3 cup chopped walnuts

In a large bowl, beat the sugar, pumpkin, oil, eggs and vanilla until well blended. Combine the flour, cinnamon, salt, baking soda and cloves. Gradually beat into the pumpkin mixture until blended. Fold in the walnuts, raisins, and cranberries.

Transfer to two greased 9x5-inch loaf pans. Bake at 350° for 60 to 70 minutes or until a toothpick inserted in the center comes out clean. Cool for 10 minutes before removing from pans to wire racks.

For spread, place cranberries in a small bowl; add boiling water. Let stand for 5 minutes, drain. In a small bowl, beat cream cheese until smooth. Beat in cranberries and walnuts until blended. Serve with bread. Yields: 2 loaves and 1 cup spread.

Dixie-Style Hoe Cakes

A Southern cornmeal pancake originally cooked on the blade of a hoe over an open fire.

2 cups fine stone-ground cornmeal

2 teaspoons baking powder

1 teaspoon salt

1 stick butter

2 eggs, lightly beaten

2 cups buttermilk

Melted butter for the griddle

CINNAMON-HONEY BUTTER (optional)

4 tablespoons honey

½ teaspoon cinnamon

Mix together the cornmeal, baking powder, and sugar in a large bowl. In a separate bowl, combine the eggs and buttermilk and beat until smooth. Stir this quickly into the dry ingredients, using as few strokes as possible.

Heat the griddle or cast iron skillet and brush it with the melted butter. Using a large kitchen spoon, take up about 2 tablespoons of the batter and pour it onto the griddle from the pointed end of the spoon. This will help insure that a round cake will form. Repeat until the griddle is full, but not crowded. Cook the cakes until the bottoms are browned and air holes form in the tops, about 4 minutes.

Turn and cook until the second side is browned - another 4 minutes. Keep in a warm oven while cooking the rest of the batter. For the cinnamon-honey butter, simply combine ingredients with a mixer and serve on hot hoe cakes.

NOTE: A great accompaniment for just about any family meal or serve 'em for breakfast with cinnamon-honey butter and maple syrup!

Photograph courtesy of Lowcountry Weekly.

Deep South Hush Puppies

1 ½ cups cornmeal

½ cup all-purpose flour

1 teaspoon salt

1 teaspoon baking powder

½ to ¾ cup whole milk

1 egg, beaten

2 tablespoons vegetable oil

½ cup minced onion, or 2 green onion tops, minced

Vegetable oil for frying

Sift cornmeal, flour, salt, and baking powder together in a large bowl. Combine ½ cup milk, egg, 2 tablespoons oil and minced onion in a separate bowl. Mix milk mixture with dry ingredients, adding up to ¼ cup more milk, if needed. Batter should be able to drip from a spoon.

Heat about 3 inches of oil in a skillet or deep fat fryer to 375°. Drop rounded teaspoonfuls of batter into hot oil. Fry 3 minutes or until golden brown. Remove from oil with a slotted spoon and drain on paper towels. Be sure oil returns to cooking temperature between batches. Serve hot. Yields: about 2 dozen.

18th at Harbour Town, oil on canvas by Ray Ellis.

*In many ways, present day Charleston, Savannah and Beaufort
have maintained their regal charms of yesteryear. They've
come through mighty wars, hurricanes, and earthquakes
and, like many women, with grit and determination,
have emerged with all their finery, stronger than ever.*

Hot from the Oven Entrees

"Only a Southerner knows instinctively that the best way to console a friend who's got trouble is with a plate of hot fried chicken and a big 'ol bowl of potato salad. If the friend is in a real crisis, they also know to add a large banana puddin'!"

HOPE YOU'RE HUNGRY! You're about to get your fill of some of my favorite entrees from the coast. If these dishes don't make you go back for seconds, I don't know what will. The Lowcountry stretches from the coastal plains of the Carolinas to the Georgia border. In food terms, Lowcountry means rice, grits, and produce paired with local crab, fish, and oysters. But we also indulge ourselves in barbecued chicken, pork, beef, and succulent meats hot from the oven.

Throughout the years, spring has always been the Lowcountry's most brilliant social season, a time for elegant private garden parties, cocktail parties after Sunday golf, outdoor concerts, and plantation tours. It's a glorious season when visitors arrive to tour the homes, and gardens come alive with the color of Formosa azaleas, wisteria and the sweet scents of jasmine.

Fall is a quieter season in the Lowcountry, punctuated by cooler temperatures, shorter lines, and spectacular autumn sunsets. It's also the time of year when area farmers begin to harvest potatoes, collards, turnips, and carrots. Delicious heirloom carrots and garden lettuces are not far behind. These pair beautifully any night of the week with these delicious entrees.

Remember that a recipe is merely words on paper to serve as a guide or a starting point from which to improvise. It cannot pretend to replace the practiced hand and telling glance of a watchful cook. For that reason, feel free to stir your own ideas into each recipe. When you cook it once. it becomes yours, so personalize it a bit. Add more of an ingredient you like or less of something you don't like. Try substituting one ingredient for another. Just remember that words have no flavor; you have to add your own!

Opposite Page: Upper King, oil on canvas by Jennifer Smith Rogers.

Magnolia, watercolor on paper by Nancy Ricker Rhett.

Deep South Buttermilk Fried Chicken

Crispy fried chicken goes to the very heart of what's great about the South! Add a little cream gravy and you'll have the perfect accompaniment to real Southern fried chicken. Though this chicken is irresistible right out of the oven, it's also the perfect picnic food since its terrific cold or at room temperature.

1½ cups buttermilk
1-2 chickens, cut into pieces
1½ cups all purpose flour
Salt and freshly ground black pepper
3 cups vegetable oil

CREAM GRAVY:
3 tablespoons drippings
3 tablespoons flour
½ cup cream
2½ cups milk
Salt and pepper to taste

Cover chicken pieces with salt and pepper and marinate in buttermilk overnight. Add enough oil to cover the bottom of a 12-inch cast iron skillet to reach a depth of ½-inch. (Cast iron will maintain a consistent temperature.) Keep the temperature of the oil at 350°. Remove several chicken pieces from the buttermilk and dip into flour mixture and turn to coat. Shake off excess.

Add chicken, skin side down, to the skillet. Reduce heat to medium low. Cover and cook until brown – about 12 minutes. Fry in batches to avoid overcrowding. Turn chicken over and cook uncovered until cooked through – about 5 minutes for breasts and 10 minutes for legs and thighs. Transfer to paper towels and repeat with remaining chicken. Add salt to taste.

Southern cooks often use a large paper grocery bag; add the flour and shake the chicken until coated. The buttermilk serves to tenderize the meat and make it moist and delicious.

CREAM GRAVY: Remember it's all in the drippings! In a medium skillet, stir the flour into the drippings until well blended. Cook several minutes. Gradually add milk and cream. Boil gently until thick and smooth, stirring constantly. Season with salt and pepper.

Lemony Chicken Piccata

This is a 3 bowl process; one for the flour, one for the egg, and one for the bread crumbs.

4 boneless, skinless chicken breasts
1 cup flour
2 medium eggs
1¾ cups seasoned dried bread crumbs
Extra virgin olive oil
4 tablespoons butter
Juice of 2 lemons
¾ cup dry white wine
Bunch of chopped parsley

Preheat oven to 400°. Using a rolling pin or a meat mallet, pound the chicken between sheets of wax paper to ¼-inch in thickness. Sprinkle the salt and pepper. Mix the flour, salt and pepper on a plate.

In a bowl beat the eggs slightly. Place the bread crumbs on a third plate. Dip each chicken breast, first in the flour, shaking off any excess, and then dip in the egg and bread crumb mixtures. (The egg adheres better to the chicken when it is first dusted in the flour.)

Heat olive oil in a large pan over low to medium heat and cook the chicken breasts for 2 minutes on each side until browned. Place them in the oven and allow them to bake for 10 minutes while you make the sauce.

SAUCE: Add 1 tablespoon of the butter over medium heat and add the lemon juice and white wine along with the salt and pepper. Boil over high heat until reduced. Add the remaining butter and stir. Serve with sliced lemon on top and a sprinkling of fresh parsley.

www.mycarolinacooking.com

Chicken Marsala with Pancetta

Just about everyone loves chicken. No other ingredient contributes so much for such little effort. In just a matter of minutes, chicken can add substance, flavor, and plenty of protein to your dinner lineup. Few other meats are as versatile. Chicken can take the spotlight as a roast at special events, but it's equally at home shredded in tostadas, grilled, fried for a picnic, or braised. Even those classics such as chili, meatballs, and one pot stews can be made with poultry instead of beef.

4 boneless chicken breast cutlets

2 ounces pancetta

2 tablespoons finely chopped onion

Olive oil

5 tablespoons butter

10 ounces mushrooms, trimmed and thinly sliced

¼ teaspoon salt

¼ teaspoon freshly ground black pepper

½ cup all purpose flour

2 tablespoons extra virgin olive oil

½ cup dry Marsala wine (good drinking wine)

⅔ cup cream

Juice of ½ lemon

Preheat oven to 200°. Coat a large skillet lightly with olive oil and set it over medium high heat. Add the pancetta and cook until crispy and lightly browned. Remove with a slotted spoon, leaving fat in the pan and set aside. Put the flour on a plate and pat the cutlets dry. Season them on both sides lightly with salt and pepper. Heat the skillet with the pancetta fat over medium high heat. Add the butter and more olive oil if needed. Dredge the cutlets in the flour and sauté until golden brown on both sides. With the pan on medium high heat, sauté the onion until translucent and cook the mushrooms until golden.

Once the pan is cooled down, add the Marsala wine and reduce. Stir in the cream and boil until the sauce thickens. Return the chicken and pancetta to the pan and cover with sauce. Allow them to reheat for a couple of minutes and squeeze lemon over them just before serving.

NOTE: When a recipe calls for wine, the best advice on the subject is to never cook with a wine you wouldn't drink. The wine should enhance the flavor of the dish and not overpower it.

Sesame Chicken Wings

Ideal for a picnic or tailgate party – sweet, spicy and tangy! Inspired by the Hilton Head Island Wingfest.

1 large garlic clove

¾ teaspoon salt

2 tablespoons soy sauce

2 tablespoons hoisin sauce

2 tablespoons honey

1 teaspoon sesame oil

Pinch of cayenne

3 pounds chicken wings

1½ tablespoon sesame seeds, lightly toasted

1 scallion (green part only) finely chopped

Preheat the oven to 425°. Adjust the oven rack to the upper third of the oven. Next line a large rimmed baking sheet (17 x 12-inches) with foil and lightly oil the foil.

Mince garlic and mash to a paste with salt using a large heavy knife. Transfer garlic paste to a large bowl and stir in soy sauce, hoisin, honey, oil, and cayenne. Add wings to sauce, stirring to coat.

Arrange wings in 1 layer on sheet pan and roast, turning over once, until cooked through, about 35 minutes. Transfer wings to a large serving bowl and toss with sesame seeds and scallions.

NOTE: I always look for the wingettes because they already have the tips discarded and the wings are halved at the joint.

Chicken Divan

This is one of the most popular casserole dishes of all time. It's one that is festive, with bright green broccoli showing through the pale yellow curry and it freezes well. So make it ahead of time and when guests drop in, you'll be ready.

4 large chicken breast halves cooked, boned and torn into bite sized pieces

2 (10 ounce) packages frozen broccoli, chopped

2 (10¾ ounce) cans cream of mushroom soup

¾ cup mayonnaise

1 (8 ounce) carton sour cream

1½ cups grated sharp cheddar cheese

1 tablespoon lemon juice

1½ teaspoons curry powder

½ teaspoon salt

¼ teaspoon pepper

¾ cup dry white wine

TOPPING

½ cup Parmesan cheese

½ cup soft bread crumbs

In a medium saucepan, cook broccoli in ½ cup salted water until hot, about 5 minutes. Drain. Mix together the soup, mayonnaise, sour cream, grated cheese, lemon juice, curry powder, salt, pepper, and wine in a large bowl. Stir well. Spread shredded chicken in bottom of a 13 x 9-inch casserole dish that you have sprayed with vegetable cooking spray. Cover with broccoli. Pour soup mixture over top of broccoli. Spread evenly to cover all of the broccoli. Or, combine chicken, broccoli, and soup mixture, mix well, and spread evenly in a 13 x 9-inch casserole dish.

Combine Parmesan cheese and bread crumbs and sprinkle over top of casserole. Cover and refrigerate.

Preheat oven to 350°. An hour before serving, remove casserole from refrigerator and allow it to sit out, covered, for 30 minutes. Bake uncovered for 30 minutes, serve.

Vegetarian Lasagna

5 quarts water

1 tablespoon olive oil

10 uncooked lasagna noodles

1 onion, minced

1 tablespoon olive oil

16 ounces mushrooms, sliced

16 ounces carrots, sliced

One 15-ounce can tomato sauce

One 6-ounce can tomato paste

1½ teaspoons oregano

½ teaspoon salt

Freshly ground black pepper

1½ teaspoons olive oil

2 cups cottage cheese

2 pounds fresh spinach, cooked and well drained

3½ cups shredded Monterey Jack cheese

3½ cups sharp cheddar cheese

2 tablespoons grated Parmesan cheese

Bring the water and 1 tablespoon olive oil to a boil in a 2 gallon stockpot. Add the lasagna noodles two and three at a time. Cook for 8 to 10 minutes or until tender, then drain. Return to the stockpot and cover with warm water to prevent sticking together.

Gently boil the carrots until softened. Sauté the onion and garlic in 1 tablespoon olive oil in a large skillet over medium heat for 2 minutes. Add the mushrooms and sauté for 12 to 15 minutes or until the moisture evaporates. Add the carrots. Stir in the tomato sauce, tomato paste, oregano, salt and pepper. Remove from the heat.

Spread 1½ teaspoons olive oil in a 9 x 11-inch baking pan. Drain the noodles and arrange five noodles in the prepared pan. Layer half the cottage cheese, half the spinach, one third of the cheese and half the vegetable mixture over the noodles. Repeat the layers and top with the remaining cheese. Sprinkle with the Parmesan cheese. Bake at 375° for 45 minutes.

Dinner on a Stick Chicken, Onion and Pineapple Kebobs

Use metal skewers to help conduct the heat to the inside of the food. Vegetables such as bell peppers and onions that take a while to cook need to be precooked before assembling the kabob.

1 boneless chicken breast, halved and cut into 1-inch cubes

1 can pineapple cuts

1 tablespoon honey

Salt and freshly ground black pepper

8 wooden or metal skewers

MARINADE

1 can coconut milk

4 tablespoons lime juice (fresh only)

8 cloves garlic, minced

1 teaspoon paprika

1 tablespoon ginger, grated

Cut chicken on a cutting board into 1-inch equal sized pieces. Place chicken in a large sealable bag. Make the marinade by combining all ingredients thoroughly. Pour ½ the marinade over chicken and refrigerate overnight.

Toss onion slices in olive oil and precook them in the oven before skewering to be sure they are tender.

Strain the chicken and discard used marinade. Arrange the chicken on skewers, alternating with a pineapple cube, then a slice of sweet onion and then a piece of chicken. Brush skewers with oil and season with salt and pepper. Oil grill to prevent sticking. Place skewers on the grill.

Cook each side of the kabob for 3 to 4 minutes. Baste with the reserved marinade throughout cooking. When chicken is golden brown and no longer pink inside, remove from the grill.

Chicken Tostadas

After biting into these crunchy, creamy, luscious layers of pure flavor, you'll want to make these again and again.

1 medium onion

1 pound tomatoes, quartered

3 large garlic cloves.

2 fresh Serrano chiles, stemmed

½ cup plus 2 tablespoons vegetable oil, divided

3 cups shredded iceberg lettuce

½ cup cilantro, divided

1 rotisserie chicken, coarsely shred the meat

Six 6-inch corn tortillas

One 1-pound can refried beans, heated

1 avocado, halved, pitted, and peeled

½ cup sour cream

½ cup aged cheddar cheese

Lime wedges

Preheat the broiler. Cut half of the onion into ¾-inch wedges, then chop remainder. Toss onion wedges, tomatoes, garlic, and whole chiles with 2 tablespoons oil on a rimmed baking sheet, spreading in 1 layer.

Broil about 4 inches from the heat until softened and charred, 10 to 15 minutes.

Meanwhile, toss together the lettuce chopped onion and half of the cilantro.

Puree tomato mixture in a blender along with the roasted serranos and a teaspoon salt until smooth. Transfer puree to a bowl and stir in chicken, remaining cilantro, and salt to taste.

Heat remaining ½ cup oil in a heavy skillet over medium high heat until it shimmers. Fry tortillas, one at a time, turning once or twice and pressing with tongs to immerse, until golden brown, about 60 seconds per tortilla. Drain briefly on paper towels, then transfer to plates.

Spread tortillas thickly with heated refried beans, then top with chicken mixture. Slice avocado over tostadas and add a dollop of sour cream. Mound lettuce mixture on top and sprinkle with cheese. Yields: 6 servings.

Turkey Deep Fried

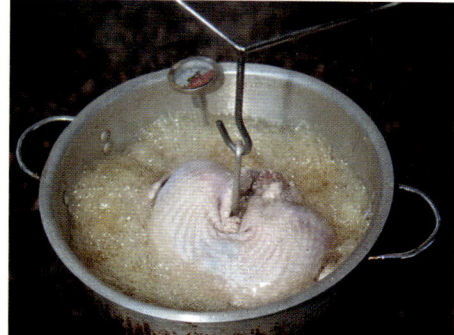

Photographs by Bob Ovelman.

DEEP FRYING WHOLE TURKEYS has become fantastically popular in the South over the past several years. I was horrified the first time I heard about it - I thought Southerners were beginning to batter and fry up anything that wasn't nailed down! Then someone told me "don't panic, there's no batter involved here, just simply the best turkey you'll ever eat in your life!"

The turkey is anything but greasy because the deep frying process seals the outside and the turkey remains incredibly juicy, while the skin gets wonderfully crispy.

In addition to a turkey, you'll need a 40-60 quart pot with a basket or turkey frying hardware, plus a propane gas tank and burner, a candy/deep fry thermometer, a meat thermometer and lots of oil. Use oils that have a high smoke point, such as corn, peanut or canola oils.

I recommend having a fire extinguisher on hand and plenty of heavy duty pot holders nearby. As far as the turkey itself goes, smaller birds work better for frying Try not to go over 15 pounds.

For the most flavorful birds, before cooking you can inject them with your favorite marinade or use a dry spice rub. You will also need about 3½ to 5 gallons of oil in which to fry the turkey.

Before you fry: Determine the amount of oil you'll need by placing the turkey in the fryer and adding enough water to cover the top of the turkey. Remove the turkey and the water line will indicate how much oil will be needed to fry your turkey. Having too much oil can cause a fire. The pot should not be more than ¾ full or the oil could overflow when the turkey is added.

RECIPE
1 (10 pound) turkey
2 tablespoons of your favorite rub
3-5 gallons oil

DIRECTIONS:
Wash turkey inside and out, and allow to drain. Pat it dry. Rub the turkey all over with the turkey rub, coating completely. Allow the bird to sit about 1 hour until it reaches room temperature.

Heat oil in the turkey fryer to 350°. Check temperature with a candy thermometer. Lower turkey slowly into hot oil, very carefully, making sure it is fully submerged. Fry turkey until an instant read thermometer inserted 2 inches into the inner thigh of the turkey registers 170° F. This should take about 3 minutes per pound. Keep a watchful eye on things because overcooking is one of the biggest mistakes beginners make. Remove turkey from oil and drain on paper towels. Let it rest for 20 minutes before carving. Yields: 6-8 servings.

Chechessee Standing Rib Roast

'T IS THE SEASON TO BE JOLLY…cook, bake, and enjoy great Carolina cuisine. When the weather outside is frightful, it's time to plan that cozy Christmas dinner you've been dreaming about. Go ahead and splurge on an expensive cut of meat. The holiday table will never be so elegant as when you serve a standing rib roast.

This sumptuous roast becomes even more luxurious with a wonderful Portobello-Marsala Sauce. Buy the best beef you can afford – at least USDA Choice, preferably USDA Prime.

Cooking this classic dish is a mystery to many home cooks, but this easy recipe creates a perfect and succulent prime rib sure to please the palates of meat lovers everywhere.

The following method for cooking works every time. I learned a few tips from an excellent cook in Atlanta years ago. Perhaps the best advice she ever gave me was to invest in a good meat thermometer. Internal temperature, not time, is the best test for doneness.

RECIPE

1 (7-8 pound) standing rib roast
1 tablespoon sea salt
2 teaspoons fresh ground black pepper

Preheat oven to 450°. Place roast ribs down (fat side up) in a heavy stainless steel roasting pan. Pat roast dry with paper towels. Generously salt and pepper the top. Insert the meat thermometer in the thickest part of the beef, being careful not to touch the bone. Brush about 2 tablespoons of butter on the cut ends of the roast. Position oven rack in the bottom third of the oven.

Roast for 20 minutes at the 450° temperature, then lower the temperature to 350° and continue to roast until the thermometer reads between 125° and 130° for medium rare. This will take about one hour and 50 minutes.

Remove from the oven and let it rest for 20 minutes. This allows the juices to redistribute throughout the roast.

NOTE: To cook evenly, the roast must not be cold. Let it stand loosely covered at room temperature for 1-2 hours before putting in oven.

It's also important to have the butcher tie your roast. If left untied, the outer layer of the meat will pull away from the ribeye muscle and overcook. Having the roast tied at both ends will prevent this problem.

While boneless rib roasts are available, roasting with the bones adds flavor. When purchasing, look for a bright red color and no dry or brown edges. Also, check for any damage to the packaging and wrapping.

PORTOBELLO MARSALA SAUCE

3 tablespoons cold butter, divided
One 8-ounce package sliced baby portobello mushrooms
3 garlic cloves, minced
2 large shallots, diced
2 cups Marsala wine
1 cup chicken broth

Melt 1 tablespoon butter over medium heat, add mushrooms and sauté 10 minutes or until browned. Add 1 tablespoon butter, garlic and shallots and sauté 5 minutes. Stir in Marsala and chicken broth, stirring to loosen any particles from the bottom of the skillet. Bring to a boil and stir constantly. Cook for 20 minutes or until reduced. Remove from heat and stir in remaining 1 tablespoon of butter. Serve with standing rib roast and garnish if desired. It's delicious every time.

NOTE: The success of a sauce lies in the sum of its parts. Choose a good Italian Marsala such as Florio or Lombardo Marsala for best results.

Here's a sauce that's also good, but a little easier.

MUSTARD HORSERADISH SAUCE

1½ cups mayonnaise
2 tablespoons Dijon mustard
2½ tablespoons whole grain mustard (don't skip this mustard – it's essential)
2½ tablespoons prepared horseradish
⅓ cup sour cream
¼ teaspoon salt

Just whisk this together and serve.

Pelican at Rest, photograph by Bob Ovelman.

Reduction Sauce, oil on canvas by Ken Auster.

Taco Salad

If your schedule gets hectic, just keep things simple. This innovative and practically effortless recipe is from Martha Nesbit, former food editor of the Savannah Morning News. Martha says whenever she needed a guaranteed hit, she turned to a recipe she's been using for over 40 years. It has never lost its appeal.

1 pound ground beef, browned, crumbled and drained

2 ripe tomatoes, diced

8 ounces sharp Cheddar cheese, diced or grated

1 large sweet onion, chopped

mixed, crisp salad greens

1 (16 ounce) bottle Catalina dressing

1 (7 ounce) bag taco flavored chips, crushed

1 (8 ounce) jar taco sauce, mild or medium

fresh cilantro, chopped

Cook the ground beef, drain, and set aside until ready to use. Chop the tomatoes, cheese, onion and lettuce and place in a large salad bowl. Stir in the ground beef and pour the entire bottle of dressing over the salad ingredients and mix well. Just before serving add taco flavored chips, tossing to combine with other ingredients. Stir in the taco sauce. Top it off with plenty of chopped cilantro. Serve immediately. Yields: 6-8 servings.

Osprey, by William Rhett, III.

Land's End London Broil

2-3 pound round steak

½ cup soy sauce

¼ cup red wine vinegar

¼ cup canola oil

3 cloves mashed garlic

Salt and fresh pepper

Make a marinade by combining the soy sauce, red wine vinegar, canola oil, garlic, salt and freshly ground black pepper. Boil the ingredients for two minutes. Remove from heat and cool. Simply place the steak in a zip top bag and pour in the marinade. Marinate the steak in the sauce overnight in the refrigerator.

The red wine has chemical properties that will tenderize and flavor the meat, making it tender and juicy through and through.

Use the marinade to baste the meat while it is cooking on the grill, 5 to 8 minutes per side depending upon the degree of doneness desired and the thickness of the steak. Discard any leftover marinade. Once off the grill, allow it to rest about 10 minutes in order for the juices to redistribute. Slice it on the diagonal in very thin slices. Yields: 4-6 servings.

HORSERADISH CREAM SAUCE

8 ounces cream cheese, softened

1½ tablespoons horseradish

1 tablespoon Dijon mustard

For the horseradish cream sauce, thoroughly combine the cream cheese, horseradish and Dijon mustard with a hand held mixer and serve on the side. This sauce is best when covered and chilled for several hours ahead of time.

Sizzlin' Flank Steak

1 flank steak (2 pounds or less)

3 cloves mashed fresh garlic

¼ cup soy sauce

3 tablespoons dark brown sugar

2 tablespoons cider vinegar

¾ cup oil

1½ teaspoons freshly grated ginger

1 small onion, chopped very fine

⅛ cup fresh parsley, chopped fine

Pinch of salt and freshly ground black pepper

Prepare the steak by scoring about ¼ inch deep on each side. Using a zip top bag, place the steak inside and pour the marinade into the bag. Marinate overnight in the refrigerator. Remove from the marinade and grill for approximately 10 minutes on each side. Once it has reached the desired degree of doneness, allow the steak to rest at least 15 minutes. Slice thinly on the diagonal. Yields: 4-6 servings.

The South, oil on canvas by John Carroll Doyle.

ADD SOME SIZZLE TO YOUR DINNER MENU with this delicious flank steak!

If you can't stand the heat — head back to your air conditioned kitchen. Otherwise, let's head out to the grill!

Warmer days mean cooking and eating outdoors and there's nothing like the aroma of steak and vegetables on the grill. That spells summer for me!

Summer is the time of year I want food that is easy to pull together, full of flavor, and lets me use what's on hand.

Your family will love this grilled flank steak, especially with some delicious potato salad and grilled vegetables.

Whether you're headed for the beach or a picnic in the backyard under a shade tree, kick back and enjoy this simple recipe you'll want to make over and over again.

We've all done it — mistaken the salt for sugar (well, it looks like sugar) and had to start all over again. Those of us who like to talk on the phone and multi-task while cooking are especially prone to a disaster now and then. I learned the hard way that even the best written recipes may not include the most important information at the beginning. Trust me, you don't want to be an hour away from your guests arriving and the last sentence of the recipe says to marinate overnight!

Next, let's look at a few common mistakes made with meat and how to avoid them. Many recipes never mention the importance of having the steak, chicken, or roast rest after cooking and before slicing. Once it comes off the heat, there needs to be a cool-off time to allow the juices to redistribute throughout. Otherwise these delicious juices will run out onto the platter or cutting board, leaving the roast or chicken dry. Even with small cuts of meat such as steak or boneless chicken breasts, the rule is an important one. They need to rest for at least 5 minutes. But if you're cooking a whole chicken or a large roast, the cool-off time is longer, about 30 minutes. Simply tent the meat loosely with aluminum foil to help keep it warm.

Slicing is another important step along the way to having a tender, fabulous slice of meat. Always slice the meat with, instead of against, the grain. This is a good idea with standing rib roasts and even poultry. With a flank steak, the grain is very obvious. For the most tender slices, look at the steak to determine the direction of the grain and cut across the grain and not with it.

There's just one more important detail! If you cook meat right out of the refrigerator while it's cold, it may not cook evenly. Allow enough time for the steak to reach room temperature before grilling or broiling. This should only take about 30 minutes.

Filet Mignon with Mushroom Marsala Sauce

Dock at Twilight, oil on canvas by Jennifer Smith.

THIS VALENTINE'S DAY, don't fret about making dinner reservations at a fancy restaurant. Enjoy a romantic dinner for two at home – one that can be on the table in no time, even at the end of a hectic day. These luxurious, quick cooking tenderloin steaks take about 20 minutes and are so tender you can cut them with a butter knife. Round out the meal with a fresh green salad, refrigerated mashed potatoes, a great bottle of Cabernet Sauvignon, and a wickedly delicious chocolate dessert!

RECIPE

½ cup beef broth

¼ cup water

2 teaspoons all-purpose flour

¾ teaspoon Dijon mustard

½ teaspoon garlic, minced

¼ teaspoon salt

Freshly ground black pepper

2 beef tenderloin steaks at room temperature

Olive oil

1 cup sliced mushrooms

½ cup sweet Marsala wine

Combine the broth, water, mustard, garlic, salt and pepper in a bowl. Heat a large cast-iron skillet over high heat. Drizzle a little olive oil in the pan, just to cover the bottom. Generously salt and pepper the steaks.

When the pan is very hot, place the steaks in the pan and sear on both sides, giving the meat a deeper flavor and a darker crust. Turn the heat to medium and cook for 5 minutes on each side or until they reach the desired degree of doneness you like. Remove the steaks from the pan. Add the mushrooms to the pan and cook for several minutes until browned. Remove mushrooms from the pan and add the Marsala wine, scraping the pan to loosen browned bits. Reduce heat to medium and add the broth mixture to the pan. Whisk in the flour until well combined. Bring to a boil. Cook about 1 minute while stirring constantly. Finally, reduce the heat back to very low and stir in the mushrooms. When purchasing the Marsala wine for this delicious sauce, choose a quality table wine. The sauce is only as good as the sum of its parts!

TIP: Be careful not to overcook; and it's important to let the beef rest about 10 minutes before slicing. This allows the juices to redistribute from the outside throughout the steak. This makes for a much juicier and tastier steak.

Squall on River Street, watercolor on paper by Ray Ellis.

Having a party during the NFL playoff games or simply having friends over for a special supper? It's as simple as firing up your gas grill. Here's a rich smoky-sweet but spicy flavored rub with a delicious apple-bacon barbecue sauce. It's the perfect complement to either spareribs or baby back ribs.

You'll need about 3 racks of baby back ribs for 6 people. Start by seasoning the ribs with this spice rub, thoroughly covering all the ribs on both sides.

Best Barbecued Ribs

SPICE RUB

3 tablespoons salt

1 tablespoon freshly ground black pepper

4 teaspoons Hungarian paprika

1½ teaspoons celery seed

2 teaspoons chile powder

Allow the ribs to reach room temperature before grilling. This helps them to cook evenly. Always place the ribs on the grill, leaving as much room as possible between each rack, with the bone side down at a temperature of 300°. The bone protects the meat from cooking too fast. Begin cooking the ribs. Your initial cooking time will be about 1 hour.

The next step is to baste the ribs with the barbecue sauce and continue to cook them for about 3 more hours, depending on their size. Allow them to cook until the meat shrinks about ¼ inch from the ends. They are done when the meat separates and tears easily near the middle of the rack. Most racks take about 4 hours total cooking time. Baste another time or two until they are finished. Allow the meat to rest for about 15 minutes before serving. The juices will redistribute and be absolutely delicious!

APPLE-BACON BARBECUE SAUCE
AND BASTING SAUCE

5 slices apple bacon, cooked crispy

1 cup apple juice

5 tablespoons vinegar (apple cider is good)

¾ cup ketchup

3 tablespoons Worcestershire sauce

½ teaspoon chile powder

½ teaspoon Hungarian paprika

¼ teaspoon celery seed

Salt and freshly ground black pepper to taste

Once bacon is cooked, drain it on paper towels. You'll not need the bacon, only the fat. Pour about ½ the bacon fat into a small saucepan and reserve the remaining fat in the skillet for the barbecue sauce.

BASTING SAUCE: To the saucepan, add ½ cup of the apple juice and 2 tablespoons of the vinegar. Warm it over medium heat. Use this to baste the ribs.

BARBECUE SAUCE: Add the remaining apple juice, vinegar, ketchup, Worcestershire sauce, chile powder, paprika, celery seed, and the salt and pepper to the bacon fat in the skillet. Cook over low heat, whisking until smooth. Let it simmer for a minute and then remove it from the heat. Apply this after the ribs are fully cooked by laying the ribs on a large sheet of heavy duty aluminum foil, lightly brushing the ribs on both sides, and wrapping each rack individually in the foil. Let them sit at room temperature for 15 minutes, then unwrap and serve. Absolutely delicious every time!

Penne with Asparagus and Prosciutto

Beached, oil on canvas by Shannon Smith.

IT'S A DAILY DILEMMA WE ALL FACE. You're finally home and hungry and someone asks, "What's for dinner?" You suddenly realize you forgot to take something out of the freezer to thaw. You want to have a nutritious meal, but you need it right away! Forget about feeling guilty about not having an over-achiever, super woman persona. Instead we'll talk about some real strategies for surviving suppertime without having to be a logistical genius.

First of all, keep it simple. Find some recipes with just a few ingredients and a few steps. Keep those ingredients on hand in the pantry and refrigerator. Basics such as good extra virgin olive oil, butter, fresh garlic, onions, balsamic vinegar, and kosher salt are all "must-haves." Great cheeses such as Parmigiano-Reggiano, capers, parsley, cream, good quality canned tomatoes, and pancetta are especially useful. The fewer steps there are in a recipe, the more important each step becomes. For weeknight speed with magnificent flavor, use the very finest and freshest ingredients.

One of my favorites for spring uses fresh sweet asparagus. Take advantage of asparagus when it is fresh and bountiful. It's a nutrient-dense food high in folic acid and a great source of potassium, fiber, vitamin B6, vitamins A and C, and thiamin.

The prosciutto in this recipe acts as a condiment with its salty flavor, while the onions become the foundation for a thick, creamy delicious sauce. Buon appetito any night of the week!

RECIPE

¾ pound fresh asparagus

½ sweet yellow onion

4 tablespoons butter

5 ounces prosciutto, sliced ⅛-inch thick

Salt and freshly ground black pepper

⅔ cup heavy cream

⅓ cup fresh Parmigiano-Reggiano

1 pound penne pasta

Fill a large pot with 8 quarts of water and bring to a boil. Next fill a skillet with water and bring to a boil. Cut off the white, woody bottom part of the asparagus spears, and then peel the remaining bottom third. Add some salt to the boiling water and add the asparagus. Cook until the asparagus is tender, 6-8 minutes, then lift it out and set aside.

While the asparagus is cooking, peel and chop the onion very fine. Put the butter into a skillet and add the onion and place over medium high heat. Sauté until the onion has turned a rich golden color.

Cut the prosciutto slices into strips about ⅛ inch wide and 1-inch long. When the onion is ready, add the prosciutto and sauté until it loses its raw color – about 2 minutes.

Cut the asparagus into 1-inch lengths and add them to the pan. Continue sautéing until the asparagus becomes lightly colored, 2 to 3 minutes.

Add 2 tablespoons salt to the boiling pasta water, add the penne and stir well. Cook until al dente.

While the pasta is cooking, add the cream to the asparagus and cook until the cream has thickened. Remove the pan from the heat. When the pasta is done, drain well, toss with the sauce and the freshly grated Parmigiano-Reggiano, and serve immediately. Yields: 4 servings.

Cat Island Marsh, oil on canvas by Peter Rolfe.

Roasted Rack of Lamb

Two 16-ounce frenched racks of lamb

3 medium fresh rosemary sprigs, leaves stripped and coarsely chopped

½ bunch fresh thyme leaves stripped and coarsely chopped

4-5 fresh garlic cloves, sliced and placed into the small incisions made in the surface of the meat

Kosher salt and freshly ground black pepper

Combine the herbs with 3 tablespoons of olive oil and rub the mixture all over the lamb. Place slivers of garlic in the small incisions made on the lamb's surface. Season well with freshly ground black pepper. Place the racks in a baking dish and cover with plastic wrap. Refrigerate at least 8 hours or overnight.

Preheat the oven to 425°. Uncover lamb and let it sit at room temperature for about 30 minutes. A piece of meat at room temperature will roast more evenly, and using a roasting rack will ensure even browning and heat circulation. Go ahead and salt the lamb just before searing. Heat a large oven safe frying pan and add about 2 tablespoons of olive oil. Place lamb racks one at a time in the pan, fat side down, and sear until browned. Remove and sear the other rack. Place the pan in the oven and roast for 15 minutes, then reduce the temperature to 325°. Continue roasting until the internal temperature is 130° for medium rare. Remove from the oven and allow the meat to rest for 10 minutes before carving. This will allow time for the juices to redistribute. Yields: 4 servings.

NOTE: The term frenched refers to a way of trimming the lamb racks so that the bone end of each chop is cleanly exposed. Your butcher will do this for you, if it has not already been done. I have recommended searing the lamb to create the perfect caramelized crust while keeping the middle tender and juicy.

FOLKS IN THE LOWCOUNTRY know they've got it good. There's sand in their shoes and a whole lot of love in their hearts for their part of the world that stays with them no matter how far away they may travel. It's a magical place with an allure that goes far beyond its beauty. For hundreds of years their land has been tilled to reap its rich bounty. From the vast tomato fields of St. Helena's Island to the abundance of blue crab and oysters, their land has yielded a rich harvest. For this is the land of fish houses with concrete walls, church homecomings with fried chicken and deviled eggs, towering coconut cakes and hot bubbly cobblers, and always, the signature of fine Southern cuisine—plenty of sweet iced tea served with lemon.

While they love a casual oyster roast and a wooden picnic table with a big pot of Frogmore Stew, they are equally at home with white linens and fine silver. With this in mind, why not polish the silver and enjoy an elegant roasted rack of lamb.

Roasted rack of lamb can be the ultimate Easter dinner dish with a real "WOW" factor when marinated in garlic, thyme, and rosemary for a subtle, yet full bodied flavor. It was while traveling through France that I first began to understand the great pride the French take in their lamb and how they enjoy eating it quite rare. Up until that time my only experience had been with well cooked, grayish lamb dishes that were somewhat dried out and served with mint sauce. When cooked properly, lamb should be crisp on the outside, and tender and juicy and rare on the inside.

The leg and rack are the most tender cuts of meat on the lamb and are flavorful enough on their own not to require much seasoning, but conversely lamb's flavor is robust and certain seasonings can be used to complement it. In the following recipe, I made small incisions in the surface of the meat and pushed slivers of garlic into the slits. You can do this right before you begin roasting or, ahead of time to create a stronger flavor. Just be sure not to salt it until just before cooking, as salt can draw moisture out of the meat.

www.mycarolinacooking.com

Rustic Chicken with Mushrooms and Gruyère Polenta

Each fall as temperatures begin to drop, I start thinking of delicious hot chicken dishes with deep, vivid flavors and wonderful savory sauces. This dish dates back to several years ago when I first tasted this fabulous flavor combination at a little restaurant in Black Mountain, North Carolina. When I returned home I tried to duplicate it and this is the recipe I came up with.

MAKE THE POLENTA FIRST

1 tablespoon butter

4 cups water

1 cup ground cornmeal

1 tablespoon chopped fresh thyme

1½ cups grated Gruyère

1 teaspoon salt

To make the polenta, heat the oven to 350°. Coat an 8 x 8-inch baking dish with butter. In a medium saucepan, bring the water and the salt to a boil and slowly whisk in the cornmeal until the mixture is smooth. Reduce the heat to a simmer and continue stirring with a wooden spoon until the mixture is thick, about 10 minutes. Take the pan off the heat and stir in the thyme and Gruyère. Pour the polenta into the baking dish and bake for 45 minutes, stirring every few minutes. Cover with foil to keep a crust from forming. Meanwhile, prepare the chicken.

FOR THE CHICKEN

2 tablespoons olive oil

8 bone-in chicken pieces

1 cup sliced yellow onions

3 cloves garlic, minced

1¾ cups portobello mushrooms

1 teaspoon salt

½ teaspoon freshly ground black pepper

⅓ cup dry white wine

1½ cups canned diced tomatoes, with their juices

½ cup chicken broth

2 teaspoons fresh thyme, minced

Heat the oil in a sauté pan, but do not let it smoke. Add as many of the chicken pieces, skin side down, as will fit without crowding and brown all sides well for about 4 minutes per side. Transfer to the plate, adding more oil if needed and brown the remaining chicken. Transfer to the plate. Reduce heat to medium; add the onion and sauté until translucent for about 4 minutes. Add the garlic and cook 2 more minutes. If the pan is dry, add a little more oil. Next add the mushrooms and cook until they release their juices and begin to brown, about 5 minutes. Add the salt and pepper. Add the wine and scrape up any browned bits in the pan. Return the chicken pieces to the pan and simmer until the wine is reduced by half.

Add the tomatoes and reduce the heat. Simmer the chicken, turning once until it is completely cooked and very tender; approximately 30 minutes. Check the pan and add broth as needed if the pan becomes too dry. Add 1 teaspoon of the thyme to the pan. Serve the chicken over the polenta, with some of the sauce and the remaining thyme sprinkled on top.

Lowcountry Chicken Parmesan

It's the cornmeal that really gives this chicken Parmesan a true Southern twist

2 large eggs

¾ cup yellow cornmeal mix

¾ cup Japanese breadcrumbs (Panko)

1 package Italian dry salad dressing and seasoning mix

4 boneless skinless chicken breasts

½ cup olive oil

One 26-ounce jar marinara sauce

1 cup Parmesan cheese

1 cup mozzarella cheese, grated

Preheat oven to 350°. In a shallow dish, lightly beat the eggs. In a separate shallow dish, combine cornmeal mix, panko and seasoning mix. Dip chicken in eggs; dredge in cornmeal mixture. In a large nonstick skillet, heat olive oil over medium heat. Cook chicken several minutes per side or until lightly browned. Place in a 13 x 9-inch casserole dish. Bake for 15 minutes. Top with pasta sauce and bake 15 minutes. Top with cheese and bake 15 more minutes. Garnish with parsley, if desired.

Egret on Log, photograph by Bob Ovelman.

Chicken Fricassee

1 tablespoon butter

2 tablespoons olive oil

1 onion, chopped

2 cloves garlic, peeled and minced

1 ½ pound skinless, boneless chicken breasts, cubed in bite sized pieces

Salt and freshly ground black pepper

3 tablespoons flour

1 cup water

½ cup dry white wine

1 pound mushrooms, cleaned and sliced

5 carrots, scraped and julienned in wide strips

3 tablespoons chopped fresh tarragon

½ cup Half and Half or cream

Melt the butter and olive oil together in a heavy large skillet on medium heat. Add the chopped onion and crushed garlic and cook for five minutes, stirring occasionally. Add the chicken and brown on all sides for about five minutes. Stir in the salt and pepper.

Sprinkle the top of the chicken with the flour and stir for 1 minute, thoroughly coating the chicken with the flour. Stir in the water and wine and then the prepared mushrooms, carrots, and tarragon. Bring to a low boil, cover and simmer on low heat for 20 minutes or just until the vegetables are cooked through. Turn off the heat and stir in the Half and Half or cream. Serve over long grain and wild rice with a salad of fresh lettuce. Yields: 6 servings.

Fixin' Up, watercolor on paper by Ray Ellis.

AS I WRITE I AM REMINDED of the incredible aroma that wafted throughout the house for the entire evening when I last cooked this marvelous fricassee. Even around 10 o'clock when I let the dogs out, I could still smell that great scent of cooked onions, carrots and chicken when I came back in.

This dish goes together very quickly, yet is rich and satisfying, even elegant. You can follow this recipe to the letter for guaranteed good results, or feel free to experiment on your own.

It's pronounced "Frihk-uh-see" and it's a loosely used term in French cooking. You will find lamb, veal, and rabbit fricassees as well as mushroom fricassee. Basically, it is a cooking method in which the meat or vegetables are browned lightly in butter, sprinkled with flour, and then cooked in bouillon or wine. As the meat and vegetables finish cooking the flour thickens the liquid and you get a sauce with absolutely no effort.

Tarragon is a common herb used in lots of French cooking and I encourage you to give it a try. Just remember this simple formula when changing herbs: One tablespoon of dried herbs usually substitutes for about 3 tablespoons of fresh.

Southern-Style Barbecued Chicken

RECIPES

2 chickens, quartered with backs removed
1 recipe for Barbecue Sauce

Marinate the chickens in ²/₃ of the barbecue sauce for a few hours or overnight in the refrigerator. Drain off the marinade and discard. Place the chicken quarters on the grill, skin side down, and cook for about 1 hour, turning once or twice to cook evenly on both sides. Continue cooking for about another 1 to 1½ hours. The chicken quarters are done when you insert a knife between a leg and thigh and the juices run clear. Baste with the remaining sauce during the last five minutes of cooking.

LOWCOUNTRY SAUCE
In a saucepan, cook ½ cup finely chopped onion and 3 cloves minced garlic in 1 tablespoon hot oil until tender. Stir in ¾ cup apple juice, ½ of a 6-ounce can tomato paste, ¼ cup cider vinegar, 2 tablespoons each packed brown sugar and molasses, 1 tablespoon each paprika and prepared horseradish, 1 teaspoon salt, and ½ teaspoon freshly ground black pepper.

Bring to a boil and reduce heat. Simmer, uncovered about 30 minutes or until sauce reaches desired consistency, stirring occasionally. Brush on chicken during the last 10 minutes of grilling.

HONEY BEER SAUCE
Cook ⅓ cup chopped onion and 1 clove garlic, minced, in 1 tablespoon hot oil until tender. Stir in 1 cup chili sauce, ½ cups beer and ¼ cup honey. Next, add 2 tablespoons Worcestershire sauce and 1 tablespoon mustard. Bring to a boil and reduce heat. Simmer uncovered until desired consistency, stirring occasionally. Brush on during the last 10 minutes of grilling.

When it's summertime and all the foods I adore are plentiful and in season, I bring home sweet corn, lush tomatoes, fresh herbs, green beans, juicy peaches, berries, and watermelon and so much more! They're just waiting to be showcased in delicious main dishes, sides, and desserts. Between my neighborhood farmer's market, roadside stands, local farms, and the local market, I am good to go.

On hot summer nights, break out the party lights, fire up the grill, and savor all the season has in store. An overflowing garden is the perfect excuse for a party! Southern-style barbecued chicken, grilled corn on the cob, and a luscious Greek tomato salad with chickpeas can be ready in no time at all.

In my experience, not as a barbecue champ, but as a dinner guest, chicken is the most abused food on the grill. The secret to changing chicken from boring to bravo — truly great barbecued chicken, one with moist, tender meat and smoky skin — is to lower the heat and leave the sauce off until the last few minutes of cooking. Most of the flavor comes through from marinating the meat overnight. Next, the smoke of the fire will fully permeate the meat during the long, slow cooking process. With low heat, and no sauce until late in the game, you don't have to keep moving chicken pieces around trying to stave off the inevitable flare-ups.

Using a temperature of about 250°, the chicken will take about 2½ hours to cook through. Slather on the sauce when the chicken is cooked. It needs only about 5 minutes to adhere nicely and since the fire isn't really hot, the chicken never gets that charred look, just a beautiful shine.

Experiment with some of these delicious sauces until you find one that pleases you. Then make it your signature sauce!

Special Attention, oil on canvas by Dan McCaw.

www.mycarolinacooking.com

Tailgate Pulled Pork Barbecue

DRY RUB

3 tablespoons paprika

1 tablespoon garlic powder

1 tablespoon brown sugar

1 tablespoon dry mustard

3 tablespoons sea salt

1 pork roast either shoulder or Boston butt

CIDER VINEGAR BARBECUE SAUCE

1½ cups cider vinegar

1 cup yellow or brown mustard

½ cup ketchup

⅓ cup packed brown sugar

2 cloves garlic, minced

1 teaspoon salt

1 teaspoon cayenne

½ teaspoon freshly ground black pepper

12 hamburger buns

Mix the paprika, garlic powder, brown sugar, dry mustard, and salt together in a small bowl. Rub the spice blend all over the pork. Cover and refrigerate for at least 1 hour or overnight.

Preheat the oven to 300°. Put the pork in a roasting pan and roast it for about 6 hours. An instant read thermometer stuck into the thickest part of the pork should register 170°. You want this roast to literally be falling apart when it is done.

While the pork is roasting, make the barbecue sauce. Combine the vinegar, mustard, ketchup, brown sugar, garlic, salt, cayenne, and black pepper in a saucepan and simmer gently. Stir until the sugar dissolves. Take it off the heat and let it rest until you're ready to use it.

When the roast is done, take it out of the oven and place it on a large platter. Allow the meat to rest for about 10 minutes. While it's resting, deglaze the pan over medium heat with ¾ cup water, scraping with a wooden spoon to scrap up all the browned bits. Reduce by half and pour that into the saucepan with the sauce and cook for 5 minutes.

While the pork is still warm pull the meat. Grab 2 forks, using 1 to steady the meat and the other to pull shreds of meat off the roast. Put the shredded pork in a bowl and pour half of the sauce over. Stir well so that the pork is covered with the sauce. To serve, spoon the pulled pork mixture onto the bottom half of each hamburger bun and top with some slaw. Yields: 12 servings.

Franklin Square, watercolor on paper by Ray Ellis.

Memories of Summer Cruises, oil on canvas by John Carroll Doyle.

Pierre's Shrimp and Crab Gravy

SportsmanPierre McGowan learned how to fix this at his friend's down-the-river camp. He's had many friends and strangers alike who, upon eating this for the first time, state that it is the best-tasting food they ever put in their mouths! This gravy will make one forget steak! Here are the ingredients:

2 pounds raw, peeled shrimp

½ pound crab meat, claw or white

1 large onion, chopped small

¼ pound good quality bacon

2 garlic cloves, sliced

½ bell pepper, chopped

Salt and pepper to taste

Flour – plain

4 drops Tabasco

¼ pound butter

2 cups water

Dice and brown bacon in a large skillet. Drain. When bacon is nearly cooked, add onions and garlic and cook 3 to 4 minutes. Set aside for adding later. Place butter in same skillet and heat to 300°. Add shrimp that have been salted, peppered and liberally rolled in flour. Shake in a brown paper bag. Do not add excess flour when frying shrimp. Brown the shrimp in butter approximately 3 minutes, turning only once. Add bacon and onions, stirring constantly. Add water, crab, bell pepper and Tabasco. Continue stirring for 5 minutes. Serve over rice or grits. May require a little more water, depending upon the desired consistency. Yields: 6 servings. Freezes well.

Oyster Roast, oil on canvas by Shannon Smith.

Shrimp Curry

Here's a savory entree that is very appealing to hostesses who like to prepare much of their dinner in advance. This is a rich shrimp curry that spills over rice for a perfectly beautiful presentation.

4 tablespoons butter

1 large yellow onion, chopped fine

½ cup apple, chopped fine

½ cup celery, chopped fine

1½ cups water

2 tablespoons curry powder

3 pounds shrimp, cleaned and deveined

1 pint Half and Half

Sauté onion, apple and celery in butter. When wilted, add water. Let simmer until apple and celery are tender and most of the liquid has evaporated. Stir in curry powder. Add Half and Half. Cook gently until cream is reduced to sauce consistency. Refrigerate. When ready to serve, bring mixture to simmer and add shrimp.

Next to the curry, place small bowls of grated coconut, chutney, and chopped almonds or other specialty relishes. Yields: 8 servings.

Serve over white rice and garnish with chopped parsley.

> The Bluffton Oyster Company actually sits on reclaimed land, built up by more than a hundred years of discarded shells from previous shucking operations. The oyster business thrived in early Blluffton and throughout the 1920s, with five different oyster operations in the area. Now, the Bluffton Oyster Company remains the last hand-shucking house in the state of South Carolina.

Scalloped Oysters

This makes a great side dish served at holiday time, or any time with either a turkey or a standing rib roast.

1 pint shucked oysters, washed and drained well

2 cups oyster cracker crumbs

¼ cup melted butter

½ teaspoon salt

½ teaspoon pepper

1 cup half and half

2 teaspoons sherry

dash Tabasco

1 teaspoon Worcestershire sauce

Preheat oven to 400°. Mix cracker crumbs and butter. Arrange a layer of half the buttered crumbs in 1 quart baking dish. Layer oysters over crackers. Season with salt and pepper. Cover with remaining crumbs. Combine Half and Half, sherry, Tabasco, and Worcestershire. Pour over casserole. Bake for about 20 minutes, or until liquid has been absorbed. Yields: 6-8 servings.

Pan Fried Steaks

July Fourth - River Street, oil on canvas by Ray Ellis.

WHEN MARSH GRASS TURNS from green to gleaming gold and brightly colored pumpkins greet us at every turn, we know autumn has arrived. I love that first day of autumn and the relief I feel after the long months of summer heat. It won't be long now until a drive through the country will show fields of neat bales of hay and pumpkins piled high at roadside stands.

The beauty and wonders of autumn are everywhere in our beloved Lowcountry, so pour yourself a hot cup of cider at the end of the day and enjoy the season!

Here's a delicious pan fried steak that's quick and easy to prepare and one you'll want to serve again and again.

RECIPE

Covering the skillet with a splatter screen will reduce the mess that pan frying inevitably makes.

2 strip steaks or rib eye steaks, or 1 sirloin
1 tablespoon vegetable oil

ROQUEFORT BUTTER
1 tablespoon butter, at room temperature
½ ounce Roquefort cheese, crumbled
¼ teaspoon brandy

Heat a 12-inch skillet (preferably cast iron or stainless steel) for 10 minutes over medium heat. Generously sprinkle each side of each steak with salt and freshly ground black pepper.

Add oil to the pan and swirl to coat the bottom. Add steaks, cover pan with splatter screen and cook until well browned on one side. Turn steaks, cook 3 more minutes for rare or more until desired degree of doneness is reached. Remove steaks from pan and make Roquefort butter.

Mash together butter, cheese, and brandy. Season with salt and pepper to taste. Top each cooked steak with a portion of the flavored butter and serve immediately. Serves 2.

From the Garden

"Only a Southerner knows how many collard greens, turnip greens, peas or beans make up a 'mess.'"

What a wonderful time of year for fresh produce from local farms. Driving the back roads to the beach, I notice the roadsides are sprinkled with handmade signs for homegrown garden vegetables. I love the smell of the great salt marsh at low tide, the summer breezes with the sound of cars and trucks whizzing by on these beach bound state roads. What I miss seeing along the roadsides are my favorite Southern peas. They show up at church picnics and family reunions and come in many varieties, shapes, colors, and names. Each farmer has his own idea of what they should be called.

Southern peas, cow peas, field peas, crowders or black-eyed peas or whatever name you call them, they are the beloved peas of the South. I haven't mentioned speckled butter beans or succotash, which is corn and butter beans, or fresh pinto beans. The "snaps" are underdeveloped pods cooked right along with the mature shelled peas. After the peas are passed around the table, pepper vinegar is not far behind, followed by the cornbread.

All those wonderful peas and corn; such humble ingredients cooked masterfully together in our home kitchens, formica diners, and barbecue huts to produce the elixir that tastes and feels like home in the South. I like to cook all of these in pure water with extra virgin olive oil, butter and a tiny bit of country ham. I give Chef Jim Nobles of Charlotte, a pioneer in the slow food movement, credit for this excellent technique. With just enough water to cover them, season with butter, salt and pepper and cook on low heat until tender. Peas have a cooking tipping point. Just under this point and they taste too green, too much and they get mushy, but cook them just right and they are sweet, nutty and healthy.

Some of my favorite childhood meals came from my grandmother's kitchen in North Carolina. Usually there were several tables of aunts, uncles, cousins, parents, and my older brother, Tom. The thing I remember most was the field peas cooking in a big pot with a chunk of pork side meat or ham hock. The liquid in the pots with the peas would turn brown. Right before everything was ready my grandmother would add several tender okra pods but not stir them in. She would just lay them on top of the peas to steam and take them out to serve separately on a plate. I considered myself lucky if I got one of those okra pods from the pot, because none of them ever made it to the table.

This simple farm produce reflects the generations of commitment to the land and devotion to the processes that yield the greatest achievements in taste. By reviving the pleasures of the table, our food heritage can be saved.

There's nothing better than a pot of Southern peas and some sliced tomato fresh from the vine out back, some spring onions, and a slice of cornbread with a side of freshly dug new potatoes – what a wonderful dinner! Bring on the sweet tea, and you have a meal that makes us uniquely Southern.

Opposite Page: Back Street in Beaufort, oil on canvas by Peter Rolfe.

Vidalia Onion Tart

5 cups sweet Vidalia onions, diced

2 tablespoons oil

1 teaspoon salt

Freshly ground black pepper

1 cup heavy cream

1 egg

1 egg yolk

1 teaspoon finely chopped flat-leaf parsley

1 teaspoon finely chopped chives

1 tart shell, partially baked

Cook the onions in the olive oil over medium heat until tender. Keep covered to seal in flavor and prevent onions from browning. Season with salt and pepper. Add the heavy cream and simmer for several minutes. Adjust seasoning, if necessary. Allow to cool slightly. Whisk the egg and egg yolk together and incorporate into the onion mixture. Finish with the chopped parsley and chives. Pour mixture into the partially baked tart shell and bake at 325° for about 20 minutes or until a toothpick comes out clean. Serves 12.

TART DOUGH

½ cup plus 2 tablespoons butter

1 teaspoon sugar

1 teaspoon salt

1 egg

1 egg yolk

1 cup all purpose flour

In a food processor use paddle attachment and cream the first three ingredients for 10 minutes on low speed. Add the eggs to the butter and process until well blended. Add the flour and mix on medium speed until incorporated. Allow the dough to rest for 30 minutes then roll out to ⅛-inch. Prick with a fork and press into a 12-inch fluted tart ring. Line with a large coffee filter or parchment paper and weight the dough with beans to eliminate any rising that may occur. Bake at 325° until light golden brown, about 10 to 14 minutes. Allow the shell to cool completely before adding the filling.

Twice Baked Potato Casserole

5 pounds Russet potatoes, peeled and cut into ½-inch cubes

3 quarts water

1 tablespoon plus 1½ teaspoons salt, divided

½ cup butter, softened

One 16-ounce container sour cream

3 large eggs, lightly beaten

1 teaspoon ground black pepper

One 8-ounce package Fontina cheese, shredded and divided

One 8-ounce package sharp Cheddar cheese, shredded and divided

12 slices bacon, cooked and crumbled

½ cup minced chives

TOPPING

Shredded Fontina cheese

Shredded Cheddar cheese

Preheat oven to 375°. Lightly grease a 3 quart baking dish and set aside.

Place potatoes in a Dutch oven with water and 1 tablespoon salt. Bring to a boil over medium high heat, cook for 10 to 15 minutes, or until tender. Drain potatoes well, and return to saucepan. Add butter; using a potato masher, mash potato mixture until butter is melted. Add sour cream, eggs, remaining 1½ teaspoons salt, and pepper, stirring to combine well.

Stir in cheeses, bacon, and chives. Spoon into prepared baking dish. Sprinkle with additional cheese, if desired. Bake for 20 to 30 minutes, or until bubbly.

> The Vidalia onion was named Georgia's Official State Vegetable in 1990. Its sweet flavor is due to the unique soil in Vidalia, Georgia.

Vinegar and Vidalias, oil on canvas by Shannon Smith.

Our Best Macaroni and Cheese

This is the full-throttle, quintessential special-occasion, Southern version of baked macaroni and cheese, loaded with flavor.

7 cups water

1 tablespoons salt

16 ounces elbow macaroni

6 tablespoons softened butter

3 eggs

2 cups evaporated milk

1 teaspoon salt

¾ teaspoon dry mustard

2½ cups sharp cheddar cheese, grated

TOPPING

15 Ritz crackers

4 tablespoons butter, melted

½ teaspoon paprika

Preheat oven to 350°. Bring water and 1 tablespoon salt to a boil in a heavy saucepan. Slowly add macaroni; return to a boil, and cook for 10 minutes or until just al dente, stirring occasionally. Strain macaroni in a colander and rinse with cool water. Place the macaroni in a bowl, mix with the softened butter, and set aside.

In a mixing bowl, beat the eggs by hand until frothy, then beat in the evaporated milk, 1 teaspoon of salt, and dry mustard. Set aside.

In a large, oiled casserole dish, spread a layer of approximately half the macaroni, and add a layer of about half the cheese. Spread remaining macaroni and top with remaining cheese. Pour egg and milk mixture slowly and evenly over the top, and tilt the casserole dish to each side until the liquid is evenly distributed.

In a separate bowl, crush the Ritz crackers with your fingers, sifting through several times to obtain a fine consistency. Add 4 tablespoons melted butter, and mix with a fork until the crumbs are uniformly moistened. Spread evenly by hand or spatula over the top of the casserole. Sprinkle top with paprika, if desired.

Bake for 40 to 45 minutes, or until the top is bubbly and well browned. Remove from oven and set on a wire rack to cool and set for 20 minutes or more before serving. Slice this incredible dish into individual servings. Its flavor and texture far exceed the sum of its parts!

Monday Morning on River Street, watercolor on paper by Ray Ellis.

WHEN IT COMES TO PLANNING side dishes for dinner, abandon all restraint. Creamy casseroles bubbling beneath blankets of melted cheese, buttered breadcrumbs piping hot from the oven, this is the food that comforts.

A big dish of macaroni and cheese can be as warm and comforting as a hug! It may be the absolute favorite among all comfort foods, not just in the South, but in all regions of our country. A great many Southern cookbooks and nearly every soul food cookbook has a special twist on this classic dish.

It's amazing to realize that Kraft sells between 1 and 2 million boxes of macaroni and cheese every day, and many devotees of the instant dinners would no doubt turn up their noses at an honest-to-goodness homemade version. "The real thing" means a casserole of macaroni and cheese that has been baked at least 30 minutes, having first been prepared by either mixing the cheese sauce into the noodles or layering it.

In both methods, macaroni is stirred into salted boiling water and cooked for about 10 minutes, or until it is just al dente – still slightly chewy. A mistake is overcooking the pasta which can nullify a lot of careful work in the later stages and produce a mushy mess. Once the pasta reaches the right texture, it should be quickly drained in a colander and rinsed with cold water.

Morning at the Fountain, watercolor on paper by Ray Ellis.

Fried Green Tomatoes

3 green tomatoes
1 ½ cups buttermilk
2 eggs, lightly beaten
½ teaspoon plus ½ teaspoon salt
½ teaspoon plus ½ teaspoon black pepper
1 tablespoon plus 1 ½ cups self-rising flour
2 cups vegetable oil

Wash and slice the tomatoes into ¼-inch slices. In a bowl mix the buttermilk and eggs. Add ½ teaspoon of the salt, ½ teaspoon of the pepper, and 1 tablespoon of the flour. Mix well. Place the tomato slices in the buttermilk and egg mixture. Set aside to rest. Preheat the oil in a heavy skillet or electric fryer to 350°. In another bowl, mix the remaining 1 ½ cups flour, ½ teaspoon salt and ½ teaspoon pepper. Remove the tomato slices from the buttermilk/egg mixture and toss them, one at a time, in the flour mixture, coating them thoroughly. Carefully place the tomato slices in the heated oil and fry until golden brown. Turn them two or three times.

Be careful not to crowd the tomatoes during frying. Do not allow them to overlap or they will stick together. Cook until crisp. Drain on paper towels. Serve immediately. Yields: 6 servings.

WHILE DRIVING DOWN Hwy. 17 through the vast expanses of marshland and centuries old Live oaks, I imagine heaven surely must be some celestial branch of the Lowcountry. For now, though, this earthly place is quite heavenly enough. It is a place where the land and the sea yield their rich bounty, year after year, as dependable as the tides. This is a place where divine food is presented with gracious hospitality in the elegant surroundings of homes built in the 1800s. Families still live in these homes; children play, go to school, and grow up. Even though Beaufort is the hometown of *The Big Chill*, *The Prince of Tides* and *Forrest Gump*, the homes are not Hollywood sets but real homes with real people.

The food culture has been passed down through the generations with meals that define Southern eating at its best, from steaming hot biscuits slathered with butter to fried green tomatoes and spoon bread and sideboards of tantalizing desserts.

Even a short visit to the Lowcountry reveals that the hospitality and manners of the old South are alive and well in the modern South. While the pace of life is a bit slower, this by no means implies that Southerners do not work as hard as those in other regions. It was Harper Lee, author of *To Kill a Mockingbird*, who explained away the perception that since Southerners do not move quickly, they do not work as hard. "We work hard, of course, but we do it in a different way. We work hard in order not to work. Any time spent on business is more or less wasted, but you have to do it in order to be able to hunt and fish and gossip."

With that being said, a recipe for one of the South's most famous specialties is in order – Fried Green Tomatoes. I've chosen the recipe for Fried Green Tomatoes loved by Lewis Grizzard, the famed columnist from the *Atlanta Journal-Constitution*. Following a visit to the Blue Willow Inn in Social Circle, Georgia in 1992, he wrote rave reviews about the food they served and especially the Fried Green Tomatoes.

Buttermilk Fried Okra

1 cup all purpose flour

½ teaspoon baking powder

½ teaspoon salt

¼ teaspoon ground mustard

1 ½ cups buttermilk

Fresh whole okra (about 24 pieces)

Oil for frying

Sift the dry ingredients together. Whisk in the buttermilk and use batter at once. In a heavy bottomed saucepan over medium-low heat, heat enough oil to submerge the okra. Dip okra into the batter one at a time, leaving the tops exposed, and coat well. Drop into preheated oil and cook for 30 to 40 seconds, until pale brown. Drain on paper towels. Serve immediately alongside a creamy herb or remoulade dipping sauce. This batter is wonderful with other garden fresh vegetables such as zucchini, squash, or eggplant, each sliced no more than a ½-inch thick to ensure the vegetable is thoroughly cooked.

REMOULADE SAUCE

1 cup mayonnaise

¼ cup chili sauce

2 tablespoons Creole mustard

2 tablespoons olive oil

Hot sauce to taste

3 tablespoons fresh lemon juice

1 teaspoon Worcestershire sauce

3 scallions, chopped fine

2 tablespoons fresh chopped parsley

1 clove garlic

Salt and pepper to taste

2 teaspoons capers

Mix together mayonnaise, chili sauce, mustard, oil, hot sauce, lemon juice, and Worcestershire. Stir in scallions, parsley, capers, and garlic. Season with salt and freshly ground black pepper. Cover and refrigerate. This is wonderful topped on crab, shrimp, lobster, salmon dishes, and even seafood po' boy sandwiches!

Lucille Wright's Tomato Pie

Lucille Wright, a legend in Savannah, was widely known as the first to ever take a pie shell, sliced tomatoes and mayonnaise, onions, and cheese, and bake it. This famous caterer became even more popular after she was immortalized in *Midnight in the Garden of Good and Evil*. Her summertime dish quickly became a regional favorite.

4 large, garden ripe tomatoes

½ cup chopped green onion

Fresh basil to taste

1 deep dish pie crust, baked

Salt and freshly ground black pepper

1 cup grated Cheddar cheese

1 cup grated mozzarella cheese

1 cup mayonnaise

Preheat oven to 350°. Layer the tomato slices, onion and basil in a baked pie crust. Season with salt and pepper. Mix cheeses and mayonnaise and spread over top of tomatoes. Bake 30 minutes or until lightly browned. Yields: 8 servings.

Putting-on-the-Ritz Pineapple

Serve with a wonderful roast or baked ham.

1 sleeve Ritz crackers, crumbled

3 tablespoons melted butter

4 ounces white sharp Cheddar cheese, shredded

⅓ cup sugar

2 tablespoons flour

One 16-ounce can crushed pineapple, drained

One 16-ounce can pineapple chunks, drained

Combine the crackers and butter in a bowl, tossing to mix. Spread on a baking sheet. Toast at 325° for 30 minutes. Next, combine the cheese, sugar, and flour in a bowl and mix well. Stir in the crushed pineapple and pineapple chunks. Spoon into a baking dish. Sprinkle with the cracker mixture. Bake at 350° for 30 minutes. Yields: 8-10 servings.

Rice Canal, oil on canvas by Ray Ellis.

Risotto with Creamy Scallops and Tomatoes

RECIPE

5 cups fish stock

½ cup chopped onion

3 teaspoons olive oil

2 shallots

1 clove garlic

1 cup Arborio rice

¾ cup dry white wine, warmed

6 large plum tomatoes

1 tablespoon chopped thyme

12 ounces fresh sea scallops

2 tablespoons ricotta cheese

¼ cup plain yogurt

1 teaspoon lemon zest

Salt and freshly ground black pepper to taste

In a heavy saucepan, heat the stock to a simmer. Chop the onion and sauté until tender. Chop the shallots and mince the garlic.

When the onion has softened, add the rice and stir to coat. Add the warm wine to the rice and let the wine cook down for several minutes.

Heat a sauté pan until it is very hot, reducing the heat to medium high. Then add the remaining oil and sauté the shallots and garlic. Add a cup of the simmering stock to the rice, and cook while stirring until the liquid is absorbed. Repeat this procedure with the rest of the stock.

Meanwhile, wash, trim and slice the tomatoes. Add them to the shallots and garlic, and cook until they soften. Add the

FORGET EVERYTHING YOU EVER HEARD about risotto being hard to make! It's just a little like riding a bicycle. It takes a bit of practice in the beginning, a little concentration thereafter and then you take off like a pro.

Head over to your local farmer's market and find the freshest and best vegetables of the season. Risottos are a delicious way to use veggies in creative and healthy ways.

The most important element is the rice itself. Arborio, an Italian rice, is better than wonderful and easy to find. The grains are short, resulting in a creamy, smooth, rich product.

This marvelous dish cannot be successfully prepared in advance, but it only requires about 20 minutes of your time. There are as many variations of risotto as your imagination will allow.

Here's the scoop on the basic how-to:

Begin by mincing a small volume of onion and whatever other herbs the recipe calls for. Sauté the mixture in olive oil and when it has browned, remove it with a slotted spoon to a plate, leaving the drippings in the pot.

Stir one cup Arborio rice into the pot with the drippings and sauté it until it becomes translucent (about 10 minutes), stirring constantly to keep it from sticking.

Return the sautéed seasonings to the pot and stir in a third of a cup of dry white wine that is warm. (Any cold ingredient will shock the rice, which will flake on the outside and stay hard at the core.)

Once the wine has evaporated, add some warm stock (about 5 cups) and stir in until the rice absorbs it all.

At this point stir in grated cheese, if the recipe calls for it, cover and let it sit for several minutes. Serve immediately for best results.

Once you've done the basics, you'll want to try this fabulous risotto with creamy scallops and tomatoes.

thyme to the tomatoes as they cook.

Wash the scallops. Whisk the ricotta and yogurt. Grate the lemon zest.

Just before the rice is tender, stir the scallops into the tomato mixture and cook. Remove from the heat, and stir the yogurt and ricotta mixture into the tomato mixture. Stir in the zest.

Remove the risotto from the heat, and stir in the scallop mixture. Season with salt the freshly ground black pepper and serve. Yields: 3 servings.

End of the Battery, oil on canvas by Jennifer Smith Rogers.

Autumn Salad with Balsamic Roasted Pears

1 pound fresh mixed lettuce

Kosher salt and pepper

6 ounces goat cheese, crumbled

FOR THE DRESSING

½ cup pecan halves

4 tablespoons red wine vinegar

1 tablespoon honey

Salt

½ cup extra virgin olive oil

Heat a large sauté pan over high heat. Add pecans and stir until almost burnt. Place pecans and vinegar into a blender and blend on high speed. Add honey and season with salt to taste. Slowly drizzle in the oil.

BALSAMIC ROASTED PEARS

4 ripe pears

Sugar

Kosher salt

1-2 tablespoons oil

1 cup balsamic vinegar

Peel and halve pears. Using a melon baller, remove seeds then season with sugar and salt. Heat a sauté pan over high heat. Add oil. When hot, add pears cut side down. Turn heat down to medium. Allow pears to caramelize, about 5 minutes. When pears are dark brown, add vinegar. Turn over and cook until fork tender, about 5 more minutes, occasionally basting them with vinegar. Remove pears and leave at room temperature. Simmer remaining vinegar until it is reduced to a glaze. Reserve the reduction.

Pour the balsamic reduction over the salad, add the pecan vinaigrette and toss. Sprinkle the goat cheese on top.

Potato Gratin with Truffle Oil

Bring your potatoes to new heights with delicious truffle oil!

3 pounds Yukon Gold potatoes, peeled and cut into ⅛ inch slices

8 ounces Fontina cheese, well chilled

kosher salt and freshly ground black pepper

1½ cups creme fraiche or sour cream

1 tablespoon white truffle oil

1 tablespoon minced fresh herbs of your choice such as basil or rosemary

Preheat oven to 400°. Butter a 9 x 13 inch baking dish. Remove rind and shred Fontina cheese using a hand grater. Place ½ the potatoes, overlapping slightly, in prepared baking dish. Salt and pepper slices generously. With a rubber spatula, spread half the creme fraiche or sour cream over the potatoes. Then sprinkle ½ the cheese over the creme fraiche. Make a second layer in the same way using the remaining ingredients.

Bake potato gratin on center rack of your oven, uncovered, for about 30 minutes. Then lower heat to 350° and bake about 30 more minutes or until potatoes are tender when pierced with a knife. Potatoes will have a golden brown crust on top. Cover with aluminum foil if potatoes become too brown. Remove from oven and let stand 10 minutes. Drizzle truffle oil over the top and sprinkle with herbs just before serving.

If you cannot find creme fraiche, make your own by whisking together 1¼ cups whipping cream and ½ cup sour cream. Let stand at room temperature until thickened, approximately 6 hours or overnight. Cover and refrigerate. Can be stored up to 1 week in the refrigerator. Makes about 1¾ cups.

Deep South Penne Pasta

8 ounces uncooked penne pasta

3 tablespoons olive oil

½ cup sweet Vidalia onions, chopped

3 cloves fresh garlic, minced

⅓ cup chopped red bell pepper

One 15-ounce can garbanzo beans, rinsed and drained

3 cups halved cherry tomatoes

¾ cup crumbled feta cheese

⅓ cup fresh basil leaves, chopped

½ teaspoon salt

½ teaspoon grated lemon rind

Freshly grated black pepper

In a large pot, cook pasta according to the directions on the box. Drain in a colander and reserve ¼ cup cooking liquid. Heat a large skillet and add the oil to the pan. Add onions and garlic and sauté about 1 minute. Stir in bell pepper and chickpeas; sauté 2 minutes. Add tomatoes; sauté 2 minutes. Stir in pasta and reserved cooking liquid. Cook 1 minute or until completely heated. Remove from the heat. Add feta and remaining ingredients and toss to combine. Yields: 4 servings.

Cranberry-Pineapple Gelatin Salad

Two 3-ounce packages raspberry gelatin

½ envelope unflavored gelatin

1 cup boiling water

½ cup ice cold water

One 15-ounce can whole-berry cranberry sauce

One 8-ounce can crushed pineapple, packed in its own juice

¼ cup finely chopped walnuts

Whipped cream (optional)

Spray a 4-cup gelatin mold or a 9-inch square pan with non stick cooking spray. In a medium glass mixing bowl, combine raspberry gelatin and unflavored gelatin. Add 1 cup boiling water and stir with a metal spoon for 2 minutes until the gelatin is completely dissolved. Stir in ½ cup cold water. Add cranberry sauce, pineapple, and walnuts.

Stir with a metal spoon until all of the ingredients are completely incorporated. Pour the mixture into the prepared mold, cover with plastic wrap, and refrigerate until firm.

About an hour before serving, invert the mold onto a serving platter and allow it to come to room temperature. The salad will release itself and come cleanly from the mold. Garnish with whipped cream if desired and surround salad with lettuce leaves.

Big Mama's Collard Greens

Slow cooked with beer, vinegar, bacon, onion, garlic, and molasses.

2 bundles of greens, including collard and/or mustard

12 ounce can of beer

3 slices of bacon

1 whole onion, chopped

1 tablespoon chopped garlic, fresh

1 tablespoon vinegar

1 tablespoon molasses

Hot sauce – about ½ teaspoon or to taste

Salt and fresh pepper

In a large pot sauté and brown bacon. Set aside. Add chopped onion and cook until soft. Prepare greens by washing, slicing off tough ends and chopping leaves into wide strips. Add garlic to sautéed onion and cook for a minute. Pour in beer, vinegar, and molasses. Bring to a boil. Reduce heat to low and press down greens into pot and cover. Cook for 15 minutes. Greens will wilt and shrink the way spinach does. Mix well so greens keep cooking down. Once well mixed, cook for an hour. Add hot sauce a little at a time until desired hotness is achieved. Check greens and add water or stock as liquid cooks out – a half cup at a time. Crumble bacon and gently fold into the greens.

NOTE: You'll find collards all year 'round, but most folks think they taste better in the winter, from about the first frost through March or April.

Beach Cottage Window, watercolor on paper by Nancy Ricker Rhett.

Savory Acorn Squash

Stoll's Alley, oil on canvas by Jennifer Smith Rogers.

As the summer months stretch into fall we begin to put away those recipes for yellow squash and think of their cold weather counterparts. Butternut, acorn, and many others just seem to get overlooked because of their large size. Their tough skin can make them somewhat intimidating because, unless you have a really sharp knife, they're a challenge to cut. Sometimes the simplest flavor combinations can be the most comforting. Take acorn squash, maple syrup, and butter for example. Whoever first put these ingredients into a hot oven on a cool autumn night many years ago knew how to make someone happy. The sweet, earthy smell of squash caramelizing in the oven is enough to get most any family to the table.

Cut in half, seeds scooped out with a spoon, an acorn squash yields two pretty cup-shaped halves. With the ends trimmed a little, the halves will stand up straight and double as their own serving bowls. Each becomes a little vessel for bubbling butter and sugar and any other seasonings you happen to like.

While a basic roasted squash with butter and maple syrup or brown sugar is hard to beat, there are a few variations and embellishments that can be added for fun. You might decide to add chopped pecans or use orange juice or apple cider with honey in place of the maple syrup. Whatever way you decide to go, serve this with a spoon. Each squash will yield two good size servings. It's best to choose acorn squash on the smaller side; they will be more tender and cook more quickly.

RECIPES

MAPLE SQUASH

1 acorn squash, cut in half and seeded

1 ½ tablespoons unsalted butter, softened

1 tablespoon maple syrup

1 tablespoon chopped pecans (add during the last 10 minutes)

Heat the oven to 400°. Butter the pan to prevent sticking. Set the halves on the baking sheet and smear the flesh all over with the softened butter. Sprinkle with salt and drizzle the remaining ingredients over the top edge of the squash and into the cavity. Roast the squash halves until nicely browned and very tender for about 1 hour and 15 minutes. Don't undercook and serve warm.

APPLE CIDER SQUASH

1 ½ tablespoons butter, softened

2 tablespoons apple cider mixed with
1 tablespoon honey and a pinch of ground cinnamon

ORANGE SQUASH

1 ½ tablespoons butter, softened

2 tablespoons orange juice mixed with
1 tablespoon honey

1 teaspoon minced fresh ginger

Be sure to spread the ingredients evenly between the two halves!

Picking Tomatoes at Dempsey's Farm, oil on canvas by Steve Weeks.

Wild Rice Salad

- ⅔ cup wild rice
- ⅔ cup brown rice
- ½ cup olive oil
- 3 tablespoons Champagne vinegar
- 2 tablespoons sugar
- 1 tablespoon curry powder
- ½ teaspoon salt
- Freshly ground black pepper to taste
- ½ cup radishes, finely chopped
- ½ cup toasted pecans, chopped
- ½ cup fresh parsley, chopped
- ½ cup red onion, finely chopped
- ½ cup golden raisins
- ½ cup currants

Cook rices in 3 quarts boiling salted water, stirring occasionally, until wild rice is tender and grains split open, about 1 hour. Drain in a sieve and rinse with cold water to stop cooking, and then drain well. Blend oil, vinegar, sugar, curry powder, salt and pepper in a blender until combined, then toss with rice and remaining ingredients in a large bowl.

NOTE: This salad can be made 1 day ahead and chilled, covered. Serve slightly chilled or at room temperature.

BEAUTIFUL, NUTRITIOUS SALADS don't have to be complicated and time consuming. Forget those tasteless winter tomatoes and get creative with some produce that's in season and delicious! Shop locally when you can for the very best and fresh.

Here's a flavorful salad I was served at 131 Main in Cornelius, North Carolina. When we asked our waitress about the ingredients, she immediately came back with the recipe! She said they have so many people ask about the recipe, they wrote it out. It's packed with nutrients and has a very unusual taste. I think you, too, will find this combination of wild and brown rice tossed with curry, pecans, onion and raisins a truly winning side dish! Once you gather all the ingredients, it all goes together in no time at all, and it even gets better after a day or two.

Crisp Tybee Salad

- 6 cups salad mix
- ½ cup mandarin oranges
- 1 red bell pepper, cut into long thin slices
- 2 avocados, sliced (½ per person)
- ¼ cup dry roasted pine nuts
- ½ cup crumbled gorgonzola cheese

In a large salad bowl, toss all ingredients together, except the gorgonzola, with the honey balsamic vinaigrette. Sprinkle gorgonzola on top. Yields: 4 servings.

NOTE: To roast pine nuts, simply place them in a dry heavy skillet over low heat until they are nicely browned.

www.mycarolinacooking.com

Egret Ready to Fly, photograph by Bob Ovelman.

For tonight's dinner make this indescribably delicious salad that can be prepared in a matter of minutes and and topped off with this rich Honey Balsamic Vinaigrette. Create your own salad mix with a combination of several leafy-green varieties of lettuce, each with its unique color, texture, and flavor. In this salad, peppery, dark-green arugula contrasts with sweet, crisp, red-leaf lettuce and dark green baby spinach. I try to stay away from iceberg lettuce as much as possible because, while it has a nice crunch, it has almost no nutritional value. Extra toppings like croutons and bacon bits pack a whole lot of calories and very little nutrition. With just a few slices of grilled chicken, you can turn this healthy salad into a healthy meal.

Honey Balsamic Vinaigrette

¼ cup aged balsamic vinegar

2 teaspoons Dijon mustard

½ teaspoon salt

¾ cup olive oil

2 cloves minced garlic

2 shallots, chopped fine

¼ to ½ cup honey – more or less depending upon taste

Whisk together the vinegar, mustard, honey, garlic, salt and pepper until the salt is dissolved and the ingredients are well blended. Gradually whisk in the oil. Toss in some shallots to the mix, which will give it a nice crunch. Cover and store in the refrigerator. If the oil hardens from being chilled, just set your jar in a pot of hot water and let it warm up while you are preparing the rest of the salad.

NOTE: Balsamic vinegar is made from white wine vinegar and gets its dark color from being aged in wood barrels for years. Just like wine, the longer it ages, the more deeply flavored the vinegar. The mustard makes this a thicker, more emulsified vinaigrette. While shopping in Salisbury I found at least nine different varieties of balsamic vinegar anywhere from $3.00 to $9.00. I recommend the ones from Modena, Italy, and there were several for about $4.00.

Asparagus and Arugula Salad with Garbanzo Beans

Asparagus is one of nature's most perfect foods, rich in flavor and high in nutrients and fiber. In fact, it's one of the most nutritionally well-balanced vegetables in existence. It leads nearly all produce items in the wide array of nutrients it supplies and can be prepared with little effort and served in this delicious salad.

6 tablespoons olive oil

½ red onion, sliced thin

1 pound asparagus, trimmed and cut on the diagonal into 1-inch pieces

1 ½ cups garbanzo beans, rinsed and drained

3 tablespoons balsamic vinegar

6 cups arugula salad greens

Kosher salt and freshly ground black pepper

½ cup feta cheese

Heat 3 tablespoons oil in a skillet over high heat and stir in the onion and cook until it starts to brown.

Add asparagus, salt and pepper and cook until asparagus is browned and tender and crisp, about 4 minutes. Stir several times and turn off the heat. Stir in the beans and transfer to a plate to cool. Whisk in 3 tablespoons oil, the vinegar, salt and pepper together until well combined. In a large bowl, toss arugula with 2 tablespoons of the dressing and divide among the salad plates.

Toss asparagus mixture with remaining dressing and place over the arugula and serve. Sprinkle feta cheese on top of each serving. Yields: 4-6 servings.

Sensational Seafood

The South is a place where ... tea is sweet and accents are sweeter, macaroni and cheese is a vegetable, front porches are wide and words are long. Pecan pie is a staple. Y'all is the only proper noun. Chicken is fried and biscuits come with gravy. Everything is darlin' and someone's heart is always being blessed.

EVERY WINTER, when waters around Lady's Island reach cold enough temperatures to produce oysters with just the right amount of salinity, there are oyster roasts. The best is usually on New Year's Day and later in the season at the fund-raiser for Ducks Unlimited — an organization dedicated to the preservation of the Lowcountry wetlands and the survival of the ducks living there. These are large social gatherings held at one of the plantations or in the front yard of an historic home in the Old Point. Everyone in town shows up and it doesn't really matter whether they care about ducks or the wetlands. It's a time for catching up on friendships, drinking a little bourbon and trying to stay warm in the glow of the fire.

From October through March oysters are found in abundance along the Beaufort coast and they are the delight of Lowcountry roasts. Anyone can buy them off the docks in burlap sacks and use them in recipes made famous at parties along the Beaufort river bluffs.

Each fall and winter, oyster beds are just ripe for gathering along the low water mark. Natives standing in ankle deep water at the break of dawn often are seen opening their sweet and succulent bounty. Throughout the salt water marshes and waterways, oysters grow in huge clusters — as many as eight stuck together in a clump.

If you've never been to an oyster roast, it's an experience that will keep you coming back again and again. It's a time to bring the whole family together — from the smallest babies to the great grandparents. As families gather by an open roaring fire, the men place a large metal sheet on blocks over the fire, while oysters are shoveled onto the metal and quickly covered with wet burlap bags.

It's a sight to behold when the oysters open from the heat and are shoveled onto high wooden tables, surrounded by folks with their oyster knives and garden gloves shucking and eating. The aroma and taste of the great salt marsh permeate the senses with every bite. The term "oyster roast" is somewhat of a misnomer, as the oysters are actually steam grilled rather than roasted. For some, a bowl of hot butter with fresh squeezed lemon juice is just right for dipping, while others prefer the succulent red sauce with ketchup, horseradish, and Worcestershire. Either way, it's a treat like no other!

While oysters take the spotlight, other delicacies such as South Carolina Brunswick stew, crab bisque, and Savannah red rice are served along side tables. The host needs only to add some beer, crackers, and the quest for the perfect oyster takes over.

Opposite Page: Oyster Boat and Blackbirds, oil on canvas by Michael Harrell.

Louis' Fried Oysters

Serves 10 to 12 people as an appetizer.

1/3 cup salt

2 tablespoons cayenne pepper

1 tablespoon plus 1 teaspoon gumbo file powder

1 tablespoon onion powder

1 tablespoon garlic powder

1 tablespoon white pepper

1 tablespoon paprika

1 tablespoon freshly ground black pepper

2 cups all-purpose flour

6 cups peanut oil

1/2 gallon select shucked oysters

Combine the salt, cayenne pepper, gumbo file powder, onion powder, garlic powder, white pepper, paprika, and black pepper. Stir to mix well. (Stored in a tightly covered container in a cool place, the spice mixture will keep for two months.)

Add 2 tablespoons of the spice mix to 2 cups of flour and stir to combine.

Heat the oil in a heavy skillet that is large enough to have the oil 1½ inches deep, but not more than halfway up the sides. Oil temperature should be 350°. Working with a dozen oysters at a time, sprinkle them with ½ teaspoon of the spice mixture and toss to distribute it evenly. Then toss the oysters quickly in the seasoned flour, coating them well, but shaking to remove any excess flour. Do not leave the oysters sitting in the flour or they will get soggy.

Drop oysters gently into the hot oil. Do not crowd the pan. Move the oysters around with a slotted spoon so they won't stick to the pan or to one another.

Fry oysters from 45 seconds to 1 minute. When they are done, they should be golden brown. Do not overcook or they will lose their delectable juices. If you suddenly hear popping and sputtering from the pan, remove the oysters immediately; they are beginning to overcook. Place them on paper towel, changing the towel if it begins to get saturated with oil. Serve immediately with your favorite sauce, or on a salad of mixed greens.

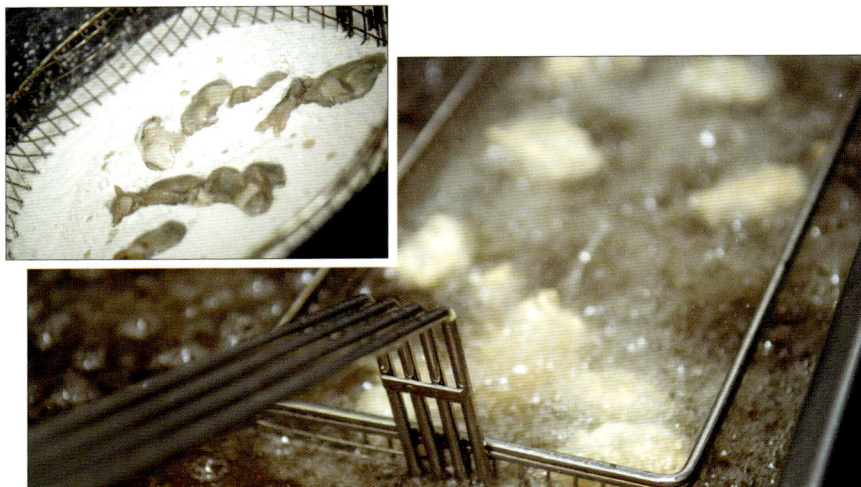

WE'LL NEVER KNOW who plucked that first wrinkled, briny oyster from the sea and had the courage to eat it, but we do know it happened a very long time ago. Ancient Romans so prized oysters that they sent slaves by the thousands to the English Channel to bring them home. Not only did they feast upon them, but they used them as the foundation for the world's first manmade oyster beds.

Throughout the world, there are over 400 varieties of oysters and all have one thing in common — that sweet, yet salty, taste of the ocean. The "season" for Lowcountry oysters begins in September just in time for those memorable outdoor roasts, and for wonderful fall casseroles and stews.

Shucking oysters continuously for nearly a century, the Bluffton Oyster Company now operates on land purchased by the Open Land Trust and the Beaufort and Bluffton governments for preservation. It is the last remaining oyster company on the South Carolina coast.

If you were to ask chef Louis Osteen, of Louis' Restaurant and Fish Camp in Pawley's Island, what is the best way to cook an oyster, he'd say, "Just cook the oysters quickly — before they start releasing their juices in the hot frying oil. Drain them ever so briefly on absorbent towels and get them right away onto toasted bread. Just top it off with a little garlic butter or your favorite red sauce." Then he'd add,"Don't forget a couple drops of Texas Pete!"

Oysters Are Ready, oil on canvas by Elaine Coffee.

Daufuskie Island Oyster Stuffing

It was Jonathan Swift who said, "He was a bold man that first eat an oyster."

2½ sticks butter

2 cups finely chopped celery

1 cup finely chopped sweet onion

2 tablespoons fresh thyme leaves

½ teaspoon sage

1 tablespoon celery seed, crushed

Salt and pepper to taste

2½ pounds toasted cornbread crumbs

1½ cups chicken broth

2 dozen oysters, shucked and liquid reserved

3 large eggs

¼ cup chopped fresh parsley

Heat oven to 350° and butter a 13 x 9 inch casserole dish. Melt 2 sticks of butter in a sauté pan over low heat. Add celery and onion, fresh thyme leaves and sage, and cook until tender about 10 minutes. Pour into a large bowl and mix in toasted cornbread crumbs. Return pan to high heat and pour in the broth. Pour hot broth over the cornbread mixture and stir until incorporated. Gently fold in the oysters and their liquid, beaten eggs, and parsley and season with salt and pepper.

Spoon stuffing into the casserole dish and dot with pieces of the remaining ½ stick butter. Cover with foil and bake 20 minutes. Remove foil and bake another 10 minutes until the top is golden brown. Yields: 8 servings.

NOTE: A Christmas dinner at my house just wouldn't be complete without a delicious serving of oyster stuffing! My dad grew up on the Chesapeake Bay and fixed oysters every way there was to fix them. He sure loved this stuffing!

The "Local" Oyster: Pat Conroy's comments on the Oyster Roast

Resident expert and adopted son, author Pat Conroy, in his cookbook, describes a proper oyster roast, "An oyster roast must take place on a cold day for it to work its proper magic…This is not a milieu that induces euphoria among highbrows and intellectuals…there will be a lot more pickup trucks than Lexuses in the parking lot…"

Mr. Conroy also is quick to tell us an amusing tale about just how seriously we take the "Local" in our oysters. Seems he was buying a few bushels from an oysterman on St. Helena Island and he asked,"Sir, are these oysters local?" To which the purveyor replied,"No, sir, Gotta be honest. I harvested these over three miles from here."

www.mycarolinacooking.com

Beaufort's Best Shrimp Burgers

Shrimp Burger courtesy of the Sweetgrass Bistro, Dataw Island, SC, photograph by Jack Howison.

The Sweetgrass Bistro on Dataw Island also serves a fabulous Shrimp Burger. Neither Nadine Awoyemi nor Hilda Upton share their secret recipes. Below is one that is known to be excellent by locals in Beaufort who absolutely love their Shrimp Burgers.

June 1 is the opening of shrimp season in Beaufort and believe me, they're serious about it! For this is the heart of shrimp burger country. While these delicious burgers are found in a few small coastal villages such as Murrell's Inlet, they are unheard of in upstate Greenville or Charlotte.

A shrimp burger is simply a cake of shrimp and seasonings served on a bun, with lettuce, tomato, and tartar sauce. Like lobster rolls or crab cakes, shrimp burgers concentrate the sweet essence of shellfish and complement it with semisweet seasonings like parsley, onion and red bell peppers. They are easy to prepare, and *absolutely delicious!*

Try it for yourself by taking a short trip from Beaufort out to St. Helena Island to the Shrimp Shack, a roadside take-out window on stilts, with just a bench and a couple of tables. It's like dining in a treehouse. The shrimp come from boats docked directly across the street at a wharf built in the 1940s by the Shrimp Shack's owner, Hilda Upton. She developed her closely guarded recipe with Martha Jenkins, another St. Helena Island native, and has been serving shrimp burgers since she opened the Shrimp Shack in 1978.

Hilda advised using only the freshest shrimp you can find. Since fresh shrimp have more natural moisture and stickiness when ground or chopped, they require less binding than frozen shrimp. Dryer, frozen shrimp don't hold together nearly as well and require large doses of breading and mayonnaise to compensate.

Local fishermen are the ones who deserve the most credit for this wonderful treat. Shrimpers are on the water for days, sometimes weeks, and they invented shrimp burgers to add variety to a diet dominated by shrimp and as a way to use any unsold shrimp at the end of the day.

RECIPE

1 pound very fresh shrimp
2 tablespoons scallions
3 tablespoons celery
2 tablespoons parsley
1 ½ teaspoons lemon zest
3 tablespoons mayonnaise
1 cup cornbread crumbs
1 egg, beaten
Salt and freshly ground black pepper
1 dash of Tabasco
3 tablespoons oil

Cook and peel the shrimp and chop coarsely. In a large bowl mix the shrimp with the scallions, parsley, and lemon zest. Stir in the mayonnaise, cornbread crumbs and the egg, and beat with a whisk or wooden spoon until evenly distributed. Season with salt, freshly ground pepper and Tabasco.

Form into patties and sauté in oil until both sides are nicely browned. Drain on paper towels. Serve on soft buns with lettuce, tomato and tartar sauce. Yields: 4 servings.

Blackened Redfish

Our South Carolina coast with its miles of rivers, creeks and estuaries is home to hundreds of species of fish, birds, and animals. The Redfish are the rulers of these waters. During high tides, the Reds take shelter amongst the spartina grass, creating hiding places from predators such as eagles, ospreys and dolphins. As the tide begins to recede, the Reds are forced out from their spartina shelter into open areas usually surrounded by mud bars and oyster mounds.

Shortly after the warming begins the larger Bull Reds start moving back into the estuaries from offshore waters. So spring is a great time of year to catch 'em and cook 'em up for supper!

Even if you don't like to fish for your dinner, incredible sight fishing adventures await you, thanks to the extreme high tides which flood our marshes. Depending on the moon phase, full or new, the gravitational pull causes these flood tides. Each month we have six to eight such tides.

As the water starts to flood the marsh, the Reds will move onto the spartina covered flats to feed on fiddler crabs. As these fish feed on the crabs, they will appear to be standing on their heads. Depending on the depth of the water, the fish may be feeding in shallow enough water to completely expose their backs and tails.

Just the sheer thought of casting a fly rod into a milling school of redfish is enough to raise the hair on the back of the neck of most anglers! The shallower the water, the more thrilling the fight.

For the finest redfish recipe ever, I turned to master chef Paul Prudhomme. I agree with everyone else who raves about his recipes. They can't be beaten.

Cypress nodules, photograph by Bob Ovelman.

RECIPE

3 teaspoons salt

½ teaspoon red pepper

½ teaspoon white pepper

¼ teaspoon black pepper

¼ teaspoon dried thyme

¼ teaspoon dried basil

¼ teaspoon dried oregano

2 teaspoons paprika

8 skinless, boneless fillets of redfish (about ¼ pound each)

½ cup melted butter

Combine the salt, red pepper, white pepper, black pepper, thyme, basil, oregano, and paprika in a small bowl. Dip the fish pieces on both sides in butter. Sprinkle on both sides with the seasoned mixture.

Heat a black iron skillet over high heat about five minutes or longer until it is beyond the smoking stage and starts to lighten in color on the bottom. Add two or more fish pieces and pour about a teaspoon of butter on top of each piece. Do not crowd them in the pan. The butter may flame up. Cook over high heat about a minute and a half. Turn the fish and pour another teaspoon of butter over each piece. Cook about a minute and a half. Serve immediately. Continue until all fillets are cooked. Yields: 4 servings.

Bateau on the May River, oil on canvas by Michael Harrell.

Lowcountry Shrimp and Mussel Paella

Have you ever had a day when time was just not on your side? Everything conspires against you to suck huge chunks of time right out of your hands. If my kitchen were in TV land there would be an assistant to instantly transform all my shrimp into a neat bowl of cleaned and peeled morsels of deliciousness. These fresh and delicate mussels would be sitting on my counter all neatly scrubbed and ready to go. This paella depends on the mussels for most of its flavor.

Historically, mussels were made into dishes for peasants. Interesting, too, that lobster used to be so plentiful, it was a main staple served to prisoners.

When it comes to mussels, always be sure to discard any that don't close when tapped sharply. Scrub and debeard them.(that's the piece of fibre hanging from the shell).

Steamed Mussels

4 pounds mussels

2 tablespoons olive oil

1 sweet onion, finely chopped

2 or 3 fresh garlic cloves, minced

½ cup dry white wine

1 lemon, juiced

1 cup chicken broth

1 tomato, peeled, seeded and diced

½ cup roughly chopped parsley

2 tablespoons butter

Rinse the mussels under cold running water while scrubbing with a vegetable brush. Discard any with broken shells. Also, be sure to discard any that don't close when tapped sharply. Scrub and debeard (the piece of fibre hanging from the shell).

Heat oil in a large stockpot and saute the shallot, garlic and thyme to create a delicious flavor. Add the mussels and give them a good toss. Add wine, lemon juice, and chicken broth. Cover the pot and steam over medium high for several minutes until the mussels open. Toss in the tomato, parsley and butter and cover the pt and steam for another minute to soften.

Serve with plenty of crunchy bread to dip in the broth.

Paella with Shrimp and Mussels

This is a quick take on paella studded with mussels and shrimp. Traditional paella made with short grain rice takes a while to cook and can be a bit tricky at times. This instant brown rice is a good shortcut and is so convenient. Make sure you use saffron, which gives this dish its distinctive yellow color and signature flavor.

1 tablespoon extra virgin olive oil

½ cup chopped onion

½ cup chopped red bell pepper

2 cloves garlic, minced

2 cups instant brown rice

1 ⅓ cups chicken broth

½ teaspoon dried thyme

¼ teaspoon salt

freshly ground black pepper to taste - about ¼ teaspoon

1 large pinch saffron

1 pound peeled and deveined raw shrimp

1 pound mussels, scrubbed well

1 cup frozen peas

Juice of 1 lemon

Heat oil in a large skillet over medium heat. Add onion, bell pepper and garlic and cook, stirring occasionally, until the vegetables are softened, about 3 minutes. Add rice, broth, thyme, salt and pepper and saffron and bring to a boil over medium heat. Cover and cook for 5 minutes.

Stir shrimp and peas. Place mussels on top of the rice in an even layer. Cover and continue cooking until the mussels have opened and the rice is tender, about 5 minutes more. Remove from the heat and let rest, covered, until most of the liquid is absorbed, about 5 minutes. Drizzle with the fresh lemon juice.

Note: Saffron is the dried stigma from Crocus sativus. It adds flavor and golden color to a variety of Middle Eastern, African and European foods. Find it in the spice section of your market. It will keep in an airtight container for several years.

> To taste right, fish must swim three times – in water, in butter and in wine.

Black Shrimpers, oil on canvas by John Carroll Doyle.

Shrimp and Crab Salad with Carolina Remoulade

SHRIMP AND CRAB SALAD

1 pound crab meat

2 cups small salad shrimp, cooked and peeled

1 cup chopped celery

½ cup Carolina Remoulade

Combine the shrimp, crab, and celery and mix with the remoulade. Chill, covered, for 1 hour.

CAROLINA REMOULADE

1 cup mayonnaise

2 teaspoons fresh lemon juice

1 tablespoon finely chopped red onion

1 tablespoon capers

1 dill pickle, finely chopped

1 teaspoon chopped parsley

1 teaspoon cayenne pepper

Whisk together the mayonnaise and lemon juice. Add the rest of the ingredients and store in the refrigerator. Great on shrimp salad and crab cakes!

Fresh, local shrimp is something we look forward to, even dream about, and with the season well underway, a lot of good eating is about to begin!

Shrimp are born in the ocean, invisible to the naked eye. They ride on top of the waves and are pulled into our marshes, inlets and tidal creeks. Once there, they sink to the bottom, where they feed and grow until they ride back out into the ocean to breed. As they develop, their flavor is influenced by the food they eat, the depth of where they live, and the water itself.

Their flavor may be influenced by the water's salinity and content and its depth. For example, there is a certain sweetness in those developed in the marsh and a distinctive iodine-like taste in those grown in the depths of the ocean. In between are all ranges of flavor, texture, and color.

When purchasing shrimp, fresh shrimp should smell like the ocean, with no strong odor of ammonia or fishiness!

Here's a recipe I think you will love from a fabulous restaurant in Beaufort, North Carolina, named "The Beaufort Grocery Company." Chef Charles Park is known for his seafood dishes and is a current member of the James Beard Foundation. He and his wife Wendy opened this lovely restaurant in 1991, and in 2003, expanded with yet another restaurant location in nearby Morehead City.

Mahi with Lemon and Capers
Ginger Glazed Mahi-Mahi

REMEMBER THE FIRST TIME YOU WENT FISHING? If not, it's possibly because you didn't catch anything. However, if you did, I imagine you're still out there today. In the Lowcountry of South Carolina, May is the month for fishing, offshore, inshore, in the sounds and everywhere in between!

Each spring Gulf Stream fishing is absolutely amazing! Wahoo, dolphin, tuna, marlin, and sails are all out there and hungry. I've fished all up and down the east coast and the Bahamas, and our South Carolina fishing in May is as good as any place I've ever been or better.

Recently I chatted with Fuzzy Davis, a world class fisherman and old friend, at the Ford Plantation in Savannah, and he says the Mahi are usually plentiful each May.

Whenever someone mentions the words Mahi-Mahi, I immediately think of some of the best fishing I've ever experienced. Mahi, also known as Dolphin, but not the bottlenose dolphin like Flipper, are great fish that make long runs often leaping out of the water as you battle them off the stern of the boat. They'll give you a fight you'll never forget! From Beaufort, it's about a three hour run to the Gulf Stream. Often we'd leave well before the crack of dawn, heading out full throttle in search of a weed line. Once there we'd lower the outriggers and anticipate the day's catch. Hooking up to one is pure excitement as they skyrocket out of the water, into the air, trying to shake the hook, changing colors from yellow to green to blue.

Here are some tried and true favorite ways to cook those delicious Mahi-Mahi.

RECIPES

MAHI WITH LEMON AND CAPERS

4 pound fresh mahi

2 cups all-purpose flour, seasoned with 1 tablespoon dried oregano

8 eggs and 1 cup milk, beaten together

1 quart Panko breadcrumbs

4 lemons

½ pound butter

3 tablespoons capers

½ bunch chopped parsley, washed, dried and chopped fine

Salt and freshly ground black pepper

2 pounds well washed fresh spinach

2 cups vegetable oil

Slice the mahi very thin, on the bias, into 16 equal parts. Dip the mahi into the flour, then dip into the egg, then dip the mahi into the bread crumbs. Set on a plate or tray and refrigerate.

Squeeze the juice from the lemons.

Just before starting to pan fry the mahi, place the butter and lemon juice in a small pan and melt over low heat. When emulsified, mix in the capers, and parsley. Set aside and keep sauce warm.

Heat oil in a large pan until fairly hot, and sauté fish in batches until nice and brown. Place on a plate in a warm oven until all are cooked.

While the fish is cooking, warm the wilted spinach in a dab of butter and season with salt and pepper. Plate a mound of spinach, and place two mahi fillets on top of the spinach. Spoon the sauce around the bottom of the plate. Repeat this process for each plate. Yields: 8 servings.

GINGER GLAZED MAHI MAHI
This recipe combines both sweet and sour taste sensations, is a snap to make and so very delicious!

3 tablespoons honey

3 tablespoons soy sauce

3 tablespoons balsamic vinegar

1 teaspoon grated fresh ginger root

1 clove garlic, crushed

2 teaspoons olive oil

4 mahi fillets

Salt and pepper to taste

1 tablespoon vegetable oil

Use a shallow glass bowl to combine the honey, soy sauce, balsamic vinegar, ginger, garlic and olive oil. Season fish fillets with salt and pepper and place them into the dish. If the fillets have skin on them, place them skin side down. Cover, and refrigerate for 20 minutes to marinate.

Heat vegetable oil in a large skillet. Remove fish from the dish and reserve the marinade. Fry fish for 4 to 6 minutes per side, turning only once. Cook until the fish flakes easily with a fork. Remove fillets to a serving platter and keep warm.

Pour reserved marinade into the skillet and heat over medium heat until the mixture reduces to a glaze consistency. Spoon glaze over fish and serve at once. Yields: 4 servings

Macadamia Crusted Mahi-Mahi with Crab Relish

RECIPE

This recipe involves a simple 3 step process; a sauce, a relish, and a baked fish.

MACADAMIA NUT
MEUNIERE SAUCE

Juice of 2 lemons

¼ cup Worcestershire sauce

1 tablespoon minced shallot

2 tablespoons heavy cream

¼ cup butter, chilled and cut into small pieces

¼ cup chopped macadamia nuts

CRAB RELISH

1 cup coarsely chopped toasted macadamia nuts

2 tablespoons chopped red bell pepper

1 tablespoon minced shallot

1 tablespoon chopped green onion

1 tablespoon olive oil

Juice of 1 lemon

½ cup crab meat

Salt and pepper to taste

MAHI MAHI

1 cup coarsely chopped toasted macadamia nuts

½ cup flour

1 tablespoon Creole seasoning

Salt and pepper to taste

1 cup flour

2 eggs

1 tablespoon milk

Two 6-ounce fillets

2 tablespoons oil

PREPARE THE SAUCE: Combine the lemon juice, Worcestershire and shallot and bring to a boil. Boil until the mixture is of a syrupy consistency and thickened. Stir in the cream and cook until the mixture is reduced by half. Whisk in the butter a little at a time until the sauce begins to emulsify; remove from the heat if the butter melts too quickly. Whisk in the macadamia nuts when the butter is fully incorporated. Adjust the seasonings and keep warm.

RELISH: Combine nuts, bell pepper, shallot, green onion, olive oil, and lemon juice in a bowl and mix well. Fold in the crab meat and season with salt and pepper.

PREPARE MAHI: Process the nuts, ½ cup flour and 1 teaspoon Creole seasoning, salt and pepper in a food processor, just until smooth, but not oily, and pour into a shallow dish. Whisk the eggs and milk in a bowl until blended. Sprinkle the fillets with the remaining 1 teaspoon Creole seasoning.

Coat fillets with the seasoned flour, dip in the egg mixture and then coat with the pecan mixture. Heat the oil in an ovenproof sauté pan until hot and add the coated fillets. Cook until golden brown and turn. Bake at 350° for 12 minutes.

To assemble, cut the fillets into halves. Ladle one fourth of the sauce on each of four dinner plates and top each with an equal portion of the fish and relish. Garnish with thinly sliced fresh chives. Yields: 4 servings

Boatyard Buddies, oil on canvas by Shannon Smith.

Seafood Ceviche on Cucumber Rounds

Heading Home, oil on canvas by Ray Ellis.

RECIPE

¼ red onion, diced very small

3 limes, juiced

1 lemon, juiced

1 mango, peeled, seeded, and diced small

½ papaya, peeled, seeded and diced small

1 tablespoon freshly chopped cilantro leaves

⅛ cup extra virgin olive oil

Salt and freshly ground black pepper

1 pound fresh mahi, grouper, or sea scallops

5 cucumbers

In a large mixing bowl, mix the onion, lime juice, lemon juice, mango, papaya, cilantro, and olive oil. Season mixture with salt and pepper, then stir in the fresh fish or scallops immersing them completely in the marinade. Cover and refrigerate for at least 8 hours. The acids in the marinade will actually "cook" the scallops.

Peel cucumbers and cut into ¼-inch thick slices. Strain scallop mixture and spoon onto cucumber disks. Delicious!

WHEN THE TEMPERATURES START REACHING INTO THE 90S, I start to think of white sand, the sound of waves hitting the shore and seagulls flying lazily overhead. An ice cold Corona with lime and a fresh bowl of ceviche sounds pretty good.

Ceviche is the perfect summertime food with tart flavors and oooh so good! When I'm not able to hang out on the beaches, I can still make this simple seafood salad and pretend I'm there. Ceviche is comprised of a mixture of one or more seafood items and a bit of lime or lemon for the marinade, complemented by fresh vegetables, fruits, and herbs.

Start with a base of raw seafood, cilantro, and your choice of veggies or fruits, and that's just about it. Refrigerate it overnight and serve it cold. Sometimes I serve it in a martini glass when I want to get a bit fancy. In this recipe I serve it on a round of cucumber, but it's also wonderful as a dip with chips. Why not just serve a big scoop of it on lettuce and have it for lunch? Anyway you decide to serve ceviche, it's healthy, low in fat and calories and delicious!

This recipe is one I treasure from my years living in South Florida, where we enjoyed the very freshest seafood the year round. Mangoes and papayas were always plentiful and yummy. However, when these fruits are not available, peaches and other seasonal fruits may be substituted and this appetizer retains its wonderful refreshing flavor! Ceviche is often eaten at lunch or brunch, and because it's so light and delicious, it's a popular appetizer along the coast. Locals say if the fish is more than a few hours old – it's not fresh enough.

www.mycarolinacooking.com

Grilled Fresh Cobia

During the summer months we see the arrival of a multitude of migratory fish in and around the water in Beaufort. Fishermen welcome the arrival of Cobia, often found near beaches, sandbars, bridges, Port Royal Sound, and the Broad River. The Broad, Chechessee, and Beaufort rivers join to form Port Royal Sound and that is where Cobia find deep saline water. They range in size from 10 to 80 pounds – one catch could feed the family for a long, long time!

One delicious way to eat this fish is really quite simple. Lightly rub the fillet with olive oil, sprinkle it with lemon pepper and garlic powder, and the charcoal grill going very hot. Put the fillet on indirect heat for about 7 minutes, turn it over and do another 7 minutes on indirect heat. You need to have a grill that's large enough and one that can be covered. Since you can literally get fish off the grill in a matter of minutes, it's the perfect after work meal.

Before you start, get prepared. Few things can be more frustrating than trying to pull your catch off the grill in one piece. But there's no shortage of equipment, gadgets, or plain old advice intended to help you get around this problem. Through lots of trials and errors, I've found that dipping paper towels in vegetable oil and rubbing the oil over the grill grates with long handled tongs, is an effective way to prevent sticking.

The hardest part of grilling fish is knowing when it's done. When fish is cooked, the meat will flake easily with a fork and will appear opaque all the way through. If any part of the meat is still glossy and partially translucent, then it's not done. If your fillet is evenly cut, the job is a lot easier, but if not, and you end up with one part much thicker than another, consider cutting the fish in two. Put the thick half on first and when it's about halfway done, put the thin half on. This way you will get the fish cooked to perfection without burning any of it.

Flip it gently and leave it there until it is ready to leave the grill. With fillets, you can tell they are ready to flip because the edges are flaky and opaque. Bring it off the grill and squeeze fresh lemon juice over the fish, allow it to rest and serve with some Lowcountry Aioli.

Carolina, oil on canvas by Shannon Smith.

RECIPE

LOWCOUNTRY AIOLI

4 cloves fresh garlic

1 teaspoon Italian herbs

1 egg yolk

½ teaspoon salt

½ cup olive oil

Combine the garlic, herbs, egg yolk, and salt in a food processor and process until smooth. Drizzle in the olive oil gradually, processing until the mixture thickens. Store in an airtight container in the refrigerator for up to one week. This is also delicious on sandwiches as a substitute for mayonnaise.

Seared Scallop Salad

The Lone Scalloper, oil on canvas by Ray Ellis.

RECIPE

4 cups lettuce

8 large fresh sea scallops

Juice of ½ lemon

3 tablespoons olive oil

pinch of ground red pepper

dash of salt

3 tablespoons whipping cream

1 clove minced garlic

2 tablespoons chopped sweet onions

4 tablespoons chopped sweet onions

4 tablespoons chopped red bell pepper

4 tablespoons chopped green bell pepper

1 cup fresh corn kernels

1 vine ripened tomato, cut into quarters

1 recipe Fresh Basil Vinaigrette

In a skillet, melt butter over low heat and add the corn, bell pepper, onions, and garlic. Cook for 5 minutes until tender. Add cream, salt and red pepper. cook for several minutes until liquid is evaporated. Remove from heat; cover to keep warm.

Salt and pepper the scallops. In a large skillet, heat the oil and add scallops. Cook for 3 minutes on each side until golden brown. Remove from heat and add the fresh lemon juice. Set aside to cool.

Place the salad greens on two plates and add ½ of the quartered tomatoes to each plate.

Next top with corn relish and drizzle with additional vinaigrette.

Garnish with fresh basil and serve immediately. Yields: 2 servings.

IT'S HOT OUTSIDE. Even the mornings send us searching out the shade. Thoughts of heating up the oven are no longer appealing. Let's look at some summer survival strategies like cool salads that are quick and easy to prepare.

When you're in the mood for a light summer supper, think of a delicious fresh salad of mesclun greens, basil vinaigrette, and delicious corn relish. Of course, there's nothing more evocative of a Southern summer than the esteemed local tomato still warm from the sun, brought in from the garden and served that same evening. These treasures are the keystone of all Lowcountry supper tables.

To ensure food safety in the summer, wash and dry veggies before adding them to a salad, use separate cutting boards for the meat and produce, and be sure your hands, work surfaces, and utensils are very clean.

BASIL VINAIGRETTE

½ cup fresh basil, chopped

¼ cup fresh lemon juice

1 tablespoon Dijon mustard

1 teaspoon sugar

¼ teaspoon salt

½ teaspoon freshly ground black pepper

½ cup olive oil

In the container of an electric blender, combine basil, lemon juice, Dijon mustard, sugar, salt, and pepper. Process until blended. With blender running, add oil in a slow, steady stream and process until blended. Cover and chill. Yields: ¾ cup.

www.mycarolinacooking.com

Crispy Oven Fried Fish

Atlantic Croaker, oil on canvas by John Carroll Doyle.

Frying fish: I adapted this recipe from several sources. Many recipes were very dated as they called for frying the fish in vegetable shortening. Most shortenings on the market have trans fats in them, which we now know is bad for us. I fry everything in grape seed oil. It's perfect for frying because you can get it pretty hot before it begins to burn.

I always use a cast iron skillet to fry foods in because of the excellent heat retention.

Just the simple thought of fried fish brings back childhood memories of gathering at the lake with family and friends while Uncle Herman fried one batch after another of incredible fresh fish, crunchy on the outside and moist on the inside. And always there were those fabulous hushpuppies you just couldn't get enough of! Just one taste of this fish and I understand why we told so many stories of the good old days at the lake and on the family farm. We'd tell enduring tales of carefree summer afternoons picking blackberries and trekking through the countryside.

I still love fried fish but often don't want to create the mess it makes to fix it just right. I've found a way to achieve a delicious crispy crust right in the oven by using crushed cornflakes. We tried it and it was scrumptious and so much healthier than deep fried. I experienced a delicious crunch with every bite!

Grape seed oil is an ideal salad dressing, cooking, frying or baking oil. It is popular because of its clean, neutral taste that allows the flavors of food to stand out.

Since grape seed oil has a very high smoke point, it can safely be used for stir-frying and deep-frying. There are many health benefits from this oil because it is rich in antioxidants and studies support the claim that it increases the good cholesterol while reducing the bad cholesterol.

RECIPE

1 cup buttermilk

Four 6-ounce fish fillets (any firm fish)

1 ½ teaspoons Creole seasoning

3 cups crushed cornflakes cereal

Cooking spray or grape seed oil

Fresh lemon wedges

Place buttermilk in a large zip top bag and add fish. Seal and chill in the refrigerator for about an hour.

Preheat oven to 425°. Remove fish from the bag and discard the buttermilk. Sprinkle with Creole seasoning.

Dredge fish in cornflakes, gently pressing the cornflakes onto each fillet. Place fish on a wire rack coated with cooking spray or grape seed oil, in a roasting pan and bake at 425° for about 30 minutes until fish is flaky.

Squeeze generously with fresh lemon juice and serve immediately.

www.mycarolinacooking.com

Shrimp Tempura with Soy Sake Dipping Sauce

Part of Beaufort's enchantment lies in its unique cuisine, which blends European, Asian, and West African customs. This marvelous cuisine is often overshadowed by that of Charleston and Savannah because much of it resides in the homes of the residents of Beaufort whose cooking and entertaining are legendary. Casual visitors may never taste it because it cannot always be found in the restaurants, but rather in the dining rooms and on the verandas of those who savor the traditions of old world elegance.

Make this recipe with the freshest shrimp you can find.

The Shrimper, photograph by Bob Ovelman.

RECIPES

DIPPING SAUCE

1 cup soy sauce

¼ cup sake

1 tablespoon sweet chili sauce (found in the Oriental section of the market)

1 tablespoon fresh ginger, grated

2 tablespoons fresh cilantro leaves

TEMPURA

1 pound large shrimp, peeled and deveined

1 cup rice flour, plus 1 cup for dusting

1 cup cold seltzer water

1 egg yolk

1 tablespoon sesame oil

Vegetable oil for frying

Make the dipping sauce by thoroughly mixing all ingredients in a bowl. Set aside to allow the flavors to develop.

Peel and devein shrimp.

To make the Tempura batter, put 1 cup of rice flour in a bowl and pour in the seltzer. Stir with a whisk to get out all the lumps. Add the egg yolk and blend it in well. The batter should be the consistency of heavy cream. Flavor with the sesame oil.

Heat about 2 inches of oil to 375° in a deep fryer. Dry the shrimp well. Dust the shrimp in flour to soak up any remaining moisture and shake off the excess. Dip the shrimp into the batter one by one. Drip 4 to 5 pieces at a time in the hot oil. Do not overcrowd the pan. Fry until golden brown, turning once, about 3 minutes. To keep the oil clean between batches, skim off the small bits of batter that float in the oil. Remove the fried shrimp from the pot and drain on paper towels. Season with salt and serve with the dipping sauce.

Ogeechee Shad Roe with Bacon

Pole Fishing, watercolor on paper by Ray Ellis.

SHAD SEASON IS AN ANNUAL EVENT eagerly awaited each spring in the Lowcountry. Atlantic shad are prized for their eggs and not their flesh. Plentiful in Savannah's Ogeechee River, they have an internal radar that allows them to return each year to their birthplace, where they will run upriver to spawn and then die. Though these fish make this same run up rivers all along the east coast, the Ogeechee is a major spawning ground. The roe fattened fish have always been plentiful there. Shad has long been savored as one of the Lowcountry's great seasonal delicacies and its arrival is a sure sign that daffodils and longer days are on their way.

Many local aficionados put shad roe on equal footing with the finest sturgeon caviar and, unlike caviar, it is quite inexpensive and enjoyed in lots of different ways. It's broiled with bacon or scrambled with eggs for breakfast or dinner. For cocktail hour it can be poached in lots of lemon juice and served like caviar. For dinner, many locals enjoy shad roe sautéed in butter and served on toast as the first course, or carefully seasoned and stuffed into a filleted fish.

RECIPE

This delightful dish is traditionally served for breakfast or supper with hot grits and for many years was a specialty of the elegant old DeSoto Hotel that once stood on Liberty Street in Savannah. This is a recipe for two, but can easily be multiplied.

1 set shad roe
Bacon drippings or butter
Salt and black pepper
Cayenne pepper
4 strips thick cut bacon
4 cups hot cooked grits

With oven rack about 8 inches below the heat source, preheat the broiler for 10 minutes. Rinse the roe, pat dry, and separate the two roe sacs. Rub a small, rimmed, metal pan such as a metal pie plate with drippings or butter. Season the roe well with salt, pepper, and cayenne. Wrap the bacon around them (2 pieces per sac) and secure with toothpicks.

Broil about 7 minutes or until the bacon is beginning to brown, turn and broil until roe is firm and bacon is browned, about 5 minutes longer. Serve at once over hot grits.

Grilled Lowcountry Shrimp

Grilled Lowcountry Shrimp. Photograph courtesy of Nobles Restaurant.

RECIPE

2 pounds large shrimp, deveined

3 cloves garlic, minced

1 onion, diced small

½ teaspoon freshly ground black pepper

¼ cup parsley

¼ cup basil, minced

2 teaspoons Dijon mustard

1 teaspoon dry mustard

Zest of one lemon

Juice of one lemon

¼ cup olive oil

1 teaspoon salt

Combine all the ingredients and allow them to marinate in the refrigerator for up to 2 days. Skewer the shrimp. Place about 4 shrimp on a 12-inch skewer for diner. Heat up the grill and brush the grill with oil to prevent shrimp from sticking. Grill the shrimp for about 1½ minutes on each side. To serve, remove from the skewer, peel the shrimp and leave on the tails. Serve with a delicious creamy risotto.

It's time to break out the bait balls and the cane poles when shrimp baiting season opens! Shrimp baiting uses a cast net, bait, and some long poles. The poles are used to mark a location and then bait is thrown into the water near the poles. After a few minutes, the cast net is thrown as close to the bait as possible and the shrimp are caught in the net. What's a bait ball? It can be made of just about anything a shrimp will eat. Most common is a mixture of powdered clay and fish meal. But flour, cornmeal, cat food or even chicken feed have all been used successfully. Better hurry and get out there because the season is short and it's officially over November 9th.

Nothing quite matches the sweet, intense, and slightly charred taste of shellfish when it's cooked on the grill. There are lots of great reasons to grill shellfish. Whether it's shrimp, lobster, clams, or oysters, grilling shellfish is simple as can be. Just a brush of olive oil and a sprinkle of salt are all you need in the way of prep – and it's a fun way to entertain!

There are just a few simple rules to go by. No matter what type of shellfish you're grilling, leave the shell on. This protects the delicate meat and keeps it moist during cooking. When cooked with the shell on, the shrimp will shrink less and the shell adds lots of great flavor.

Look for jumbo shrimp, about 16 to 20 count, which means there are 16 to 20 of them in one pound. Devein the shrimp in their shell and rinse under cold running water. Dry them off with paper towels and toss them in olive oil to coat. Season with kosher salt.

The next step is to grill over a medium-high direct heat and cover the grill to keep the heat in. If the cooking time is too long, the shrimp will get tough and chewy. Use long handled tongs to put the shrimp on the cooking grates, arranging them across the grates so they don't fall through. Turn about halfway through the cooking process until the shrimp curl and become pink, about 3 minutes per side. When the entire outside surface of the shrimp has changed color, they are done. They'll continue cooking for a short time after they are taken off the grill. If you take them off just before the center is completely cooked, they should be done to perfection!

www.mycarolinacooking.com

SENSATIONAL SEAFOOD

Early Biker, watercolor on paper by Ray Ellis.

THE ABUNDANT HARVEST OF THE SEA has long been a basis for Lowcountry cooking since the days when the Indians harvested oysters, clams, shrimp, and crabs. No one visiting the coastal areas of South Carolina can resist the okra and seafood gumbo, oyster or crab stew, seafood au gratin, and the succulent flavors of fish fresh from the ocean. In the Lowcountry, we're fortunate to have wonderful seafood markets, which not only carry fish fresh each day, but offer them beautifully, completely filleted!

Fish are delicate creatures, and begin to deteriorate as soon as they're brought out of water and into the boat. Obtaining the freshest fish possible makes all the difference. It should look as if it's about to swim away with bright, shiny skin and close-fitting scales. Dry, dull flesh is a sign of age. Beautiful food doesn't have to be complicated. If you use quality ingredients, you'll create a quality product.

Fish Casserole Au Gratin

2 pounds fish fillets, crab meat, scallops or shrimp (or use ¼ pound of each)

2 tablespoons chopped onions

2 tablespoons chopped celery

Salt and freshly ground black pepper to taste

2 tablespoons lemon juice

2 tablespoons butter

2 tablespoons flour

1 cup evaporated milk

½ cup grated cheddar cheese

½ cup plain bread crumbs

In a saucepan, melt butter over low heat. Add onions, celery, salt, pepper, lemon juice and grated cheddar cheese. Add each ingredient while stirring constantly. Slowly add the milk. Combine thoroughly.

Place the seafood in a deep casserole dish, and pour mixture of ingredients over the top evenly. Sprinkle with breadcrumbs. Bake at 350° for 45 to 50 minutes. Serve over rice.

Grilled Shrimp Savannah Salad

6 heads Bibb lettuce (one small head per serving)

16 ounces canned artichoke hearts, drained and halved

2 avocados, sliced

2 pounds large shrimp, grilled (about 1½ minute per side)

4 hard cooked eggs, quartered

Wash and dry lettuce; gently separate leaves. Combine with other ingredients and toss lightly.

DRESSING

½ teaspoon salt

Freshly ground black pepper to taste

½ teaspoon prepared mustard

1 small clove garlic, minced

¼ cup tarragon vinegar

1 egg yolk

1 cup oil

½ teaspoon sugar

1 tablespoon Worcestershire sauce

¼ cup chili sauce

Make a paste of salt, pepper, mustard, garlic, and a small amount of vinegar. Blend in the egg yolk until smooth. Start adding oil very slowly until the dressing is the consistency of mayonnaise. Continue adding oil alternately with remaining vinegar. Beat in sugar and Worcestershire sauce; fold in chili sauce and chill thoroughly. Serves 6.

Lowcountry Shrimp and Grits

Adapted from Craig Claiborne

1½ pound shrimp, peeled, halved lengthwise and deveined

Juice of 1 lemon

Dash of hot sauce

Kosher salt to taste

1½ cups stone ground grits

6 slices thick bacon, chopped

1 small onion, finely chopped

¼ cup finely chopped green bell pepper

1 garlic clove, minced

½ cup thinly sliced scallions

1 cup mushrooms, sliced

2 tablespoons all purpose flour

1 cup chicken stock

1–2 tablespoons butter

1 cup grated sharp Cheddar cheese

Combine the shrimp with the lemon juice and a splash or two of hot pepper sauce and set aside.

FOR THE GRITS: In a large, heavy saucepan, bring 6 cups of water and a teaspoon of salt to a boil. Whisk in the grits a few handfuls at a time. Reduce the heat to a very low simmer and cook over low heat for about 40 minutes. Stir occasionally at first and more frequently toward the end.

FOR THE GRAVY: While the grits are simmering, fry the bacon in a medium skillet until brown. Stir in the onion, green pepper, and garlic and continue cooking until the onion and pepper are soft, about 5 minutes. Add the scallions and mushrooms, sprinkle the flour over the mixture, and continue sautéing for 5 minutes longer. Stir in the stock and remaining salt and cook for 5 minutes longer. Remove from the heat while you finish the grits.

When the grits are thick and creamy, stir in as much of the butter as you wish, followed by the cheese. Add a splash of hot pepper sauce

Lowcountry Shrimp and Grits. Photograph courtesy of Nobles Restaurant and Chef Phil Barnes.

THERE'S A CERTAIN AMOUNT OF TRUTH in the saying that for any true Southerner "a day without grits is a day without sunshine." For the grits purist, real Old South flavor and texture are only found in old fashioned stone ground grits cooked ever so slowly.

The first published recipe for shrimp and grits was called Hominy and Shrimp and is found in "200 Years of Charleston Cooking." According to Nathalie Dupree, whom Pat Conroy calls the "queen of the Southern kitchen," the man to whom it was credited said he had been making it all his life and he was 70. The book was published in 1934. Nevertheless, during shrimp season in Charleston, it was not unusual for shrimp with hominy to be eaten for breakfast seven days a week in many families.

While this dish had somewhat humble beginnings, it was Craig Claiborne, with his 1985 article in the *New York Times*, who launched it into the signature dish of sophisticated Southern cuisine. The shrimp and grits that fired Claiborne's imagination came from Crook's Corner restaurant in North Carolina. This recipe featured a spicy sauté of shrimp over cheese grits loaded up with bacon, mushrooms, and scallions. Since that time every Southern chef has felt obligated to come up with a new spin on this classic favorite.

The first time I tried the much-ballyhooed shrimp and grits was back in the '80s at the Charleston Yacht Club. Their recipe was deliriously good but if you're not a fan of stone ground grits, feel free to use quick cooking grits and follow the cooking directions on the package.

and more salt if you like. Cover the grits while you finish the gravy. Return the gravy to medium heat and stir in the shrimp. Cook until the shrimp are opaque throughout, about 5 minutes. Serve immediately, mounding the grits in large shallow bowls or on plates and covering them with shrimp and gravy. Serves 4.

www.mycarolinacooking.com

Baked Mackerel With Herb Crust

1 pound baby new potatoes, halved

4 mackerel fillets

1 ounce ciabatta bread

Grated zest and juice of 1 lemon

4 tablespoons chopped chives

2 teaspoons olive oil

²⁄₃ cup plain yogurt

2 teaspoons wholegrain mustard

1 teaspoon honey

2 cups salad greens

Place potatoes in a saucepan of boiling water and cook until tender.

Line a large baking sheet with parchment paper. Rinse the fillets, drain them well and place them, skin side down, on the paper.

Tear the bread into small pieces and place them in a food processor to make coarse crumbs. Mix with the lemon zest and juice, chives, and a little pepper. Spoon over the top of the fish fillets, then drizzle with the oil.

Bake in a preheated oven, 425° for 10 minutes until the fish flakes easily when pressed with a knife and the crumb mixture is golden and crisp.

Meanwhile, mix the yogurt, mustard, honey, and a little pepper together in a salad bowl. Drain the potatoes and add them to the dressing. Toss together, and gently spoon onto the mixed greens. Add the mackerel to the plate and serve immediately. Plan on serving about ½ pound of fish per person.

Wing Away, oil on canvas by John Carroll Doyle.

Capt. Woody's King Mackerel Tournament is held the last part of June on Hilton Head Island. Although I haven't been king mackerel fishing in years, reading about it brought back a lot of great memories of time spent fishing for them from Florida to North Carolina. But as is the case with so many types of fishing, the method of catching kings has changed dramatically.

Oldtimers often trolled using drone spoons and ballyhoo, but about the 1980s, someone figured out that live bait, mainly mullet, were far more effective.

One benefit to king mackerel fishing is that you really don't have to go far to find them. In fact, many tournaments have been won five miles from shore. Big kings are normally solitary fish and can be caught within sight of land.

Searching for them can be lots of fun because they're noted for their remarkable leaps, often clearing the water by 10 feet or more.

If you have a chance to go out there and land some big ones, here's a recipe I've used often that is absolutely delicious! The fillets are topped with a tangy lemon and chive ciabatta crust and served with baby new potatoes tossed in a wholegrain mustard dressing.

Tideland Soft-Shell Crabs

SOMETHING TRANSFORMING happens when you drive down Hwy. 17 through Yemassee and on into Beaufort. Turn your radio off, open the windows and inhale the pungent aroma of the salt marsh while you enter the world of towering Live oaks and endless water. Step back in time and become one with the land, the water, and the seafood.

Enjoy the best menus of spring by dining on the season's finest. If you travel here or live here in April, you'll be here just at the right time for the yearly arrival of the soft shelled crabs. The sweet and subtle briny flavor of soft shelled crabs is like tasting a piece of the ocean itself. In their natural environment, blue crabs begin shedding their outgrown shells about mid-April. The process, called molting, allows these sideways scurrying creatures to grow larger. In this unprotected state, they become soft shell crabs, a delicacy often described as succulent. But — better be alert, because you can only enjoy them fresh for two or three weeks. Local fishermen say they come and go fast, and then it's another year before they become available again, fresh from the sea.

As the catch begins to come in along the coast, festivals spring up in celebration and one of the season's first takes place in the little village of Port Royal, just outside Beaufort. Each year locals set up up their folding chairs along Paris Avenue for the Port Royal Soft Shell Crab Fest, with performances by local bands and the Lowcountry Shag Club. But the real stars of the day are the sensational soft shelled crabs!

Timing is everything. If the crabs are left in the water, this blissful "soft shell" state lasts only a few hours before they begin growing another hard shell. To prevent this, they are caught just prior to losing their shells and closely monitored in holding tanks until the molting is complete. At that time they are whisked from the tank and either frozen at once, or packed in wet paper or straw and shipped live, via seafood purveyors, to restaurants and markets. All this must happen quickly as these crabs can only survive a few days out of water.

These delicious crabs are one of the most popular restaurant items each spring, but because of the need for precise harvesting and shipping, the markup is huge by the time they are plated at a restaurant. Fortunately, these delicate creatures are available right here in Beaufort and are easy to prepare and cook at home.

They're at their best simply fried or sautéed and take only minutes to prepare.

RECIPE

A magnificent meal served with hollandaise, remoulade, tartar sauce or Lowcountry aioli! You'll experience a taste of the sea with every bite.

- 8 cleaned soft-shell blue crabs
- 2 cups buttermilk
- 1 tablespoon Tabasco
- 1 cup yellow cornmeal
- 1 cup flour
- ½ teaspoon baking soda
- 1 ¼ teaspoon salt
- 1 ¼ teaspoon freshly ground pepper
- 1 tablespoon dried tarragon
- 1 ½ sticks of butter
- ¼ cup fresh chopped parsley
- Juice of one lemon

SOAKING THE CRABS: soak crabs in the herb-milk mixture. This makes them extra plump and sautéing them in the butter makes them extra crispy. Combine buttermilk and tarragon and place crabs in a glass dish in a single layer. The crabs should soak at room temperature for about 2 hours. Cover with plastic wrap and refrigerate, turning the crabs occasionally. Then drain the crabs and throw away the milk.

SAUTÉ: Dredge each crab with the flour and cornmeal mixture seasoned with Tabasco, salt and pepper. Melt half the butter in a shallow pan and sauté crabs about 2 minutes per side until they are a nice golden brown, adding more butter as needed. Squeeze lemon juice over them and add capers and sprinkle with parsley just before serving. To serve, arrange two crabs on each plate.

> Be sure crabs are alive when you buy them. Have them cleaned and bring 'em home to cook the same day. They are a real Lowcountry delicacy. Soft-shells are crabs caught in the spring just after shedding or molting their hard outer shell. Pull up a folding chair and plan on attending the Soft Shell Crab Festival held each April in the little town of Port Royal.

Blue Crabs, photograph by Bob Ovelman.

Grouper Oscar

This recipe is from the marina at Singer Island in West Palm Beach, Florida. Sport fishing boats would bring in their catch in the late afternoon and the restaurant there would cook it to perfection – delicious! This was always their most requested recipe.

1 stick butter

Juice of 1 lemon

8 grouper fillets

1 pound fresh crab meat, carefully checked to remove all cartilege

Salt and pepper to taste

2 bunches fresh asparagus

2 cups Bearnaise Sauce

Wash fillets. Melt the butter in a Pyrex baking pan. Pour juice of 1 lemon into the butter and mix. Place fillets on top of butter; turn over in butter to coat. Bake at 350° for about 20 minutes until fish is white when separated with a knife and fork.

Remove from the pan and place on top of asparagus which has been steamed gently until tender. Sprinkle crabmeat evenly over the 8 fillets.

Top it off with the Bearnaise sauce just before serving.

BEARNAISE SAUCE

1 ½ cups butter

3 egg yolks

2 tablespoon white wine

Juice of 1 lemon

4 dashes of hot sauce or to taste

1 tablespoon dried tarragon

1 teaspoon chopped shallots

Bring the butter to a boil in a saucepan. Remove from the heat and let it stand for 5 minutes. Combine the egg yolks, wine and lemon juice in a blender and process until smooth. Add the hot butter gradually, processing constantly to form an emulsion. Season with the hot sauce.

This sauce can be held in a warm place for about two hours, but will separate if maintained at too hot or too cold a temperature.

> Our Sea Islands are forever linked with two of the most famous and valuable agricultural crops in history: Sea Island rice and Sea Island cotton.

Charleston Crab Au Gratin

Ah, autumn in the Lowcountry! The humidity and heat of August has passed. Dining must be simple, yet grand, with fresh seafood the order of the day.

1 pound crab meat

2 tablespoons butter

1 tablespoon cornstarch

1 cup Half and Half

1 egg yolk

Salt to taste

¼ cup Parmesan cheese, grated

¼ cup Swiss cheese, grated

Paprika

Sauté crab in butter for 3 minutes. Mix cornstarch, Half and Half, egg yolk, and salt. Gently stir into the crab until thickened.

Mix in cheese and pour into buttered 2 quart baking dish. Heat at 350° for 20 minutes. Serve on avocado, toast, or in pastry cups. Sprinkle lightly with paprika on top for color.

Crab Ogeechee

½ cup butter, melted

4 shallots, finely chopped

¼ cup cider vinegar

½ teaspoon salt

Dash of Tabasco

Sprinkle of white pepper

1 tablespoon parsley, chopped

1 pound lump crab meat

Sauté shallots in butter until transparent. Add vinegar, salt, Tabasco, pepper, and parsley and simmer for several minutes. Add crab meat. Stir mixture carefully so that it remains in lump form. Pour into oven-proof ramekins.

Broil 3 inches from the heat for about 8 minutes or until just browned. Serve with rice to absorb the delicious juices. Yields: 4 servings.

Gullah Fixin's

Today, the descendants of West Africans brought in bondage to the coastal islands are striving to preserve a way of life. Theirs is a story of struggle, spirituality, perseverance and tradition.

"IF YOU DON'T HAVE A HORSE to ride, take a cow!" In Gullah, this would sound like, "Ef oonah yent hab hawss fuh ride – ride cow!"

Shortly after settling into our house on Lady's Island, I was sitting on the porch watching the shadows of evening fall across the land. The sound of cicada-filled trees and the soft flow of the river as waves hit the shoreline was restful and serene. Then, in the distance I began to hear the sound of drums beating rhythmically, the cadence drifting across the marsh on the gentle breeze created by the changing of the tides.

That next day I set out to discover what this might be all about. These sounds seemed to be coming from the direction of St. Helena Island. Driving down the dirt and gravel roads of this rural island off the Atlantic Coast, I passed by small clusters of houses, many painted blue, where women sat on porches wearing head wraps and aprons and weaving baskets from seas grass. I later learned St. Helena had been a point of entry for slaves who worked the rice and cotton fields in the years before they were freed. These sweetgrass baskets were used as a tool in the production and processing of rice back when slaves made large, round ones to clean off the rice husks. It was a centuries old tradition brought to America by these enslaved Africans from the Windward and Rice Coasts of West Africa in the 17th century.

The drums were being played by the descendents of the thousands of enslaved Africans who survived the rough passage in the bowels of overloaded ships to reach the sea island shores. Many had died along the way in horrid conditions where disease and death were common place. But in the souls of those who managed to come ashore, came the heart of the African culture.

Along with a rich dialect, these slaves brought with them customs, and beliefs that helped shape the history and culture of the seas islands into what it is today. Their world was rich in spirits such as ghosts, boo-daddies and other creatures that roamed the cemeteries, marshes and woodlands.

The High Sheriff of the Lowcountry

These were the days when the great High Sheriff of the Lowcountry, Ed McTeer, held the power of the law in his hands. J.E. McTeer, a witch doctor, lived on Coffin's Point Plantation in Frogmore, S.C., the very heart of the voodoo belt. He often spoke of his mother and grandmother who had been gifted with extra sensory perception, saying that he had inherited their talent. His grandmother, Louisa Guerard Heyward, was the wife of a rice planter and had observed slaves brought from Africa. She had made a study of their use of hexes and spells and she didn't overlook any of the slave secrets, scorned by most. McTeer observed her and his Uncle Tony who practiced Voodoo and learned their secrets from an early age.

Decked out in a crisp white linen suit and a white fedora hat with a dark trim, he greeted me cordially as I came through the door of his office located on an alley way just off Bay Street. His manner was proud as he told me his story and spoke of how he became the top lawman in the county at the age of 23 when he replaced his father.

Opposite Page: Charleston Nobility, oil on canvas by John Carroll Doyle.

For 37 years, McTeer tackled everything from Prohibition-era rum runners, a nudist colony on Cat Island in the early 1930s, voodoo inspired murderers, mannered Southern politicians and local root doctors. With his own brand of Voodoo, also known as conjure, he governed Beaufort County, and as a result never had to carry a gun during his long tenure.

"Whether or not Sheriff McTeer had any spiritual force as a conjurer is very debatable, but the fact that he respected that power and acknowledged it made him very influential," according to local historian Larry Rowland.

During the time he served as sheriff, McTeer sometimes joined forces with Dr. Buzzard, a witch doctor of national fame, in order to solve crimes committed in the county. McTeer estimated that more than five thousand people came to him for help after he became involved in the supernatural. "I'm more of a poor man's psychiatrist," he told me. One thing's for sure, McTeer was a man of his times and an American original.

This was the 70s, and in this corner of the deep South, black folks were lucky to have any kind of job and were kept in line by the secrets of black magic. Their culture embodied the essence of struggle, spirituality, perseverance, and tradition. I could see their strength in the Gullah folks who worked on our land, Miss Dora, Elmo, and Joe. Elmo could skin a raccoon faster than any man in Beaufort County, an art passed down through the generations of men who hunted each day to feed their families. His forefathers were people of their environment, with deep spirituality and happiness and love of God and all his creation. He was rooted and grounded in his environment and his food was a reflection of those values.

Having to reap from the land whatever they could made folks like Elmo resourceful as they learned to cook rabbits and squirrels and to gather what they could along the shoreline.

Miss Dora lived in a tiny two room wood framed house, painted blue to ward off evil spirits, and cooked on a wood stove. She was the happiest woman I ever met. Each Sunday she'd be out on the winding narrow road that ran in front of her house, walking to church. Her suit, hat, and shoes matched just right and her black handbag hung by her side. Barely five feet tall, she moved with authority and pride. The rest of the week she cleaned, sang hymns, washed clothes, and cooked the best collard greens, black-eyed peas, and sweet potato corn bread you ever ate.

What it Was was Witchcraft

WHILE TODAY the infiltration of Northerners has somewhat blurred the sharp edges of what is the true essence of the Lowcountry, there are still some customs and beliefs as reliable as the coming and going of the tide.

One morning, most unexpectedly, I experienced a strange story, an occurrence most common in those days but certainly not to a newcomer like me.

Humidity hung heavy in the air that July morning. Al-

Open for Business (Flowers for Sale), oil on canvas by John Carroll Doyle.

though it was barely 8 a.m. the temperature was hovering in the 90s and the scorched earth beneath my feet was cracked and parched from lack of rain.

I drove down to the edge of the property to pick up Miss Dora. On this particular day she had plenty to say about what was goin' on. Her eyes were large with fear and her voice was fast and loud as she spoke about a strange phenomenon that took place in the night down the road with her friend Miss Flowers. "Ohhh," she moaned, "Miss Flowers – why she so sick, she near death's door. She got the evil 'blue root' – she got the curse put on her."

I soon learned Ed McTeer had been on a mission that night above and beyond his normal legal and civic duties. He had gone out there to perform an exorcism. Unusual for a white sheriff, McTeer was also a "conjure man," or practitioner of Hoodoo. He had studied black magic in the 1920s in order to learn the ways of the local black population with whom he came into contact every day as a young law enforcer. Once he'd mastered the basics of the subject, however, he'd declared himself a practitioner and soon earned himself a reputation as a powerful conjure man.

"I could feel it in ma bones. There was evil workin' in dat place. When ta sheriff come, he goes round and round in da yard, his legs and arms just a tremblin. He howled and leapt in ta air and come up under some steps with ta blue root, wavin' in the air and showin' it to all us. Den he throw it in ta creek. All tis time he in a trance just a circlin' round. Wid tat, why, Miss Flowers, she sat up in da bed a wantin ta eat. She done been cured of da root. Hallelujah!"

After hearing the story I went to talk with Roger Pinkney, the coroner of Beaufort County and local historian who knew everything about everything. Sitting on his porch as he carved a walking cane from the branch of a myrtle tree, he explained to me how McTeer was more than a retired sheriff. He was the celebrated white witch doctor of Frogmore. When folks needed a curse removed or were looking for a protective amulet, they went to see McTeer.

In his 37 years as sheriff, McTeer also called on his gift of second sight to help solve crimes. "I know for a fact," said Pinkney, "many of the criminals he arrested while sheriff were more afraid of the harm he could do them as a witch doctor, with the power to put a 'black root' on them, than the power of the law. It sure suited his purpose to let the belief stand."

There were different types of roots. "Why, I knew of him selling one fella a root to bring him luck in gambling. Cost him 'bout fifteen dollars," Mr. Pinkney leaned forward in his seat as his eyes gained a new intensity. He put down the cane. "On the other hand, the price of a death root will depend on how much the traffic will bear. I'd say five hundred dollars is not unreasonable, well, cause it may take a few trips, and preparation of the root could take considerable time. Why, it could even entail making a 'hex doll' to hide on the intended victim's premises, or a trip to a local graveyard at midnight to get dirt from a criminal's grave.

"You know, a root buried in your yard will cause you untold pain in your limbs. Everything you plant in your yard will die and you need another witch doctor to find and get rid of the hex if you ever want to be cured."

That's how much power and authority witchcraft held over the people.

Gullah Food Culture

Many of the foods now associated with the Gullahs are based on the customs brought to this country by these enslaved Africans. The climate and soil of the Lowcountry were similar to that of the African coast, so the field laborers produced some of the same crops they did in their native land.

Rice, one of the crops produced along the African coast, is recognized as one source of the areas' original wealth. In fact, a number of our favorite seafood and vegetable stews can be traced directly to the meals that were served on the dining tables of wealthy plantation owners as their cooks stirred up the conventional recipes with new combinations of spices. Their skills translated into delicious new ideas for the families they served.

Today Penn Center, established on the site of an early mission school on St. Helena Island, is devoted to advising Gullah people and houses a museum to display their arts and crafts and is dedicated to preserving their folklore and language.

Gullah Festivals

Today throughout the Lowcountry there are festivals in celebration of the Gullah Heritage. One of the most popular is held in Beaufort every Memorial Day weekend.

You might say there's a lot of razzle-dazzle goin' on in Beaufort that weekend.

Each year during the Memorial Day weekend, Gullah folks and folks from all over gather for the annual Gullah Festival at the Henry Chambers Waterfront Park. It's a celebration of the Gullah culture and a tribute to their forefathers. Their history chronicles the enslavement of tribes from West Africa and their relocation to southern plantations.

Their rich dialect has been passed down through the generations, extolling the virtues of spirituality rooted in nature and family. Here at the festival, the food of the Gullah people is expressed not only with clarity but pure passion.

Catfish stew, shrimp gumbo, frogmore stew, and chicken bog are high on everybody's list, but it's the chicken bog that steals the show.

Chicken bog is chicken, rice, and anything else they can throw in the pot. It's appropriately named because there's not a better word for it than bog, which simply means it's a soggy, cloggy, noggy, foggy mess. Often the chicken and rice will also have sausage and seasonings. Sometimes people add a few carrots and celery and sometimes they don't. Any way they fix it, it's been a real attraction for years at church suppers, fundraisers and now the Gullah Festival.

People are zealous about it and opinionated, even bullheaded about chicken bog. It reminds me of the way folks are about their barbecue. While walking through the crowd, I heard one gentleman talking about how it was a major calamity to have either bone or gristle in chicken bog – or skin for that matter! "Maybe I'm just not country enough," he muttered, "but that's just the way I am."

Types of bog vary. There are dove, quail, and duck bog, although they are more commonly called perlo. Mighty men from Coosaw and the surrounding areas have built solid reputations on the birds they hunt and add to rice before inviting others to partake. There's a whole lot of pride involved in the process.

Now don't get confused about the difference between bog and perlo, because I've thoroughly checked this out. I can tell you what a city policemen said about it all. "The only difference I can tell you is in a perlo, the rice don't stick together too bad." He continued, "In a bog, you can sorta throw it up against a wall and it will hang there for awhile." A gentleman from Yemassee overheard us talking and couldn't wait to tell me about a political cookout where squirrel bog was served.

No matter how exotic the bog may be, rice is the one constant ingredient. It is inescapable in the Lowcountry, where plantations made South Carolina one of the largest producers in the world at one time. Folks mixed rice with everything whether it be beans, peas, okra; you name it, and ate it with every meal.

You talk about being shocked and amazed, the first time I went into a grocery store in Beaufort, I

Conference on Church Street, oil on canvas by John Carroll Doyle.

saw hundred pound bags of rice for sale. Where I came from people didn't eat rice all that much, but around here it was pretty much rice with everything.

A lot of good ol' country cookin' was there at the Gullah Festival that day. That means biscuits, country fried steak, cream gravy, cantaloupe, and green beans that have been cooked in a big black pot for hours. They even ate gravy on their cantaloupe! While I could see that all this food was popular, it was the chicken bog that brought in the crowd! I learned that from a lady under a tent in a red apron wearing black tennis shoes. She stood there stoking her chicken bog, made from a century's old recipe, served all the way – with sausage, skin, and bone!

"Why, even some rich folks eat bog," she said. "Once the smell of this bog hits the air, people start comin' over." It was hard to fathom the depth and soul of this woman as she stood there that day, let alone the legends and lore of the times she grew up in.

Looking back, I think the whole experience was more about the memories of how things used to be and the spirit of times gone by. These old recipes originated in the days of milk and bread suppers, rice and cotton plantations – a time when men worked all day in the fields and women stayed home wearing aprons, cooking and canning food for the winter months ahead.

Mullet, Protein Staple from the Sea

IN THIS CHAPTER I've included a Gullah recipe for Mullet Stew because mullet was a principal source of protein for the slaves and for blacks after the Civil War who had access to saltwater estuaries. Many lived on land near the Coosawhatchee, Waccamaw, and Combahee rivers and would catch mullet with nets and cane poles. When this fish is rolled in corn meal or cracker crumbs and pan fried in butter within several hours of being caught, its flavor is exceptional. In the fall, the fish are full of roe and many folks on the islands believe that the roe of the mullet is by far the best.

Since it is one of the most oily fish, it is an excellent choice for smoking. Smoking not only enhances the flavor, but this

Mullet Fishing, oil on canvas by John Carroll Doyle.

salting and curing process prolongs the time that the fish can be kept for future enjoyment. Many years ago out on St. Helena Island, it was not unusual to be driving along Seaside Road and see the heavily salted fish on roof tops of fishermen's houses receiving the direct rays of the sun for as long as one week. The mullet could then be stored without refrigeration for several months. Prior to cooking, the fish would be soaked in fresh water, which would not only soften it but would remove most of the salt used in the "curing" process.

Mullet Stew

Louise Miller Cohen, Hilton Head Island Storyteller

1 mullet, 1½ to 2 pounds, cleaned
1 yellow onion
2 tomatoes
Salt and pepper
Cayenne pepper
All-purpose flour
½ cup vegetable oil
½ cup fish stock

Chop the onion; peel and chop tomatoes. Rinse the mullet and pat dry with paper towels. Cut the mullet into quarter and season the fish with salt, pepper and cayenne pepper. Place the flour in a brown paper bag. Add the fish pieces two at a time and shake the bag to coat the pieces evenly. In a large skillet over high heat, warm the oil. Add the fish pieces and fry, turning once, until golden on both sides - about 5 minutes. Return the fish pieces to the skillet and add the tomatoes and stock. Cover and simmer over low heat until the fish flakes easily, about 10 minutes. Taste and adjust seasonings. Goes well over rice.

Hoppin' John

Julia Ferguson of Beaufort

1 gallon of water
2 cups dry black-eyed peas or field peas
2 tablespoons bacon drippings
¼ pound fatback
2 ham hocks
1 pound white rice
Salt and pepper
Season-All

Rinse peas and clean. Discard any peas that float to the top of the water. Place peas in water and bring to a boil adding the bacon drippings, and the ham hock or fat back and the salt and pepper. Simmer on low, stirring often for about an hour.

Serve over your favorite rice. This is a traditional New Year's Day dish said to bring good luck all year long for those who partake! This recipe is typical of the one-pot cooking of the Lowcountry and is said to have come directly from West Africa to America.

Weaving a sweetgrass basket, photograph by Bob Ovelman.

Gullah Lowcountry Shrimp Pilau

Anita Singleton-Prather (Aunt Pearlie Sue)

1 pound medium size shrimp
2½ cups water
2 tablespoons Bay Seasonings
1 small yellow onion
3 cloves garlic
2 tomatoes
3 thick slices bacon
1 cup long grain white rice
Salt and pepper to taste

Peel the shrimp, reserving the shells. Make a shallow incision along the back of each shrimp, deveining and cleaning well. Cover and refrigerate the shrimp. Place the shrimp shells in a saucepan, add water and Bay Seasonings. Bring to a boil, reduce the heat to medium boil and simmer, uncovered for 15 minutes. Remove from heat and strain the stock through a fine mesh sieve into a measuring pitcher. Set the stock aside. Chop onion and mince the garlic. Peel and chop the tomatoes. In a heavy skillet over medium high heat, cook the bacon until crisp, 3 to 5 minutes. Using a slotted spoon, remove to paper towels to drain. Add the onion, garlic, and rice to the bacon drippings remaining in the skillet and cook, stirring frequently, until all the ingredients are coated with the oil and the rice is beginning to turn opaque. Add the tomatoes, salt, pepper, and the reserved 2 cups of stock. Bring to a boil over medium heat. Stir in the shrimp, re-cover and cook until the shrimp turn pink and the liquid is full absorbed - 5 to 8 minutes. Transfer to a serving dish, crumble the bacon over the top and serve.

www.mycarolinacooking.com

Mama's Sweet Potato Poon

3 or 4 sweet potatoes, grated

3-4 tablespoons sugar

½ cup all-purpose flour

2-3 teaspoons vanilla extract

¼ cup butter

2 cups Karo syrup

Preheat oven 350°. Blend all ingredients together. Bake 10 to 15 minutes and allow to cool. If desired, cinnamon, ground allspice, and dark or golden raisins may be added.

NOTE: Often served as a side dish but can easily be a dessert - just add the whipped cream!

Harold's Country Club, watercolor on paper by Nancy Ricker Rhett.

Broomfield Cabbage Soup

Broomfield is located on Lady's Island and has been home to Gullah folks for generations.

1 fresh green cabbage, sliced thin

2 shallots

8 strips of bacon, cooked until crispy

4 potatoes, cubed

1 liter chicken stock

Light cream to taste

Olive oil

Salt and fresh pepper

Sauté the cabbage and shallots in olive oil without browning until soft. Cover with a liter of chicken stock. Add the potatoes with the seasoning and cook for 20 minutes on medium heat uncovered. Puree the soup and add some cream, salt, pepper and olive oil. Pass through a fine sieve. Serve with crumbled bacon bits. Yields: 6 servings.

Fresh Specker Butter Beans

This recipe is courtesy of *Dye's Gullah Fixin's*, by chef Dye Scott-Rhodan.

4 ham hocks (smoke)

2 quarts fresh specker butter beans

½ onion, chopped

1 teaspoon salt

1 ½ tablespoons suga (sugar)

¼ teaspoon black pepper

Get up ta boiling for 1 hour or til tender. Gotta add water, wen good clouded water add specker butter beans, put cover over um, cover wit water, bring ta boil for 30 minutes or pat ya foot 200 times. Put in suga, pepper and boil for 10 minutes. Enjoy!

Dye's Country Corn Pone

Dye Scott-Rhodan. Recipe is presented Gullah-style.

3 cups fresh cut corn

2 tablespoons suga (sugar)

2 cups milk

¼ cup melt butter

2 eggs

½ tablespoon salt

Dash pepper

½ teaspoon baking soda

1 cup cornmeal (yellow)

1 cup Cheddar chez (optional)

Dump all in a bowl and mix and dump in a baking dish big enough ta hold. Bake until done 30 minutes.

Carolina Cottonfields, oil on canvas by John Carroll Doyle.

Buttermilk Hush Puppies with Onions and Bell Peppers

Submitted by a Gullah friend

1 quart peanut oil

2 cups self rising cornmeal mix

½ cup all purpose flour

1 teaspoon baking soda

1 large egg

1 cup buttermilk

1 small onion

3 tablespoons finely chopped red pepper

Heat oil in deep fryer or very deep heavy pot to 365°. Combine cornmeal mix, flour, and baking soda in a medium bowl. Whisk together egg, buttermilk, onion and bell pepper in a small bowl. Add dry ingredients, stirring just until moistened

Be sure oil is at correct temperature before adding batter. If you do not have a thermometer, you can test using a cube of bread. The bread will brown within a few seconds, without absorbing very much oil.

Drop batter by rounded tablespoonfuls carefully into hot oil. Fry 2 to 3 minutes or until golden brown, turning once.

Batter will rise to the surface when done.

Remove hush puppies with metal tongs or metal slotted spoon; turn onto paper towels to drain. Allow oil to return to the right temperature before repeating with additional batter.

Daufuskie Crab Fried Rice

Daufuskie Island is a sea island located at the southern tip of Beaufort County and it's pronounced "das-fus-cay," meaning "the first cay" or island, by the Gullah natives. Here is the home of Sallie Ann Robinson, who has preserved much of her homeland's culinary heritage and lore in two cookbooks, *Gullah Home Cooking The Daufuskie Way,* and *Cooking the Gullah Way.* She's one of those infectiously joyful people and her cooking is a reflection of her love for life and great cuisine.

4 strips thick cut bacon, diced

1 medium yellow onion, trimmed, split lengthwise, and chopped

1 medium green bell pepper, stemmed, cored, seeded and chopped

1 rib celery, strung and chopped

1 large clove garlic, minced

1 pound crabmeat

3 cups steamed rice

Salt and freshly ground black pepper

Put the bacon in a large, deep skillet over medium high heat. Sauté, tossing often until the fat is rendered and it's golden brown. Add the onion, pepper, and celery and sauté, tossing until it is softened and the onion is golden, about 5 minutes. Add the garlic and crab and sauté, tossing, until the crab is hot through and golden brown, about 5 minutes.

Add the rice and toss until it is well coated and the crabmeat is evenly distributed. Season it liberally with salt and pepper, if needed. Toss well, lower the heat to medium low, cover, and let steam gently for about 10 minutes. Taste and adjust the seasonings, toss well, and serve hot. Serves 4.

www.mycarolinacooking.com

Basket weaver, watercolor on paper by Nancy Ricker Rhett.

Purloo (pronounced PUR-low)

A Lowcountry dish thought to have come to the South by way of African slaves.

3 slices bacon, chopped

1 medium onion, chopped

1 medium green pepper, chopped

1 cup thinly sliced okra

1 clove minced garlic

1 cup cooked ham, in thin slices

3 cups cooked rice

1 medium tomato, seeded and chopped

1 teaspoon dried thyme

½ teaspoon salt

½ teaspoon dried basil

⅛ teaspoon red pepper flakes

Cook bacon over medium heat in large skillet until brown; drain fat. Stir in onion, pepper, okra and garlic; sauté several minutes until the onion is tender. Heat thoroughly and serve as a side dish or as a main dish.

Boiled Peanuts

"Official Snack Food of South Carolina"

1 pound green peanuts

1 quart water

Salt

Wash peanuts with their shells on and place them in a large kettle. Add water until the water is an inch above the floating peanuts. Push the peanuts down with your hand to make sure the water is at the right level above the peanuts. For each quart of water, add a well rounded tablespoon of salt. Bring water to a rolling boil. Turn down the heat and allow peanuts to simmer, as long as two hours or more, depending on how crunchy you like your peanuts. Allow peanuts to sit in the brine as they cool to eating temperature.

Best enjoyed outdoors with sweet tea!

Lowcountry Red Rice

Eleanor Howard of Beaufort

Two large 15-ounce cans Italian-style stewed tomatoes, undrained

4 green onions, sliced

1 large green bell pepper, diced

2 garlic cloves, pressed

1 tablespoon vegetable oil

1 pound Polish sausage, cut into ¼-inch pieces

2 cups uncooked rice (white or brown)

1-2 tablespoons Tabasco

¼ teaspoon salt

¼ teaspoon pepper

Drain tomatoes, reserving liquid. Add enough water to liquid to equal 2 cups. Sauté sausage, green onions, bell pepper, and garlic in hot oil until tender. Stir in tomatoes, 2 cups reserved liquid, salt and pepper. Bring this to a boil then simmer a few minutes. Cover and cook rice according to the directions on the rice package. Add tomato mixture to the rice and stir together. Serves 6-8.

For Lowcountry Rice with Ham: Sauté 2 cups diced cooked ham with green onion mixture.

Okra was introduced to this country in the 1700s by African slaves. In Africa, the pods were eaten cooked, and the seeds were toasted and ground - used then and now as a coffee substitute. When cut these pods release a sticky substance with thickening properties, quite useful for soups and stews.

The Old Crab Factory, watercolor on paper by Ray Ellis.

Carolina Country Hobo Bread

1 ½ cups raisins

2 teaspoons baking soda

1 cup boiling water

1 cup sugar

½ cup chopped nuts

3 tablespoons shortening

1 egg, beaten

2 cups flour

⅛ teaspoon salt

Pour the boiling water over the raisins and baking soda and let stand until cool. Combine the other ingredients with the raisin mixture and bake in a greased loaf pan at 350° for 60 minutes or until done.

Corn Skillet Fritters

2 eggs

½ cup milk

1 teaspoon salt

1 tablespoon sugar

1 cup sifted all-purpose flour

2 tablespoons bacon drippings or oil

2 cups whole kernel corn, drained

Combine all ingredients except corn. Beat until smooth; blend in corn. Drop spoonfuls of batter in hot fat in skillet (⅛ to ¼ inch deep. Brown lightly on both sides. Serve hot with butter and syrup.

Bald Eagle, photograph by Bob Ovelman.

Pounding Rice, etching on paper by Alfred Hutty.

Buttermilk Pie

Ervena Faulkner, popular columnist for the *Beaufort Gazette*.

1 cup butter

2 cups sugar

3 eggs

3 tablespoons flour

¼ teaspoon salt

1 cup buttermilk

Cream butter and sugar, pouring ½ cup sugar at a time. Add eggs, one at a time. Combine flour and salt. Add to butter/sugar mixture in small portions. Add buttermilk. Batter should look like a cake mix that needs more flour. Cook in an unbaked pie shell at 300 degrees for 1½ hours until pie is golden. Delicious!

NOTE: Ervena is a retired educator and columnist for the *Beaufort Gazette*. She has always had an interest in food and nutrition, and we thank her for gathering the recipes for this section from her Gullah friends who live and work on the islands in the Lowcountry.

Old Country Pound Cake (Suga Cane)

This recipe is three or four generations old by Dye Scott-Rhodan, presented Gullah style.

1 cup milk

3 cups all-purpose flour, sifted

3 cups suga (sugar)

1½ cups room temperature butter

¼ cup suga can syrup

1½ teaspoons vanilla

6 eggs

½ teaspoon baking powder

Cream suga an butter for 1 minute. Put eggs one at a time, beat after each one. Put flour a little at a time in between. Put in milk and the rest. Beat 3 minutes. Pour in a regular sized bundt pan. Bake for 45 minutes.

Benne Seed Cookies

1 cup Benne seeds

1½ cup dark brown sugar, packed firmly

1 cup all-purpose flour

¼ teaspoon baking powder

¼ teaspoon salt

¼ cup butter, melted

1 egg

1 teaspoon vanilla

Known as sesame seeds in most of the country, "benne" is the name the Gullah people learned to call these seeds, which were brought from Africa by the slaves. Toast benne seeds on ungreased baking sheets until light brown, 10-12 minutes will bring out their flavor and give cookies a slightly crunchy texture. Heat oven to 375° Mix all ingredients in a large bowl. Drop by ½ teaspoonfuls 1½ inches apart onto greased baking sheets. Cool about 2 minutes before removing from baking sheets to a wire rack to cool completely.

NOTE: According to Lowcountry legend, benne brings good luck to those who eat or plant it in their gardens. These seeds arrived in America on the necks of African slaves, who wore them for good luck and planted them near their quarters on the plantations.

www.mycarolinacooking.com

Sweet Splurges

*Cooking at home nourishes the body, comforts the soul and brings loved ones together.
I appreciate the generations of women in my life who have inspired
my culinary imagination and nurtured me with stockpots of love.*

THERE'S SOMETHING MAGICAL about the aroma of fresh baked cakes and cookies. It conjures up visions of Grandma's kitchen and recipes you know are out-of-this world good because the recipe card wears evidence of the luscious ingredients like a badge of honor. Keeping the cookie jar filled at my house is a challenge — not because cookies are hard to make, but because they disappear with lightning speed once they come out of the oven.

Each year as Christmas rolls around, I anticipate gathering together with friends and family to celebrate this season filled with joy and love. Often these celebrations draw from warm childhood memories when every color, fragrance, and sound appeared larger than life and positively magical. While we turn to memories for inspiration, the reality of the moment is one of limits: finances, time, and our own sense of confidence. Most folks have a need to simplify, and they want to capture the spirit of the season without the fuss and stress. The recipes presented here are intended to be easy, quick, yet elegant.

After all, we need time to bring every branch and twig of Southern greenery into the house for decorations. Our Lowcountry gardens overflow with magnolias, camellias, and ruby colored berries dripping from nandina hedges. Armloads of fresh holly, boxwood for the topiary, baskets of pecans, and beautiful paperwhites all need to be arranged and displayed. These are the elements that feel like home — that welcome friends, show hospitality and are so Southern. These are the things that give us our sense of place and remind us how rich Christmas in the South really is.

Cold, snowy winter days conjure up memories of taffy pulls and mint pulls that served as fun for the entire family. A cold marble slab, buttered hands, and lots of muscle are all that is needed to make the most delicious handmade mints you've ever tasted. Southern luncheons, teas, bridal showers and wedding receptions all feature a bowl of handmade mints. It's just expected!

Finally, don't forget to brighten your home with the extraordinary things you can't see, the most important elements — laughter, lots of good cheer, love, and music!

Opposite Page: Keats, oil on canvas by Joe Bowler.

Peach and Blueberry Trifle

RECIPE

CUSTARD

One 14-ounce can sweetened condensed milk

½ cup water

¼ cup cornstarch

2 eggs

3 cups milk

½ cup butter

1 teaspoon vanilla extract

1 teaspoon almond extract

TRIFLE

¼ cup sugar

8 large fresh peaches, peeled and sliced

¾ cup blueberries

1 pound cake, cut into ½ inch cubes

¼ cup Amaretto

Single Peach, oil on canvas by Loren Speck.

Combine the condensed milk, water, cornstarch, and eggs in a bowl and mix until smooth. Combine the milk and butter in a saucepan and heat until the butter melts. Add the egg mixture gradually and cook over low heat for 20 minutes or until thickened, stirring constantly. Remove from the heat and stir in the vanilla and almond extract. This is delicious all by itself!

Sprinkle the sugar over the peaches and blueberries in a bowl and let it stand until the sugar dissolves.

Brush the pound cake cubes generously with the liqueur, and layer them into the Mason jars. Layer one third of the peaches and berries, then one third of the custard and then the cake. Repeat the layers until all the cake, peaches, blueberries, and custard are used.

Place lids on the Mason jars and refrigerate several hours before using. If desired, decorate with brightly colored ribbons and fabric. Serves 10.

EVERYONE LOVES TO MAKE TRIFLE because it's one of the prettiest desserts you can pull together. And even better, it's a cinch to make. The multiple layers delight the senses with so many colors, textures and flavors. Although the dictionary defines "trifle" as something insignificant, this dessert is anything but.

It makes a big show at a party; however, often it is staid and stuffy and offers little in terms of real taste. Now's the time to turn up the flavor in this old-fashioned dessert by using the wonderful summer peaches and blueberries available right now. Let's turn it into the delicious and elegant offering we know it can be.

While we're at it, let's try a unique presentation idea. Layer this lusciousness into Mason jars topped with pretty fabrics and tied with bright ribbon — perfect for any backyard or poolside gathering! You'll need 3 or 4 jars for this recipe, depending on the size you choose.

> Make peaches simple to peel by tossing them into boiling water for 30 seconds. Then pour the water off and place in a cold water bath for a minute and the peeling will slide right off.

www.mycarolinacooking.com

Blueberry and Peach Crisp

Blueberries, oil on canvas by Joe Bowler.

SUMMER IN THE SOUTH sings with the sweetness of fresh blueberries and peaches. In the summer blueberries and peaches are abundant and at their freshest, bursting with flavor and guaranteed to make for big smiles on all the little faces in your life.

Nothing says summer like the sight and smell of baskets of fresh blueberries and peaches at a roadside stand. And what better way to showcase them than with an old fashioned crisp topped with creamy vanilla ice cream.

Inspiration for this recipe comes from lazy summer afternoons when my son Andrew and I stopped at the blueberry patch located between Beaufort and Hilton Head, picked baskets of fresh berries and rushed home to make this fabulous crisp!

Magnolia Blossom, photograph by Bob Ovelman.

RECIPE

12 large ripe peaches

1 orange, zested

1 ½ cups granulated sugar

1 cup light brown sugar, packed

1 ½ cups plus 3 tablespoons all-purpose flour

½ pint fresh blueberries

Pinch of salt

1 cup quick-cooking oatmeal

½ pound cold butter, diced

Before you get started, here's a great tip on making peaches simple to peel. Just immerse the peaches in boiling water for 30 seconds, and then place them in cold water. The skin slides right off – so easy!

Preheat the oven to 350°. Butter the inside of a 10x15-inch oval dish. Peel peaches. Slice peaches into thick wedges and place them into a large bowl. Add the orange zest, ¼ cup granulated sugar, ½ cup brown sugar, and 2 tablespoons of flour. Toss well. Gently mix in the blueberries. Allow the mixture to sit for 5 minutes. If there is a lot of liquid, add another tablespoon of flour. Pour the peaches into oval baking dish.

Combine 1 ½ cups flour, 1 cup granulated sugar, ½ cup brown sugar, salt, oatmeal, and the cold, diced butter in the bowl of an electric mixer. Mix on low until the butter is pea sized and the mixture is crumbly. Sprinkle evenly on top of the peaches and blueberries. Bake for 1 hour until the top is browned and crisp and the juices are bubbly. Serve at once or store in the refrigerator and reheat later at 350° until warm. Top it off with some real French vanilla ice cream.

There's something magical about the aroma of fresh baked cookies! So preheat your oven, pull out your mixing bowls and try one of these favorite recipes.

One of the most joyous aspects of Christmas cooking is sharing your specialties with friends and loved ones. I've put together some very old and dear recipes with this gracious goal in mind. Many of the selections found here can also serve as hostess gifts and homemade presents and teacher gifts. Even a luscious Huguenot Torte or layer cake hand delivered to the neighbors is a wonderful way to pass along holiday cheer.

Coconut-Pecan Chocolate Bars

½ cup butter, softened

¼ cup butter flavored shortening

¼ cup plus 3 tablespoons sugar

2 teaspoons heavy whipping cream

½ teaspoon vanilla extract

¼ teaspoon salt

1¾ cups all-purpose flour

½ cup chopped pecans

1 cup toasted sweetened flaked coconut, divided

Ten 1-ounce squares baking chocolate, melted and divided

¼ cup sweetened condensed milk

½ teaspoon coconut extract

Half of a 16-ounce package vanilla flavored candy coating

In a large bowl, combine butter and shortening. Beat at medium high speed with an electric mixer for 1 minute.

Add sugar, cream, vanilla, and salt, beating until combined. Add flour, pecans, and ¼ cup coconut. Mix at low speed until combined.

Remove dough, and divide into 2 portions. Wrap dough in plastic, and refrigerate for at least 2 hours.

In a small saucepan, combine 7 squares chocolate and condensed milk. Cook over low heat, whisking constantly until melted. Remove from heat. Add coconut extract, stirring to combine. Cool slightly.

Preheat oven to 350°. Line a baking sheet with parchment paper. Set aside.

On a lightly floured surface, roll half of dough into a 10 x 8-inch rectangle approximately ¼-inch thick. Place on top of chocolate covered dough, and gently press edges with fingers to seal. Transfer to prepared baking sheet.

Bake until light golden brown, 15 to 20 minutes. Cool completely.

Transfer to a cutting board. Cut into 2¾ x 1¼-inch bars. Set aside.

Place candy coating in a microwave safe bowl. Heat coating in a microwave in 30 second intervals until melted, stirring between each interval.

Dip bottoms of bars in melted coating. Place bars coated side up on parchment paper to dry.

Melt remaining 3 squares chocolate in the same manner as candy coating.

Spoon a strip of melted chocolate across each bar. Sprinkle with remaining ¾ cup coconut. Let dry for about 30 minutes. Yields: 2½ dozen

Cranberry Toffee Walnut Tarts

One 14.1 ounce box refrigerated pie crusts

⅔ cup sugar

¼ cup butter, melted

2 large eggs

1 teaspoon vanilla extract

1 cup dried cranberries

¾ cup toffee bits

¾ cup chopped walnuts

Preheat oven to 325°. Spray a 24 count mini muffin pan with nonstick baking spray with flour. Using a 2¾-inch round cutter, cut 12 circles from each pie crust. Press crusts into the bottom and up sides of each cup of muffin pan.

In a medium bowl, combine sugar, melted butter, eggs, and vanilla, whisking to combine. Stir in cranberries, toffee bits, and walnuts.

Spoon about 1 tablespoon mixture into each prepared crust. Bake for about 25 minutes, or until lightly browned. Let cook in pan for 10 minutes. Remove to wire racks to cool completely.

Photograph by Ed Funk.
www.edfunkphotos.com

www.mycarolinacooking.com

Christmas Divinity

Make this recipe on a sunny day; rain and dampness will cause it to be chewy.

2½ cups sugar

½ cup water

½ cup light corn syrup

¼ teaspoon salt

2 egg whites

1 teaspoon vanilla extract

1 cup chopped pecans, toasted

Garnish: pecan halves

Coat a large sheet of wax paper with butter; set aside. Cook first 4 ingredients in a heavy 2 quart saucepan over low heat about 15 minutes or until sugar dissolves and a candy thermometer registers 248°. Remove hot syrup from the heat.

Beat egg whites at high speed with an electric mixer until stiff peaks form. Pour half of hot syrup in a thin stream over egg whites, beating constantly at high speed, about 5 minutes.

Cook remaining half of syrup over medium heat, stirring occasionally, 4 to 5 minutes or until a candy thermometer registers 272°. Slowly pour hot syrup and vanilla extract over egg white mixture, beating constantly at high speed 6 to 8 minutes or until mixture holds its shape. Stir in 1 cup chopped pecans.

Drop mixture immediately and quickly by rounded teaspoonfuls onto lightly greased wax paper. Garnish with a pecan half on top. Cool. Yields: 4 dozen.

NOTE: The syrup mixture should bubble on the surface. Be sure to keep an eye on the thermometer because the temperature of the syrup rises quickly. The process used when beating egg whites is as important as cooking the ingredients to the proper temperature. Start with a clean bowl. Any greasy residue in the bowl can reduce the volume of beaten egg whites. When egg whites are beaten properly, stiff peaks will form.

For Chocolate Marble Divinity: omit pecans and fold in 1 cup semisweet chocolate mini-morsels.

For Peppermint Divinity: omit pecans, and fold in ¾ cup crushed hard red or green peppermint candies and, if desired, 2 drops liquid food coloring.

Mocha Surprise Truffles

One 11.5 ounce package milk chocolate morsels

½ cup sweetened condensed milk

2 tablespoons coffee liqueur

4 teaspoons instant coffee granules

⅛ teaspoon salt

30 chocolate-coated coffee beans

Chocolate sprinkles, cocoa, or sifted powdered sugar

Microwave chocolate morsels in a glass mixing bowl at high 1½ minutes, stirring after 1 minute. Stir until smooth. Add condensed milk and next 3 ingredients, stirring well. Shape 1 level tablespoon chocolate mixture around each coffee bean. Roll in chocolate sprinkles, cocoa, or powdered sugar. Place truffles in miniature paper liners; chill. Store in refrigerator. Yields: 30 truffles.

Double Treat Toffee

2½ cups semisweet chocolate morsels, divided

2 cups finely chopped pecans

2 cups sugar

1 cup butter

¼ cup water

1 teaspoon pure vanilla extract

Bake pecans in a shallow pan at 350°. Stir occasionally, 5 to 10 minutes or until toasted. Set aside.

Combine sugar, butter, and water in a 3 quart saucepan. Cook over low heat, stirring gently, until sugar dissolves. Cover and cook over medium heat, 2 to 3 minutes. Uncover and cook, without stirring, until mixture reaches the hard crack stage or a candy thermometer registers 300°. Remove from heat, and stir in vanilla. Pour mixture into a greased 15 x 10-inch jelly roll pan, quickly spreading to edges of pan.

Sprinkle 1¼ cups chocolate morsels over toffee; let stand 1 minute or until chocolate begins to melt and spread evenly over candy. Sprinkle with half of pecans; let stand until set.

Melt remaining 1¼ cups of morsels in a saucepan over low heat, stirring often.

Run a sharp knife around edge of toffee, and carefully invert onto a wax paper lined baking sheet. Spread with melted chocolate, and sprinkle with remaining pecans. Let stand until set. Break into pieces; store in an airtight container. Yields: 2 pounds

Shaker Lemon Pie

The pie's flavor is bright and tart. Try a scoop of vanilla ice cream or some crème fraiche with it! This pie is easy, easy, easy!

4 large lemons
4 cups granulated sugar
9 eggs, well beaten
Pinch of salt (optional)
2 egg whites, beaten with a fork

Wash and cut 2 of the lemons into paper thin slices using a very sharp knife. Remove the peel and pith of the two other lemons. Slice the flesh very, very thinly, and put it with the other slices in a large mixing bowl. Add sugar, and toss well to coat. Cover bowl with plastic wrap, and let the mixture rest overnight, stirring occasionally.

The next day, preheat the oven to 450°. Press one circle of pastry into an 11-inch pie plate and chill. Either make your own pate brisee for a double crust or purchase at the market. You will need two pastry rounds.

Add beaten eggs to the lemon mixture, and mix well. Turn the mixture into prepared pie shell, neatly arranging some of the lemon slices on top. Cut long, even slashes 1 inch apart in the other pastry round, and place on top of the filling. Crimp edges of the pie to seal. Brush top and edges with the egg-white glaze. Bake for 15 minutes. Reduce oven temperature to 375° and continue baking for 30 minutes, or until the crust is golden brown and shiny. The pie is done when an inserted knife comes out clean. Let it cool on a rack before serving.

Three of a Kind, oil on canvas by John Carroll Doyle.

PUCKER UP WITH CITRUS! I grew up with lemon meringue pies and later tried lemon tarts, lemon curd and lemon chiffon pies. It wasn't until I attended a Quaker prep school in Providence, Rhode Island (no, I'm not Quaker) that I started experiencing Shaker lemon pies. This style of lemon pie is a specialty of a small religious group known as the "Shaking Quakers" from Manchester, England. The Shaker lemon pie recipe, which wastes none of the fruit, is one of their more enduring legacies.

This recipe dates back to my high school days and was served on all important occasions. Unlike other lemon pies, which are mixed from lemon juice with perhaps a bit of the zest, whole-lemon pie includes the peel and all. Slicing the lemons paper thin provides a potent, appealing mix of sweet and tart flavors. If you are comfortable with a mandoline, you might try using one of those. Be careful of your fingers! Folks are astounded when they find out just how easy this is to make and how good it is to eat. It's light and creamy and melts in your mouth like a lemon cloud.

Mama Green's Banana Puddin'

CUSTARD

3 eggs

3 cups milk

1½ cups sugar

3½ tablespoons cornstarch

1 teaspoon pure vanilla extract (no imitation vanilla please!)

6 medium bananas

One 12-ounce package Vanilla Wafers

Beat the eggs until fluffy. In a heavy saucepan, combine the eggs, sugar, and milk, mixing well. Cook over medium heat, stirring constantly with a whisk. Once custard starts to bubble, add cornstarch mixed with a little water to thicken. When custard is thickened to the consistency of pudding, remove from heat. Strain custard through a fine mesh sieve to remove lumps. Add vanilla and set aside.

Slice bananas. In a 3-quart baking dish, arrange ⅓ of the bananas in a single layer on the bottom. Top with ⅓ of the vanilla wafers. Pour ⅓ of the custard over the bananas. Repeat layering process two more times. Top with meringue.

MERINGUE

3 egg whites

6 tablespoons sugar

3/8 teaspoons cream of tartar

Add cream of tartar to unbeaten egg whites. Whip using mixer to medium soft peaks. Beat in sugar until egg whites are glossy and hold a firm peak. Be careful not to over beat. Top banana pudding, sealing the edges with the meringue and bake at 350° until golden.

Chef Nadine Awoyemi of Sweetgrass Bistro, Dataw Island, SC. Photograph by Mark Shaffer, LowcountryWeekly.

"AS EASY GOING as a marsh breeze on a balmy day" are words used to describe Chef Nadine Awoyemi of Dataw Island's Sweetgrass Bistro. This Sea Island native has been cooking for folks in Beaufort for a long, long time. While I've been eating banana pudding since childhood, never have I tasted one so marvelously, deliriously delicious as Nadine's. Owner Lauren Tilapaugh attributes this delectable dessert recipe to her great grandmother who passed it down through the generations. Lauren remembers, while growing up, eating this warm, right out of the oven, with a perfect golden meringue on top. So, while many are used to chilled banana pudding, Sweetgrass serves theirs warm with whipped cream and extra wafers.

Mama Green's Banana Pudding. Photograph by Mark Shaffer, Lowcountry Weekly.

Luscious Lemonade Layer Cake

1 1/3 cup granulated sugar

6 tablespoons butter, softened

1 tablespoon grated lemon rind

3 tablespoons lemonade concentrate

2 teaspoons vanilla extract

2 large eggs

2 large egg whites

2 cups all purpose flour

1 teaspoon baking powder

1/2 teaspoon salt

1/2 teaspoon baking soda

1 1/4 cups buttermilk

FROSTING

2 tablespoons butter

2 teaspoons grated lemon rind

2 teaspoons thawed lemonade concentrate

1/2 teaspoon vanilla extract

8 ounces cream cheese

3 1/2 cups powdered sugar

Bake at 350° for 20 minutes. Grease and flour two 9-inch cake pans. Place the first 5 ingredients in a large bowl and beat with a mixer at medium speed until well blended. Add eggs and egg whites, one at a time, beating well after each addition.

Lightly spoon flour into dry measuring cups. Combine flour, baking powder, salt, and baking soda and mix well. Add flour mixture and buttermilk alternately to sugar mixture, beginning and ending with flour mixture.

Beat well after each addition.

Divide batter evenly into the prepared pans. Sharply tap pans once on counter to remove any air bubbles from the batter. Bake until wooden pick inserted in center comes out clean.

Cool in pans for 10 minutes on a wire rack.

FROSTING

Place 2 tablespoons butter and the next 4 ingredients in mixing bowl and beat well. Add powdered sugar and beat at low speed just until blended. Chill for an hour. Place cake layer on a plate and spread with 1/2 cup frosting. Place next layer on top. Spread remaining frosting over the top and sides of cake. Store in the refrigerator.

Caramel Crème Brûlée

1 cup plus 6 tablespoons of sugar

1/2 cup water

2 cups whole milk

1 cup whipping cream

1 tablespoon vanilla

Pinch of salt

8 egg yolks

Preheat the oven to 325°. Make a caramel with 1 cup of sugar and the water in a large sauce pot and bring to a boil without stirring. The sugar will dissolve and begin to bubble. Let it boil for about 5 minutes, watching carefully as the water boils off and it begins to turn yellow. Gently swirl until the sugar turns an even golden. Take it off of the heat before it gets brown. Quickly pour the milk and cream into the caramel along with the vanilla and salt, and whisk until incorporated. Whisk eggs and then slowly pour the caramel mixture into them, a little at a time, whisking constantly.

Pour into crème brûlée dishes and bake in a hot water bath in the oven for 30 minutes, or until edges are set and center is slightly jiggly. Just prior to serving, sprinkle with the remaining sugar and caramelize with a blowtorch. Serves 6.

Huguenot Torte

Considered Charleston's most famous dessert — almost every restaurant in the area serves this wonderfully delicious apple and nut torte. The truth of the matter is that it's neither — Huguenot nor a torte! Instead, it's a kind of pecan pie without the crust.

2 eggs

1/4 cup white sugar

2 teaspoons pure vanilla extract

1 teaspoon freshly squeezed lemon juice

1/4 cup all purpose flour

1/2 teaspoon freshly grated nutmeg

2 teaspoon baking soda

1/4 teaspoon salt

1 1/2 cups toasted, chopped pecans, divided

1 cup peeled and chopped tart apples

Whipped cream

To toast pecans, spread shelled, whole pecans in a shallow pan and toast in a 275° oven for about 20 minutes.

Preheat oven to 325° and butter a 13 x 9-inch baking dish.

In a large bowl, beat eggs until very frothy and lemon colored. Add sugar, vanilla extract, lemon juice, flour, nutmeg, baking soda, and salt. Stir until well combined. Fold in 1 cup toasted pecans and apples. Pour batter into the prepared baking dish. Bake 30 to 35 minutes or until the top is brown and crusty. Remove from the oven.

Serve warm with whipped cream and chopped nuts on the top. Yields: 8 servings.

> It's amazing to realize that a single lemon tree can produce 1,000 to 2,000 lemons every year! Zest is the perfumy outer skin which is removed with the aid of a zester, paring knife or vegetable peeler. Only the yellow portion of the skin, not the white pith, is considered the zest. The aromatic oils in the zest add so much flavor to all kinds of food dishes.

Maple Sweet Potato Pie

2 large sweet potatoes

4 tablespoons butter, melted

1 teaspoon pure vanilla extract

3 eggs

1 egg yolk

¾ cup cream

¼ cup plus 2 tablespoons maple syrup

¼ cup plus 1 tablespoon brown sugar

¼ cup bourbon

¼ teaspoon kosher salt

¼ teaspoon freshly grated nutmeg

¼ teaspoon ground cinnamon

⅛ teaspoon ground cloves

A dash of freshly ground black pepper

One 9-inch pie crust, baked blind (Make your own or use one purchased in the market. To blind bake, simply preheat the oven to 375°, line the shell with foil and fill with dry rice or beans. Bake for 20 minutes. Remove foil and beans before filling.)

Preheat the oven to 425°. Pierce the sweet potatoes at each end with a fork and place them on a foil lined baking sheet. Roast until the potatoes are soft, about 1 hour, turning them over halfway through the baking time. Cool, peel and put the flesh through a food mill or mash smoothly with a potato masher. You should have 2 cups of puree.

Turn oven down to 375°.

Combine the puree with all the remaining ingredients for the filling. Whisk until well combined and smooth. Pour the filling into the partially baked pie shell. Bake for about 45 to 50 minutes, until the filling is just barely set. When the rim of the pie plate is nudged, the very center of the filling should barely move.

Cool the pie to room temperature. It can be made several hours or up to 1 day in advance. Just be sure to refrigerate it.

Stealthy Egret, photo by Bob Ovelman.

THE SOUTH'S BELOVED SWEET POTATO enjoys a place of prominence during November and December. This marvelous, sugary root vegetable captures fall's colors and heralds the advent of the holiday season.

Back in the 1800s the sweet potato was used to augment slave diets, and when rations were scarce during the Civil War, sweet potatoes were dried and ground to make a substitute for coffee.

While today there are more than 100 varieties, American growers stick to about a dozen, ranging in color from whitish to deep reddish-orange and varying widely in taste and consistency. And in addition to being virtually fat-free, cholesterol-free, and very low in sodium, the complex carbs in sweet potatoes make them acceptable even with today's low-carb diets.

This dessert is always one of my favorites at Thanksgiving. It's a little denser and creamier in texture than pumpkin pie. This is like a sweet potato custard, and you'll need to take care not to overbake the filling. Check it frequently as it nears the end of its baking time. It's delicious served with some lightly whipped cream!

BASIC PIE CRUST

2 ⅔ cups all purpose flour

¾ teaspoon kosher salt

¾ teaspoon sugar

4 ounces chilled butter, cut into pieces

4 ounces (½ cup plus 1 tablespoon plus 2 teaspoons) chilled vegetable shortening, cut into pieces

¼ to ½ cup cold water, as needed

Place the flour, salt, and sugar in the bowl of a food processor with a steel blade. Pulse to combine. Add the chilled butter and shortening; pulse until the fat is evenly cut in and the mixture resembles coarse cornmeal. Remove to a mixing bowl.

Working quickly, gradually add enough cold water, while tossing and stirring with a fork, until the dough just begins to come together. Divide the dough into two even portions, flatten into rounds, wrap in plastic, and chill for a few hours or overnight.

Roll out one portion and fit it into a 9-inch pie pan. Crimp edges. Reserve remaining portion for another use. Line shell with foil or parchment paper and fill with dry rice or beans. Blind bake for 20 minutes at 375°.

Out on Folly, oil on canvas by Jennifer Smith.

REMEMBER THE STRAWBERRIES of your childhood, fresh-picked in the early morning and served with whipped cream and shortcake in the evening? Take a trip to the farmer's market and re-create the experience with some of the finest berries you'll ever eat, fresh picked from the farms nearby. Or maybe you prefer to go out and pick your own. Whatever you decide, you'll want to eat one or two on the ride home — a taste of spring with every bite!

Can there possibly be too many ways to enjoy strawberries? I don't think so. I've included just a few of my all time favorites. Choosing which ones was the hard part because there are just so many creative, delicious desserts, salads and breads to make with this versatile red berry.

Here's a super easy strawberry torte. A torte is a cake made mainly of eggs, sugar and ground nuts instead of flour. In this recipe, I made it even simpler by substituting ladyfingers for the crust. Use only the freshest and the best strawberries, discarding any that are mushy or bruised.

Strawberry Cream Pie

One 9-inch deep dish pie shell

1 cup whipping cream

4 ounces cream cheese

One 14-ounce can of sweetened condensed milk, well chilled

1½ cups pureed strawberries

¼ cup sugar

Bake and chill the pie shell. Make sure the ingredients are well chilled. Whip the cream until stiff peaks form. Set cream in the refrigerator to keep cold. Whip the cream cheese. Beat in the condensed milk and the strawberries. Gently fold in the whipped cream. Pour the filling into the pie shell. The pie shell will be very full and will overfill to a slight mound. Put the pie into the freezer right away to set. Freeze for several hours and serve frozen.

Strawberry Torte

11 ounces cream cheese, softened

¾ cup sugar

2 teaspoons pure vanilla extract

1 pint whipping cream

Two 12-ounce packages Ladyfinger cookies

1 pound fresh strawberries, sliced

2 tablespoons cornstarch

Place the sliced strawberries and ¼ cup of the sugar in a bowl and stir. Set aside for at least an hour to allow the berries to macerate. This process allows the fruit to form a syrup. Pour the strawberry syrup in a pan with the cornstarch over medium high heat and bring to a gentle boil to dissolve the cornstarch.

Add the berries and cook over medium heat until softened. Cool down. Place this mixture in the blender and blend together.

Whip cream cheese, the remaining ½ cup of sugar and vanilla together. In a separate bowl, beat whipping cream until stiff peaks form. Fold whipped cream into the cream cheese mixture. Arrange ladyfingers around the sides and bottom of a 9-inch springform pan. Stand ladyfingers lengthwise around the sides. Pour ½ of this cheese filling into the pan, and then place a layer of ladyfingers on top of the filling. Pour remaining filling over ladyfingers.

Spread strawberry sauce over the top of the cake and place some whole strawberries on top for garnish. Refrigerate for 24 hours and remove from the pan once it is thoroughly chilled. Add a sprig of fresh mint for decoration.

This is a fabulous, easy to make dessert. Select a crust of your choice. A graham cracker crust is the classic but you can use a baked pastry crust or even a nut crust.

www.mycarolinacooking.com

Pumpkin Mousse Parfaits

14 gingersnaps

One 15-ounce can of canned pure pumpkin (not pie filling)

4 tablespoons dark rum

1 pack of unflavored gelatin

½ cup granulated sugar

½ cup light brown sugar

2 large egg yolks

¼ teaspoon freshly grated nutmeg

½ teaspoon cinnamon

1 teaspoon pure vanilla extract

1 ½ cups heavy cream

Sweetened whipped cream

Crystallized ginger, for decoration, optional

Place the rum in a heat proof bowl and sprinkle the gelatin over it. Set aside for 10 minutes for the gelatin to soften. In a large bowl, whisk together the pumpkin, granulated sugar, brown sugar, egg yolks, cinnamon, nutmeg, and set aside.

Set the bowl of gelatin over a pan of simmering water and cook until the gelatin is clear. Immediately whisk the hot gelatin mixture into the pumpkin mixture. In the bowl of an electric mixer fitted with a whisk attachment, whip the heavy cream and vanilla until soft peaks form. Fold the whipped cream into the pumpkin mixture.

To assemble, spoon some of the pumpkin mixture into parfait glasses, and add a layer of whipped cream, then some chopped cookies. Repeat, ending with a third layer of pumpkin. Cover with plastic wrap and refrigerate for several hours or overnight. To serve, decorate with whipped cream and slivered crystallized ginger. Yields: 8 to 10 servings.

If you don't have parfait glasses, simply layer the mixture in tall, clear glassware.

Soda Cracker Bark

This recipe shows up every Christmas and for oyster roasts and tailgates. It is marvelous and simple to make.

1 sleeve Saltine crackers, or more

1 cup butter

1 cup packed light brown sugar

1 (12 ounce) package semi sweet chocolate morsels

Preheat oven to 400°. Line a large cookie sheet with foil. Lay crackers on foil in a solid cover with crackers touching. If your pan is large, you may need more than one sleeve of crackers touching.

In a medium saucepan, boil butter and brown sugar for 3 minutes, stirring constantly. Pour over crackers, spreading to cover them all. Bake for 5 to 7 minutes but do not allow the sugar mixture to burn.

Remove from oven and allow to sit undisturbed about 3 minutes. Sprinkle chocolate chips evenly over candy and spread with a spatula as chocolate begins to melt.

Refrigerate. Chocolate will harden in about 30 minutes to an hour and candy can be broken into pieces. If weather is hot enough to melt chocolate, keep chilled until ready to serve.

Spirit in the Sky, oil on canvas by Karin Jurik.

Holiday Party Fare

Surrounding ourselves with loved ones is the perfect way to celebrate the holiday season. From the rich colors and traditions of Thanksgiving to the magical moments and memories of Christmas captured in our imaginations, it's the time of year to savor every fragrance, every act of kindness and every meal shared with family and friends. So pull up a chair and gather around the table for some holiday delights. You'll for sure want to include these decadent Chocolate Chip Pecan Pie Bars in your cookie baking repertoire. It's just like eating pecan pie in an easy bar cookie. This is from my collection of Blue Ribbon Winners!

Bite Sized Peppermint and Chocolate Chip Cheesecakes

CRUST:

1 cup chocolate wafer crumbs

2 tablespoons sugar

2 tablespoons butter, melted

Cooking spray

FILLING:

12 hard peppermint candies, divided

⅔ cup block style cream cheese, softened

½ cup cream cheese, softened

¼ cup sugar

2 tablespoons flour

2 large egg whites

1 large egg

1 (8 ounce) carton sour cream

¼ cup semisweet chocolate mini chips

¼ teaspoon peppermint extract

1 cup frozen whipped topping, thawed

2 tablespoons chocolate sprinkles

Preheat oven to 325°.

To prepare crust, combine the first 3 ingredients in a small bowl. Press about 1½ teaspoons crumb mixture into the bottom of each of 48 mini muffin cups coated with cooking spray. Bake at 325° for 5 minutes.

NOTE: A baton-like device called a "tamper" makes pressing dough evenly into muffin cups easy and fast.

To prepare the filling, place 6 candies, cream cheese and the next 6 ingredients in a food processor; process until smooth. Stir in mini chips and peppermint extract. Divide the filling evenly among prepared crusts. Bake at 325° for 12 minutes or until done. Cool in pans on a wire rack for 30 minutes. Remove mini cheesecakes from pans, and cool completely. Top each mini cheesecake with 1 teaspoon whipped topping. Crush the remaining 5 candies, sprinkle the crushed candies and chocolate sprinkles over the cheesecakes. Yields: 4 dozen.

Sweet Potato Streusel Tarts

CRUST:

1 cup all purpose flour

2 tablespoons granulated sugar

⅛ teaspoon salt

2 tablespoons vegetable shortening

3 tablespoons ice water

FILLING:

¼ cup maple syrup

2 tablespoons brown sugar

¾ teaspoon ground cinnamon

½ teaspoon ground allspice

¼ teaspoon salt

1 large egg

1 cup cooked, mashed sweet potatoes

¼ cup evaporated milk

STREUSEL

2 tablespoons finely chopped walnuts

2 tablespoons brown sugar

1½ teaspoons chilled butter, cut into small pieces

To prepare crust, lightly spoon flour into a dry measuring cup and level with a knife. Place the flour, sugar, and salt into a food processor, pulse 2 times or until combined. Add 2 tablespoons butter and shortening, and pulse 4 times or until mixture resembles coarse meal. With processor on, add ice water through the food chute, 1 tablespoon at a time, processing just until combined but does not form a ball. Shape mixture into a 6 inch log. Wrap in plastic wrap coated with cooking spray. Freeze 30 minutes.

Shape the dough into 24 balls, and place 1 in each of 24 miniature muffin cups coated with cooking spray. Press dough into the bottoms and up the sides of the muffin cups.

Preheat the oven to 425°.

To prepare the filling, place syrup and the next 5 ingredients into a bowl. Beat with a mixer for a few minutes until well blended. Add sweet potatoes and milk; beat until well blended. Spoon about 4 teaspoons filling into each muffin cup.

Prepare streusel by combining nuts and 2 tablespoons brown sugar in a small bowl. Cut in 1½ teaspoons butter with a pastry blender until mixture resembles coarse meal. Sprinkle streusel evenly over tarts. Bake at 425° for 10 minutes. Reduce heat to 350° (keep tarts in the oven and bake for 12 more minutes until the filling is set. Cool; run a knife around the outside edges and remove tarts from the pan. Place on a wire rack until completely cool. Yields: 2 dozen

Palm Beach Brownies

I make no apologies for writing to you about my own magical weapon of mass destruction, the Palm Beach Brownie. When it's deep in the heart of winter with its grey skies and cold temperatures, I throw all caution to the wind.

During these dark days, just pull out one of these velvety chocolate, pepperminty gems, sit back with a cup of expresso and life is good. Best of all you can stash some away covered in the refrigerator or freezer for up to a month.

I learned all about it from Maida Heatter, now in her 80s, as energetic as ever and still cooking in her kitchen in Miami. Maida is the divine diva of desserts. Heatter's Palm Beach Brownies are legendary. When she tossed handfuls of them to a crowd at the James Beard Foundation awards dinner several years back, the formally dressed guests went nuts trying to catch one.

Without a doubt they are the biggest, thickest, gooiest, chewiest, darkest, brownie you can imagine with a fudgey middle and crisp crunchy top. What's the catch? You must follow the recipe exactly and they're best if they can sit for up to a day before cutting. They're too sticky to be cut into bars when they are just out of the oven.

8 ounces unsweetened chocolate

8 ounces butter, unsalted, plus more for buttering pan

2 generous cups walnuts

5 large eggs

2 teaspoons vanilla extract

½ teaspoon almond extract

¼ teaspoon salt

1 teaspoon powdered instant espresso

3 ¾ cups granulated sugar

1 ⅔ cups sifted unbleached flour

Two (14-15 ounce) bags chocolate covered peppermint patties, wrappers removed

Adjust oven rack one third up from the bottom and preheat the oven to 425°. Line a 9x13x2-inch pan as follows: Invert the pan and center a 17-inch length of aluminum foil, shiny side down, over the pan. With your hands, press down on the sides and corners of the foil to shape it to the pan. Remove the foil. Turn the pan right side up. Place the foil in the pan, and very carefully press it into place in the pan. Now, to butter the foil, place a piece of butter in the pan and put the pan in the oven. When the butter is melted use a pastry brush to spread the butter all over the foil. Set the prepared pan aside.

Place the chocolate and 8 ounces butter in the top of a large double boiler over hot water on medium heat, or in a 4 to 6-cup heavy saucepan over low heat. Stir occasionally until the chocolate and butter are melted. Stir to mix. Remove from the heat and set aside.

Break the walnuts into large pieces; set aside.

In the large bowl of an electric mixer, beat the eggs with the vanilla and almond extracts, salt, espresso, and sugar at high speed for 10 minutes. On low speed add the chocolate mixture and beat only until mixed. Then add the flour and again beat on low speed only until mixed. Remove the bowl from the mixer. Stir in the nuts.

Pour half the mixture into the prepared pan and smooth the top. Place a layer of the mints, touching each other and the edges of the pan, all over the chocolate layer. Cut some mints to fill in large spaces on the edges. Pour the remaining chocolate mixture all over the pan and smooth the top. Bake for 35 minutes, reversing the pan front to back once during baking to ensure even baking. At the end of 35 minutes, the cake will have a firm crust on top, but if you insert a toothpick in the center it will come out wet and covered with chocolate. Nevertheless, it is done. Do not bake any longer.

Remove the pan from the oven; let stand until cool.

Cover the pan with a cookie sheet and invert the pan and the sheet. Remove the pan and the foil lining. Cover the cake with a length of wax paper and another cookie sheet and invert again leaving the cake right side up. Now the cake must be refrigerated for a few hours or overnight before it is cut into bars.

When you are ready to cut, use a long, heavy knife with a sharp blade either serrated or straight. Cut into quarters and cut each quarter in half, cutting through the long sides. Finally, cut each piece into 4 bars, cutting through the long sides. These are better in narrow bar shapes than in squares.

Pack in an airtight box or wrap individually in clear cellophane, wax paper or foil. They will freeze perfectly.

Chocolate Chip Pecan Pie Bars

1 ½ cups Original Bisquick mix

1 cup powdered sugar

¼ cup firm butter

4 eggs

1 cup dark corn syrup

¼ cup butter, melted and cooled

1 teaspoon pure vanilla extract

1 cup semisweet chocolate chips

1 ½ cups chopped pecans

Heat oven to 350°. In a medium bowl, mix Bisquick mix and powdered sugar. Cut in firm butter, using pastry blender until crumbly. Press firmly in bottom of a 13 x 9-inch pan. Bake 15 minutes. Cool.

In a large bowl, beat eggs, corn syrup, melted butter and vanilla with a spoon until smooth. Stir in chocolate chips and pecans. Pour over crust.

Bake 25 to 30 minutes or until golden brown and set. Refrigerate at least 2 hours until chocolate is firm. For bars, cut into 6 rows by 6 rows. Makes 36 bars.

Chocolate Raspberry Truffle Torte

1 stick butter

½ cup sugar

¾ teaspoon vanilla extract

Salt to taste

1 cup all purpose flour

⅓ cup baking cocoa

1 cup heavy cream

12 ounces bittersweet chocolate, chopped

1 teaspoon butter

1 cup seedless raspberry preserves

Beat ½ cup butter with the sugar, vanilla, and salt in a mixing bowl until light and fluffy. Add the flour and baking cocoa and mix well. Shape into a ball and wrap in plastic wrap. Chill for 1 hour. Roll the dough ⅛-inch thick on a lightly floured surface. Fit into a tart pan and trim. Prick the surface with a fork. Bake at 350° for 15 minutes or until set. Cool to room temperature on a wire rack. Bring the cream just to a boil in a saucepan. Pour over the chocolate and 1 teaspoon butter in a mixing bowl. Let stand for 5 minutes to melt the chocolate and butter. Whisk until smooth. Stir in the preserves. Spoon into the tart shell and chill for 2 hours or longer.

Not So Humble Fudge Pie

A most wickedly delicious dessert!

¾ cup butter

Three 1-ounce unsweetened chocolate squares

1 tablespoon instant espresso powder

3 large eggs

1½ cups sugar

¾ cup all-purpose flour

1 teaspoon pure vanilla extract

¾ cups chopped pecans, toasted and divided

Cook butter and chocolate in a double boiler over low heat, stirring often until melted. Beat eggs with an electric mixer for 5 minutes and gradually add espresso and sugar, beating until well combined. Gradually add chocolate mixture, flour, and vanilla, beating until blended. Stir in ½ cup pecans. Pour into a lightly greased 9 inch pie plate. Bake at 350° for 40 minutes until the center is firm. Cool and add your favorite topping such as vanilla ice cream and chocolate syrup. Sprinkle remaining chopped pecans over the top - WOW!

NOTE: Dark chocolate is high in antioxidants and delivers a nutritional wallop. Just 1 to 2 ounces eaten every day can reduce risk of blood clots, lower blood pressure, increase indurance, and improve skin quality. It's even been proven to help sharpen problem solving skills.

Key Lime Pie with Grand Marnier Whipped Cream

A very special dessert

1 graham cracker crust

1 teaspoon unflavored gelatin

2 tablespoons cold water

2 egg yolks

½ cup Key lime juice, freshly squeezed

One 14-ounce can sweetened condensed milk

GRAND MARNIER WHIPPED CREAM

½ pint heavy cream, chilled

2 tablespoons sugar

1 tablespoon Grand Marnier liqueur

Bake pie crust for 10 minutes until lightly brown and set aside. Dissolve gelatin in cold water, stir, and set aside. In a heavy saucepan, combine egg yolks and lime juice and stir over medium heat for 10 minutes or until slightly thick and very hot. Be careful not to bring to a full boil. Add softened gelatin to lime juice mixture. Whisk well for 1 minute or until gelatin is dissolved. To quickly cool, place saucepan in a large bowl filled with ice. When cool, whisk in condensed milk. stirring until blended well and mixture becomes thick. Spoon into crust and spread evenly. Cover filling with plastic wrap and refrigerate.

GRAND MARNIER WHIPPED CREAM

In a stainless steel mixing bowl combine cream, sugar and liqueur. Whip with an electric mixer on high until cream holds peaks. Be careful not to over-whip cream or it will separate. Cream is properly whipped when you can drag a finger through it and a trough remains.

NOTE: For quicker results, chill the stainless steel bowl and beaters before whipping the cream.

Oystercatchers, watercolor on paper by Nancy Ricker Rhett.

www.mycarolinacooking.com

Benne Wafers

In Beaufort and throughout the Lowcountry, you will find a number of variations of these traditional cookies. Some are more like brittle candy than cookies and others are more light and delicate. These tend to be light, delicately scented and yet intensely flavored. You will want to purchase white sesame seeds often found in bulk at Asian markets.

¾ cup white sesame seeds

¾ cup all purpose flour

¼ teaspoon salt

¼ teaspoon baking powder

¾ cup unsalted butter

1 ½ cups light brown sugar

1 large egg, lightly beaten

grated zest of 1 lemon

2 tablespoons freshly squeezed lemon juice

With rack in the center of the oven, preheat the oven to 350°. Spread the sesame seeds on a 9-inch metal pie plate or cake pan and put them in the oven. Toast, stirring frequently until they are a rich golden brown. Let cool. Reduce the oven temperature to 300°. Line 2 large cookie sheets with cooking parchment. Whisk or sift together flour, salt and baking powder.

In a separate bowl, cream the butter and sugar until light and fluffy. Beat in the egg, and then mix in the flour, sesame seeds, lemon zest, and lemon juice. Drop by scant half teaspoonfuls onto the parchment, leaving at least an inch between them. (These cookies spread a good deal.)

Bake in batches about 10 minutes until lightly browned. Place the pans on wire cooling racks and let them cool completely before peeling them off the parchment. Store in airtight tins. Yields: 14 dozen.

Polenta Pudding with Caramel

Add a caramel sauce and you have an incredible, scrumptious dessert! Some have called polenta "Italian Grits."

2 cups whole milk

2 cups Half and Half

1 cup granulated sugar

1 cup yellow cornmeal (stone ground, if you can find it)

¼ cup butter

1 cup coconut

½ cup dried cherries or craisins

½ cup golden raisins

½ cup chopped pecans or walnuts

HEAVENLY CARAMEL SAUCE

1 stick of butter

1 cup granulated sugar

½ cup heavy cream

2 tablespoons light corn syrup

Pinch of salt

To make the pudding, start with a 2-quart saucepan over high heat. Bring the milk, Half and Half, and sugar to a boil. Do not stir. Reduce heat to low and whisk the cornmeal into the liquid, stirring constantly to prevent lumping. Stir in the butter, coconut, dried cherries, raisins, pecans and salt until thoroughly combined. The mixture will be thick. Spoon the mixture into silicone muffin baking molds. Press the mixture firmly into the molds to release air and ensure that when inverted, the pudding does not have big holes on the surface. Chill for about an hour. Release from molds and place on a dessert platter for serving.

To make the caramel sauce, chop up the butter and place in a small saucepan. Add sugar, cream and corn syrup. Stir to combine. Cook over low heat until the sugar dissolves and the mixture begins to boil. Increase the heat to high and boil, stirring just a little, until the mixture begins to turn light brown. (between 200° and 220° degrees on a candy thermometer) Remove from the heat and drizzle over polenta.

NOTE: Invest in a good candy thermometer before attempting this sauce. You may keep this caramel sauce covered in the refrigerator for as long as 6 months. You'll find plenty of uses for this sauce - over ice cream, cake and homemade breads, or share it with a friend!

Rhett Gallery, Beaufort, watercolor on paper by Nancy Ricker Rhett.

INDEX

A
appetizers
- Bay Street Mushroom Puffs, 36
- Caramel Pecan Brie, 45
- Cheese en Croute, 38
- Goat Cheese & Truffle Oil Crostini, 44
- Great Bruschetta Caper, The, 38
- Meeting Street Crab Tassies, 35
- Sea Island Crab Stuffed Mushrooms, 36
- Savannah Cheese Straws, 40
- Stuffed Artichoke Bottoms, 40

apple
- Apple Fritters for Fall, 51
- Hot Baked Fruit with Granola Nut Topping, 51
- Puffed Apple Pancake, 50

Apple Bacon Barbecue Sauce, 68
Apple Bacon Sausage Balls, 48
Apple Fritters for Fall, 51

artichokes
- Stuffed Artichoke Bottoms, 40

Asparagus and Arugula Salad, 89
Autumn Salad with Balsamic Roasted Pears, 85

B
Bacon-Mushroom Dip, 43
Baked Mackerel with Herb Crust, 109
Balsamic Roasted Pears, 85

banana
- Mama Green's Banana Pudding, 131

Basil Vinaigrette, 102
Bay Street Mushroom Puffs, 36

beans
- Fresh Specker Butter Bean, 119
- Hoppin' John, 118
- Tuscan Bean Soup, 32

Beaufort's Best Shrimp Burgers, 94

beef
- Chechessee Standing Rib Roast, 62
- Filet Mignon with Mushroom Marsala Sauce, 67
- Land's End London Broil, 65
- Pan Fried Steaks, 77
- Sizzlin' Flank Steak, 66
- Taco Salad, 65

Benne Seed Cookies, 123
Benne Wafers, 139
Best Barbecued Ribs, 68
Best Ever Queso Dip, 45

beverages
- Perfect Mint Julep, 40
- Wassail Punch, 40
- Sweet Tea, 41

Big Mama's Collard Greens, 86
Black-Eyed Pea Hummus, 42
Blackened Redfish, 95
Blueberry and Peach Crisp, 127
Boiled Peanuts, 121

breads
- Buttermilk Hush Puppies, 120
- Cheddar Bay Biscuits, 55
- Deep South Hush Puppies, 57
- Dixie-Style Hoe Cakes, 57
- Dye's Country Corn Pone, 119
- Fruit Nut Pumpkin Bread, 56
- Mama's Sweet Potato Poon, 119
- Pecan-Apple Bread, 50
- Spoon Bread, 54
- Sweet Potato Biscuits, 54
- Sweet Potato Cornbread, 54
- Zucchini Pineapple Bread, 55

Broiled Figs with Prosciutto and Gorgonzola, 42
Broomfield Cabbage Soup, 119
Buttermilk Fried Okra, 83
Buttermilk Hush Puppies with Onions and Bell Peppers, 120
Buttermilk Pie, 123

C
cakes
- Peppermint & Chocolate Chip Cheesecakes, 136
- Gullah Delicious Carrot Cake, 122
- Lucious Lemonade Layer Cake, 132
- Old Country Pound Cake (Suga Cane), 123

Caramel Crème Brûlee, 132
Carolina Country Hobo Bread, 122
Carolina Pickled Shrimp, 37
Carolina Remoulade, 97
Charleston Crab Au Gratin, 111
Chechessee Standing Rib Roast, 64
Cheddar Bay Biscuits, 51

cheese
- Cheese en Croute, 38
- Pimento Cheese, 34
- Savannah Cheese Straws, 40

chicken
- Chicken Divan, 61
- Chicken Fricassee, 72
- Chicken Marsala with Pancetta, 61
- Chicken, Onion and Pineapple Kebobs, 62
- Chicken Tostadas, 62
- Deep South Buttermilk Chicken, 60
- Lemony Chicken Piccata, 60
- Lowcountry Chicken Parmesan, 71
- Rustic Chicken, 71
- Sesame Chicken Wings, 61
- Southern-Style Barbecued Chicken, 73

chocolate
- Chocolate Chip Pecan Pie Bars, 137
- Chocolate Raspberry Truffle Torte, 138
- Coconut-Pecan Chocolate Bars, 128
- Valentine's Day Fudge Pie, 138

Christmas Divinity, 129
Cider Vinegar Barbecue Sauce, 74
Coconut-Pecan Chocolate Bars, 128

cookies
- Benne Seed Cookies, 123

Corn Skillet Fritters, 122
Corn Strata, 53
Cowan Creek Sweet Potato Cornbread, 54

crab
- Charleston Crab Au Gratin, 111
- Crab Bisque, 33
- Crab Ogeechee, 111
- Crab Relish, 99
- Daufuskie Crab Fried Rice, 121
- Meeting Street Crab Tassies, 35
- Pan-Seared Lowcountry Crab Cakes, 36
- Sea Island Crab Stuffed Mushrooms, 36
- Seafarer's Oyster and Crab Bake, 37
- Seafood Gumbo, 30
- She Crab Soup, 39
- Shrimp and Crab Salad, 97
- Tideland Soft-Shell Crabs, 110

Cranberry-Pineapple Gelatin Salad, 86
Cranberry Toffee Walnut Tarts, 128
Cream Cheese Frosting, 122
Creamy Mushroom Soup, 35
Crisp Tybee Salad, 88
Crispy Oven Fried Fish, 103

D
Daufuskie Crab Fried Rice, 120
Daufuskie Island Oyster Stuffing, 93
Deep South Buttermilk Fried Chicken, 60
Deep South Hush Puppies, 57
Deep South Penne Pasta, 86

dips
- Bacon-Mushroom Dip, 43
- Best Ever Queso Dip, 45
- Vidalia Onion Dip, 40

Dixie-Style Hoe Cakes, 57
Double Treat Toffee, 129

dressing
- Basil Vinaigrette, 102
- Honey Balsamic Vinaigrette, 89

Dye's Country Corn Pone, 119

F
Farm Stand Peach Freezer Jam, 49

figs
- Broiled Figs with Prosciutto and Gorgonzola, 42

Filet Mignon with Mushroom Marsala Sauce, 67

fish
- Baked Mackerel with Herb Crust, 109
- Blackened Redfish, 95
- Crispy Oven Fried Fish, 103
- Fish Casserole Au Gratin, 107
- Ginger Glazed Mahi-Mahi, 98
- Grilled Fresh Cobia, 101
- Grouper Oscar, 111
- Macadamia Crusted Mahi-Mahi, 99
- Mahi with Lemon and Capers, 98
- Mullet Stew, 118
- Ogeechee Shad Roe with Bacon, 105
- Seafood Ceviche on Cucumber Rounds, 100

Fish Casserole Au Gratin, 107
Fresh Specker Butter Beans, 119
Fried Green Tomatoes, 82
Fried Okra Pancakes, 54
Frogmore Stew, 29
Fruit Nut Pumpkin Bread, 56

G
Garden Fresh Tomato Basil Soup, 33
Ginger Glazed Mahi-Mahi, 98
Great Bruschetta Caper, The, 38

greens
- Big Mama's Collard Greens, 86

Grilled Fresh Cobia, 101
Grilled Lowcountry Shrimp, 105
Grilled Savannah Salad, 107
Grouper Oscar, 111
Gullah Delicious Carrot Cake, 122
Gullah Lowcountry Shrimp Pilau, 118

H
Heritage Breakfast Puffs, 48
Honey Balsamic Vinaigrette, 89
Honey Beer Sauce, 69
Hoppin' John, 118
Hot Baked Fruit with Granola Nut Topping, 51
Huguenot Torte, 132

K
Key Lime Pie with Grand Marnier Whipped Cream, 138

L
lamb
- Roasted Rack of Lamb, 70

Land's End London Broil, 65
Lemony Chicken Piccata, 60
Louis' Fried Oysters, 92
Lowcountry Aioli, 101
Lowcountry Chicken Parmesan, 71
Lowcountry Red Rice, 121

Lowcountry Sauce, 73
Lowcountry Shrimp and Grits, 108
Lowcountry Shrimp Cocktail, 45
Lucille Wright's Tomato Pie, 83
Lucious Lemonade Layer Cake, 132

M
Macadamia Crusted Mahi-Mahi, 99
Mahi with Lemon and Capers, 98
Mama Green's Banana Pudding, 131
Mama's Sweet Potato Poon, 119
Maple Sweet Potato Pie, 133
Meeting Street Crab Tassies, 35
Mocha Surprise Truffles, 129
Mullet Stew, 118
mushroom
    Creamy Mushroom Soup, 35
    Bay Street Mushroom Puffs, 36
    Sea Island Crab Stuffed Mushrooms, 36

N
Not So Humble Fudge Pie, 138

O
Ogeechee Shad Roe with Bacon, 105
okra
    Buttermilk Fried Okra, 83
    Fried Okra Pancakes, 54
Old Country Pound Cake (Suga Cane), 123
onion
    Vidalia Onion Dip, 40
    Vidalia Onion Tart, 80
Our Best Macaroni and Cheese, 81
oysters
    Daufuskie Island Oyster Stuffing, 93
    Louis' Fried Oysters, 92
    Oyster Bisque Savannah Style, 31
    Scalloped Oysters, 76
    Seafarer's Oyster and Crab Bake, 37

P
Palm Beach Brownies, 137
Pan Fried Steaks, 77
Pan-Seared Lowcountry Crab Cakes, 36
peanuts
    Boiled Peanuts, 121
pasta
    Deep South Penne Pasta, 86
    Our Best Macaroni and Cheese, 81
    Penne with Asparagus and Proscuitto, 69
    Vegetable Lasagne, 62
Peach and Blueberry Trifle, 126
peaches
    Farm Stand Peach Freezer Jam, 49
pears
    Autumn Salad with Balsamic Roasted Pears, 85
peas
    Black-Eyed Pea Hummus, 42
Pecan-Apple Bread, 50
Peppermint and Chocolate Chip Cheesecakes, 136
Perfect Mint Julep, 40
Penne with Asparagus and Proscuitto, 69
Pierre's Shrimp and Crab Gravy, 75
pies
    Basic Pie Crust, 133
    Buttermilk Pie, 123
    Key Lime Pie Grand Marnier with Grand Marnier Whipped Cream, 138
    Maple Sweet Potato Pie, 133
    Shaker Lemon Pie, 130
    Strawberry Cream Pie, 134
    Valentine's Day Fudge Pie, 138
Pimento Cheese, 34
pineapple
    Putting-on-the-Ritz Pineapple, 83
Polenta Pudding with Caramel, 139
pork
    Best Barbecued Ribs, 68
    Tailgate Pulled Pork Barbecue, 74
potato
    Potato Gratin with Truffle Oil, 85
    Twice Baked Potato Casserole, 80
pudding
    Mama Green's Banana Pudding, 131
    Polenta Pudding with Caramel, 139
Puffed Apple Pancake, 50
pumpkin
    Fruit Nut Pumpkin Bread, 56
    Pumpkin Mousse Parfaits, 135
Purloo, 121
Putting-on-the-Ritz Pineapple, 83

R
rice
    Lowcountry Red Rice, 121
    Purloo, 121
    Risotto with Creamy Scallops and Tomatoes, 84
    Wild Rice Salad, 88
Rise and Shine Breakfast Strata, 53
Risotto with Creamy Scallops and Tomatoes, 84
Roasted Rack of Lamb, 70
Roasted Vegetable Frittata, 52
Rustic Chicken with Mushrooms and Polenta, 71

S
salads
    Asparagus and Arugula Salad, 89
    Autumn Salad with Balsamic Roasted Pears, 85
    Cranberry-Pineapple Gelatin Salad, 86
    Crisp Tybee Salad, 88
    Grilled Savannah Salad, 107
    Shrimp and Crab Salad, 97
    Wild Rice Salad, 88
sauces
    Apple Bacon Barbecue Sauce, 68
    Carolina Remoulade, 97
    Cider Vinegar Barbecue Sauce, 74
    Honey Beer Sauce, 73
    Horseradish Cream Sauce, 65
    Lowcountry Aioli, 101
    Lowcountry Sauce, 73
    Mustard Horseradish Sauce, 64
    Remoulade Sauce, 83
    Soy Sake Dipping Sauce, 104
sausage
    Apple Bacon Sausage Balls, 48
    Heritage Breakfast Puffs, 48
    Savory Acorn Squash, 87
Savannah Cheese Straws, 40
scallops
    Risotto with Creamy Scallops and Tomatoes, 84
    Seafood Ceviche, 38
    Seared Scallop Salad, 102
    Shellfish Chowder, 28
Scalloped Oysters, 76
Sea Island Crab Stuffed Mushrooms, 36
Seafarer's Oyster and Crab Bake, 37
Seafood Ceviche, 38
Seafood Ceviche on Cucumber Rounds, 100
Seafood Gumbo, 30
Seared Scallop Salad, 102
Sesame Chicken Wings, 61
Shaker Lemon Pie, 130
She Crab Soup, 39
Shellfish Chowder, 28
shrimp
    Beaufort's Best Shrimp Burgers, 94
    Carolina Pickled Shrimp, 37
    Frogmore Stew, 29
    Grilled Lowcountry Shrimp, 106
    Grilled Savannah Salad, 107
    Gullah Lowcountry Shrimp Pilau, 118
    Lowcountry Shrimp and Grits, 108
    Lowcountry Shrimp Cocktail, 45
    Pierre's Shrimp and Crab Gravy, 75
    Seafood Gumbo, 30
    Shellfish Chowder, 28
    Shrimp and Crab Salad, 97
    Shrimp Curry, 76
    Shrimp Tempura/Soy Sake Dipping Sauce, 104
Sizzlin' Flank Steak, 66
Soda Cracker Bark, 135
soups
    Broomfield Cabbage Soup, 119
    Crab Bisque, 33
    Creamy Mushroom Soup, 35
    Frogmore Stew, 29
    Oyster Bisque Savannah Style, 31
    Tuscan Bean Soup, 32
    Garden Fresh Tomato Basil Soup, 33
    Seafood Gumbo, 30
    She Crab Soup, 39
    Shellfish Chowder, 28
Southern-Style Barbecued Chicken, 73
Soy Sake Dipping Sauce, 104
Spinach Cheese Strata, 53
Spoon Bread, 54
squash
    Savory Acorn Squash, 87
strawberry
    Strawberry Cream Pie, 134
    Strawberry Torte, 134
Stuffed Artichoke Bottoms, 40
sweet potato
    Cowan Creek Sweet Potato Cornbread, 54
    Mama's Sweet Potato Poon, 119
    Maple Sweet Potato Pie, 133
    Sweet Potato Biscuits, 54
    Sweet Potato Streusel Tarts, 136
Sweet Tea, 41

T
Taco Salad, 65
Tailgate Pulled Pork Barbecue, 74
Tideland Soft-Shell Crabs, 110
tomato
    Fried Green Tomatoes, 82
    Garden Fresh Tomato Basil Soup, 33
    Lucille Wright's Tomato Pie, 83
Turkey Deep Fried, 63
Tuscan Bean Soup, 30
Twice Baked Potato Casserole, 80

V
Vegetarian Lasagna, 62
Vidalia Onion Dip, 40
Vidalia Onion Tart, 80

W
Wassail Punch, 40
Wild Rice Salad, 88

Z
zucchini
    Roasted Vegetable Frittata, 52
    Zucchini Pineapple Bread, 55

The Artists

Ken Auster

A native Californian, Ken Auster grew up with his feet deeply planted in the surfing culture. While studying illustration at California State University, Long Beach, he expressed his art through silkscreen and graphic design. In the mid 1990's Ken moved to a more serious art level, involving himself with the immediacy of oil paints as opposed to the process-burdened medium of printmaking.

Auster is a signature member of the Plein Air Painters of America, a founding signature member of the Laguna Plein Air Painters Association, and a signature member of the California Art Club. He consistently walks away with gold medals and first place awards at juried exhibits and his work is collected by patrons across America. Ken is represented by Morris & Whiteside Gallery, 220 Cordillo Parkway, Hilton Head Island, SC 29928

Joe Bowler

As an illustrator, the pictures by Joe Bowler have graced the covers of major magazines and national ad campaigns. As a fine artist, Joe Bowler is widely recognized for his premier portraits. He enjoys rock star-like success in both the commercial and fine art arenas.

Portraits have become the prime focus of his career, which began when he was seventeen. Born in Forest Hills, New York in 1928, he began to draw when he was three. His first illustration for a national magazine was published by *Cosmopolitan* when he was nineteen working as an apprentice at the prestigious Charles E. Cooper Studios, Inc. There he had the opportunity to learn the craft from the finest artists in the profession who were generous in sharing their knowledge.

The Artists' Guild of New York named him their Artist of the Year in 1967. By this time magazines were commissioning him to do portraits of well known people. These included a 1968 *McCall's* fashion article portraying eight presidential candidates' wives; the August 1971 issue of *Ladies' Home Journal* cover portrait of Rose Kennedy and the *Saturday Evening Post* cover of Julie and David Eisenhower.

In 1972, seeking a milder climate, the Bowler family moved to Hilton Head Island, SC. For more information visit www.morris-whiteside.com.

Elaine Coffee

A keen observer of the human figure, Coffee depicts the body language of people in a wide range of environments. However, she intends her paintings as much more than figural compositions in familiar settings; more than mere snapshots of time and place. She strives for expressions of attitudes and atmospheres; spontaneous gestures with endless possibilities for interpretation.

A New Jersey native, Elaine Coffee completed her formal training at the School of Visual Arts in New York City and has traveled throughout the United States and Europe gathering inspiration for her contemporary genre paintings.

Elaine Coffee is a member of the National League of American Pen Women, The Arizona Artists Guild and the Sonoran Arts League, and her paintings may be found in public and private collections throughout the United States and Europe. For more information visit www.morris-whiteside.com.

John Carroll Doyle

Born in Charleston in 1942, John Carroll Doyle is nationally known for his energetic, light filled paintings of subjects as diverse as Gullah people, blues musicians, blue marlins and blue hydrangeas. The artist got his start with his distinctive sport fishing paintings which have graced the covers of many popular sport fishing magazines in the late 1970's and early 1980's. He continued to make a name for himself throughout the 1980's with his now famous and large scale commissioned paintings that can be seen on the walls of many of downtown Charleston's beloved restaurants, as well as clubs and restaurants as far afield as Chicago, Illinois and Alexandria, Virginia.

With a career that spans four decades, John has become a seasoned American Impressionist whose muse has always been Charleston and the surrounding Lowcountry. From wildlife to still life, John Doyle paints with a passion and understanding that makes it hard to believe he is self taught.

His gallery is located at 125 Church Street in Charleston. For more information visit: www.johncdoyle.com.

Ray Ellis

Ray Ellis has been painting for over seventy years on all seven continents. The Telfair Museum of Art in Savannah, Georgia in 2004 honored the depth and breadth of his career with a major traveling exhibition titled *Ray Ellis in Retrospect: A Painter's Journey*. He subsequently was awarded the Salmagundi Club's Medal of Honor for lifetime achievement in the Arts.

Born in Philadelphia, Ellis attended the famed Philadelphia Museum School of Art. In 1969, he was able to devote all his time to painting. Later he moved south to Hilton Head Island, South Carolina and then to Savannah, Georgia. He later resettled on Martha's Vineyard where he maintains a home and studio.

In the 1980s, Ray Ellis and Walter Cronkite collaborated on a series of fine art books which celebrate America's coastlines. His 15th and most recent book, *By the Light of the Moon*, showcases a theme that has captivated him for many years – moonlight.

For three consecutive years beginning in 1998, Ellis was commissioned by the President to paint scenes of the White House to be reproduced as the official Christmas card.

Today Ellis is represented in fine galleries across the country. His works have been exhibited in U.S. Embassies in Geneva, Vienna and London. Ray Ellis paintings are in the permanent collections of the White House, museums across the country and private collections worldwide. For more information visit www.rayellis.com. The Ray Ellis Gallery is located on Congress Street in Savannah, Georgia

Michael Harrell

Florida native Michael Harrell received his BFA in graphic design from the University of Georgia. Following graduation, he was a freelance illustrator for MasterCard, American Express and Paramount Pictures and exhibited with the Society of Illustrators at the Museum of American Illustration in New York.

From Nantucket, Massachusetts to the far reaches of the Florida panhandle and the Bahamas, Michael Harrell is almost always close to the water. Observing from shore, sailing on the bay or deep in the marshes at low tide with a third generation oysterman, Harrell moves quietly among the timeless moods of coastal living, recording real people in real environments with a depth of perception well beyond his years. For more information visit www.morris-whiteside.com.

Alfred Heber Hutty

Hutty was born in Grand Haven, Michigan in 1878 and moved to Charleston to teach classes in art for the Carolina Art Association in 1919. He was forty years old and his move was destined to begin a love affair with the city as well as a new chapter in his life and art.

His move to Charleston marked the beginning of his most productive and significant period. It was there that he learned etching and established a print studio. It is noted that he and his wife were among the first to try and preserve historic Charleston.

Hutty holds the honor of being the first American elected to the British Society of the Graphic Arts. For more information visit www.morris-whiteside.com.

Karin Jurick

Karin is a self taught artist whose work is held in private collections all over the country. She attributes her talent and exposure to different mediums to her mother, Lee, an artist who sold her works at traveling art shows in the Northeast. As a child, Karin's family traveled to many countries, living in Thailand, Philadelphia, and Chicago, before settling in Atlanta in 1979. There her parents opened a picture framing shop and art gallery. It was Karin's intention to pursue a career as an illustrator, but the unexpected deaths of her parents led her to continue running the family business. Not until several years ago did she begin painting with oils - observing works done by such artists as Wayne Thiebaud, Lucian Freud, and Ken Auster as a starting point for her pursuit to paint with courage and skill. For more information visit www.morris-whiteside.com.

Nancy Ricker Rhett

Nancy is a Beaufort native and fourth generation artist whose work is known nationally and abroad in both private and public collections, including the Ronald Reagan Presidential Library. Although she works from her studio at home on Lady's Island, her artwork, including the many books she has illustrated and written, can be seen at the Rhett Gallery on Bay Street in Beaufort. Here she shares space with four generations of family artists. Her husband, Bill, is a renowned wood sculptor and painter and their son William paints in watercolors and oil just like his great grandfather, James Moore Rhett, whose prints typify life in the Carolina Lowcountry.

Morris & Whiteside Galleries

Morris & Whiteside Galleries is an American fine art firm specializing in representational paintings and sculpture by the nation's leading artists. Housed in the historic Red Piano Gallery (South Carolina's oldest professional art gallery) at 220 Cordillo Parkway on Hilton Head Island, SC, the cordial partners Jack A. Morris, Jr., J. Ben Whiteside and David G. Leahy provide over 70 years of experience for individual collectors, corporations and institutions.

Featured artists include Ken Auster, Joe Bowler, Elaine Coffee, Jane DeDecker, Kim English, Glenna Goodacre, Jonathan Green, Walter Greer, Michael Harrell, Clark Hulings, Karin Jurick, Michael Karas, Milt Kobayashi, Dan McCaw, Dean Mitchell, Pino, Sandy Scott, Loran Speck, Linda St. Clair, and Stephen Scott Young among others.

For more information visit www.morris-whiteside.com.

Marilyn Simandle

"Perfectionism is the enemy of great art." Marilyn says she knew she wanted to be an artist since she was 6 years old. "My journey as an artist has changed many times over the years. My reason for painting has changed, too. I have always loved the process of putting paint to paper and canvas making shapes and values into beauty. Out of my love for God and His creation, my relationship with Him and painting His creation has become more important than painting. My painting has become an act of worship."

Marilyn's artwork reflects locales from around the world. She and her family reside in California and she is an avid traveler with a special interest in the subtlety of light. Over the past thirty years, Simandle has exhibited more than sixty-five one woman shows. She won the People's Choice Award at the Oil Painters of America National Show in 1998. For more information visit www.morris-whiteside.com.

Betty Anglin Smith

A native of the Carolinas, Smith has firmly established herself in Charleston's artistic community. With a style consisting of large brush strokes and bold, vibrant colors, Smith has grown exceptionally accomplished at capturing the expansive marsh vistas, beaches and waterways that are such an integral part of the Lowcountry landscape. Her work is shown in many places throughout the United States from New York to California. Smith says, "I want my work to be expressionistic, whilst also remaining in the realm of reality."

Not only is she an accomplished artist but her three children, who are triplets, have incredible talent and each are accomplished artists in their own right. For more information visit: wwwsmithkillian.com. Their work is on display at Smith Killian Fine Art of Charleston

Jennifer Smith Rogers

Jennifer is a native of Charleston well known for her themes of architecture and vistas seen from towering over the city. Her works weave together the themes of light and architecture, portraying a near symbiotic relationship between the two. Raised in a household of artists, she began painting at a very early age. Throughout the years her work has been sought by galleries all along the Eastern Seaboard, from Charleston, SC to Martha's Vineyard. While she paints all over the world she is always drawn back to her beloved Lowcountry. For more information visit: wwwsmithkillian.com.

Shannon Smith

Her sister, Shannon, has established a solid reputation within the fine art community. Regardless of what subject she chooses to paint, Smith has proven she possesses an unusually keen eye and an unrivaled sensitivity to light. Shannon is noted for strong contrasts of color, with dramatic darks and subdued grey tones juxtaposed with warmer, more radiant hues. But her main focus is capturing light. She has been honored by the Oil Painters of America and she is a signature member of the Plein Air Painters of the Southeast. Her brother, Tripp, is an accomplished photographer. For more information visit: wwwsmithkillian.com.

Loren Speck

Loren Speck is a California born painter known for his still life works that echo the techniques of the great Masters. Speck has been featured in national publications including U.S. Art, American Artist and Art of the West and Southwest Art. He has been exhibiting his work for over 25 years.

Peter Rolfe

Peter Rolfe is a Portland, Maine native and has an unusual formal education for an artist. He studied mechanical and industrial engineering at the University of Illinois, graduating in 1965, and also holds a Master's Degree in Business Administration. He worked for Westinghouse and USM until late 1970 when he began to dabble in painting. He sailed as first mate on a private yacht in 1971 and started to paint seriously later that year. He spent a year painting before opening his gallery in Wiscasset, Maine in 1972. Rolfe is a self-taught artist who paints primarily in oil, but also uses watercolor, gouache, acrylic and pastels.

Steve Weeks

Steve Weeks of Beaufort, SC has spent a lifetime around tidal waters and is quick to say he is invigorated by the Lowcountry. For 25 years he studied art at the Pennsylvania Academy of Fine Art and the University of the Arts in Philadelphia. Nature's breathing in and breathing out in the form of the ebb and flow of tides is somehow comforting and a necessary thing for Steve to experience. Steve's work may be viewed at the I. Pinkney Simmons Gallery on Bay Street in Beaufort.

The Photographers

Bob Ovelman

Bob Ovelman of Hilton Head has turned his hobby of picture taking into a career. He is a professional photographer, corporate photographer and a photo-journalist. Bob moved from Philadelphia about 10 years ago and is an Indigo Run resident and member of the Camera Club of Hilton Head.

Ed Funk

Photographer Ed Funk of Bluffton, SC is a chemist by trade who practiced photography as a hobby through his career at Sun Chemical Corporation, a manufacturer of printing inks and pigments in New Jersey and Chicago. Ed is a former president of the Hilton Head Camera Club and a founding member of the Photography Club of Beaufort.

Jack Howison

Jack Howison of Beaufort, SC is a photographer for BeaufortTribune.com who rises early each morning to capture the days sunrise.

Resources

Nancy Ricker Rhett, *Beaufort and the Lowcountry*
Bill and William Rhett of the Rhett Gallery, Bay Street, Beaufort, SC
Ben Whiteside of the Morris and Whiteside Gallery, HHI, SC
Lee Limehouse, Director Smith-Killian Fine Arts, Charleston
John Carroll Doyle Gallery, Charleston
Steve Weeks, I Pinckney Gallery, Beaufort, SC
Bob Ovelman Photography, Hilton Head, SC
Ed Funk Photography of Hilton Head, SC
Jonathan Green
Nathalie Dupree
George Trask- BeaufortTribune.com, and *Beautiful Beaufort By the Sea Guildebook*
Martha Nesbit, *Savannah Celebrations*
Pierre McGowan, *Tales of the Barrier Island*
the late Roger Pinkney
the late Sheriff Ed McTeer
Lawrence S. Rowland, Professor of History University of South Carolina, Beaufort
The Historic Beaufort Foundation
The Historic Charleston Foundation
The Historic Savannah Foundation
Sweetgrass Bistro, Dataw Island
Nadine Awoyemi, chef and Jeff and Lauren Tillapaugh, owners of Sweetgrass Bistro, Dataw Island
Lowcountry Weekly
The Hilton Head Monthly
the many friends and acquaintances who have opened their recipe files and kitchens
Chef Phil Barnes of Nobles Restaurant, Winston Salem, NC
Annie Sergent of Wren Bistro, Carteret Street, Beaufort, SC
Ervena Faulkner of *The Beaufort Gazette*
Damon Lee Fowler, nationally known authority on Southern cooking from Savannah
Jenny and Wilber Roller of Hilton Head's Sea Trawler Restaurant
The Chive Blossom Cafe, Pawley's Island
Fuzzy Davis, sportsman, and Executive Chef Juan Carlos of the Ford Plantation
Lynn McLaren, *Ebb Tide-Flood Tide*
Charlie's L'etoile Verte, Hilton Head, S.C.
Dr. C. Thomas Anderson and Anne Anderson
the late Mr. and Mrs. C.T. Anderson
The Sea Shack, Hilton Head, S.C.
The Kitchen Crew of St. Helena's Church, Beaufort, S.C.
Larry and Tina Toomer, operators of the Bluffton Oyster Company
Chef Louis Osteen, Louis Restaurant and Fish Camp, Pawley's Island
The Beaufort Grocery Company, Beaufort, N.C.
Matt and Carol Jording, The Sage Room, Hilton Head Island

www.mycarolinacooking.com